18 MONTHS:

A Memoir of a Marriage Lost
to Gender Identity

18 MONTHS:

A Memoir of a Marriage Lost
to Gender Identity

SHANNON THRACE

FIRE
BUSH

Author's Note:

The following narrative is based on a true story, and the events herein are relayed as I remember them. I recognize that memory is unreliable and that others may remember the events differently.

Names, places, and other details have been changed to protect the anonymity and privacy of those involved. Some events have been collapsed and some characters are composites of multiple individuals.

18 Months is, unavoidably, set in the past. The identities of Eddie Izzard, Andrej Pejić, and others reflect how they were known at the time.

Published in the United States by Firebush Books.

ISBN: 979-8-9866938-0-4 (Paperback)

First paperback edition October 2022

Cover design © Firebush Books
Cover illustrations:
© Photos77777 | Dreamstime.com
© Renata Kuthanova | Dreamstime.com
© Sylverarts | Dreamstime.com

www.firebushbooks.com
www.shannonthrace.com

For the women
who walk in these shoes

TABLE OF CONTENTS

THE SEVENTEENTH MONTH

"I am *literally* a woman," you say, your expression suggesting you've just chewed up an aspirin. "And *not* someone who identifies as one."

Though you stand a few feet from me in the foyer of our Indianapolis home, you couldn't be further away. For most of our fifteen years we've shared an unassailable, easy intimacy, and my heart aches to reach you, to bring you back, to talk with you. Instead I stare down a yawning chasm that can't be breached. Sometime within the past few months, talking with me became a thing you no longer do.

"Jamie—" I call, stepping forward and offering my hand. But you move toward the door. Towering in high-heel boots and a dress too slinky for the cold November air, you scarcely resemble the person who proudly identified as a man only months ago. "Why would I call myself a woman?" you'd asked, when someone suggested you reevaluate your gender identity. "That would just legitimize the binary that forces people into outdated sex roles." The shift in your position is written all over you: the dress ill-suited for winter; the layers of pasty foundation; the fussed-with, sprayed hair.

You turn back to glare at me, pulling your coat tightly around you in defense against some invisible barrage. "Trans women are women," you add, with a tone that suggests insider access to a secret I could never understand. You smirk as you pull your scarf from the hook, but without amusement; it's as if you've learned you must cut me out of your life, but find the obligation distasteful.

PART I

REJECTING GENDER

DAY ONE

"A hard cock peeking out of tight lace panties?" I ask, making sure I understand your request. "Is *that* the sort of thing you're looking for?"

Your eyes widen—you're the proverbial deer in headlights. But you can't hide that I've piqued your interest and a faint smile crosses your lips.

"Yes," you say, with a self-conscious shrug. "That would be *perfect*, actually."

You lean toward me from your end of the couch to glimpse my laptop screen, blond hair falling across wiry, heavily inked shoulders. Your recent forty-pound weight loss, and now the glow of curiosity, knock several years off your middle-aged face.

We're enjoying a Saturday evening in our little fixer-upper in rural Ohio. The windows are open to the summer heat—we're still enamored with the idea of living more naturally—and the pair of swallows are feeding their hatchlings under the eave. I was reading some piece about dinosaurs on *McSweeney's* when you sprang the question on me, about an hour ago: could we share some porn with each other tonight? You'll find something for me, you said, and I'll find something for you. It was out of character for you—you browse the shady side of the web less often than I do.

I know your sexual tastes like I know the creases in your calloused hands, the pattern of moles on your back. But my attempts fall flat tonight.

I start with a photo of two bearded hippies in denim making out. You've always liked scenes of men together as long as they're not "too gay." No hairless, oiled pretty boys for you. No leather chaps. No sass, no slapping, no sadomasochism. Just regular-looking men getting it on.

But you aren't in the mood for guys kissing tonight.

I move on to amateur porn. I find a clip of a straight couple performing for their female videographer, who's purring bawdy suggestions off-screen. It's natural and candid—they don't seem like actors. You always like that, and I do too. But that isn't doing it for you either.

How about women in schoolgirl uniforms, their bare thighs peeking between short skirts and tall socks? That often works, but not tonight. I cycle through your usual themes and even some of mine, but nothing is quite right.

Tonight, it turns out, you want to see masculine men in feminine clothing. An erect penis straining against lingerie. "Crossdressers," you say. "Tranny porn." You're not interested in anything else.

And that's how this chapter of our relationship—this final chapter—begins.

The day starts auspiciously enough. I awake to the sun streaming into our tiny attic bedroom, warming the cake-batter beadboard we installed over every mouse-eaten surface. I stretch and breathe in the room's scent: clean and dusty all at once. The way my grandma's house used to smell. Like books shelved in a small-town library. Like my ionizing flat iron, or that ozone smell after it rains.

The sun is barely over the horizon but since you started teaching you've made an early riser of me. I let you sleep and make my way downstairs to our oversize country kitchen. I fill Carrot's bowl, then start the pot of boiling water we'll share—some for my Earl Grey, some for your French press. "Carrot Top," I call, until the aging tabby saunters in. "My Baby Carrotine." I sit down at a dining room table that's much too big for the two of us but perfect when we host family Thanksgivings. Outside the window hummingbirds flit around the feeder, reminding me of the song you recently wrote about them. For an acoustic, folksy album, you said. About how they can't rest, like you.

It isn't long before you join me.

We take our drinks outside, as we do on temperate Saturdays. Though the front porch needs a paint job and nails creep treacherously from loose boards, its south-facing view of rolling farmland is breathtaking. We sit in the Adirondack chairs your dad made, watching a calf romp and play on the neighboring farm. As city transplants several years into our largely unsuccessful stab at homesteading, we still find the wobbly little creatures charming.

"They look like work to me," the farmer said once. He wasn't impressed with the Queen Anne's lace I'd cut to tuck into a bouquet for the table, either. "Whaddaya want with that wild carrot?" he wondered aloud.

We sip our beverages and discuss our plans for the year. Will we make it to Tennessee Fall Homecoming, our favorite place for amateur bluegrass and Appalachian pottery? Should we order tickets for Quafftoberfest, that new craft beer festival? And what will we do for vacation? We could return to the Sanibel Island resort where we spent our honeymoon. We want to see Europe but it always seems out of reach.

You're ready to plan our annual fall bonfire. We'll get straw for the hayride from those kids up the street whose little roadside greenhouse provides them with money for college. You'll make spiced cider and bratwurst and kraut. You want to stuff cellulose casings with a cheese, apple and rye bread filling for our vegetarian friends. I'm skeptical, but you say you have a vision.

We revisit moving back to Indianapolis, the city we once called home, where your family and so many of our friends reside. Our fixer-upper needs constant repairs, so country life hasn't put money in our savings. We don't have much in common with our conservative neighbors, and I've moved on to a different job than the one that lured us here. We brave the two-hour drive on special occasions but we miss grabbing Indian food with friends on a lazy Sunday or joining board game nights at your brother's. We miss sushi, too. And mom-and-pop coffee shops smelling of nutmeg and artisan toaster pastries.

But it's hard to contemplate leaving our little country sanctuary after all the work we put into it. We replaced each appliance with an energy-efficient one, constructed built-in bookcases, ripped up carpets and patched walls and floors. We spent a weekend razing a massive barn, bringing down towering hardwood poles with ropes tied off to your overworked little pickup truck. It was a beautiful, century-old structure we were loath to destroy—lovingly built of rough-hewn timber, its fiery red paint faded to a rusty brown. But our homeowner's insurance wanted it gone. A demolition service quoted several grand to do the job, but we did it for the cost of our sweat and a home-cooked meal for the friends who helped. For months afterward the two of us stacked wood, cleared brush, and hauled away junk.

You used the barnwood to build raised beds for a vegetable garden, filling them with store-bought dirt and composted kitchen scraps. You planned every detail, designing a crop rotation that would fix nitrogen and reduce plant disease, leaving me little room to contribute. So I took over the landscaping, adorning the yard with meandering patches of black-eyed Susans and coneflowers edged with creeping Jenny and shored up with bricks from Freecycle.

We're falling behind on our gardening, we admit, as we finish our second cup. Unharvested tomatoes crowd serpentine zucchini vines, and the painted daisies bend under their own weight. It's a good day to catch up. We better start early before the midday sun renders the job unbearable.

We walk to the shed, where you grab a plastic colander the size of a wading pool that we found at the international grocery in the city. You head to your vegetable plot and start harvesting at one end, working your way to the other, gathering far more produce than any two people should ever need: lettuce, peppers, tomatillos, herbs. You pick each vegetable carefully, deliberately, now and then pinching off a dead leaf or retying the strip of bandanna holding up a sagging tomato vine. You're right at home, capable and content, and for a moment you seem like part of the garden itself, the two of you primitive and timeless.

I grab a trowel and head toward my flower beds, but you call me over. We watch a cute little garter snake weave around the cilantro and slither out of sight. You know catching a glimpse of a critter is one of my favorite things.

It gets hot, despite our early start, but I don't mind. For me, summer's unpopular facets are part of its charm: the scratchiness of daisy stems as I deadhead, biting ants emerging from dew-dampened bricks, the honeyed scent of bees hovering close to my face. Hours pass easily as I dig in the cool dirt, pulling up dandelions, turning the mulch, retraining a clematis.

The bounty of the harvest inspires our dinner plans—salad and ratatouille. I wash the vegetables as you pair your phone with the speaker and queue up *This American Life*. "I'll start with the carrots and you chop the *pommes de terre*," you say with a fake accent, handing me a potato.

"Apples of the earth," I acknowledge, recalling my high school French. I position the cutting boards on the kitchen island and grab a couple of chef's knives from the magnetic strip behind the stove.

The dinner we pull together is big, as always, served on the good dishes and accompanied by baked bread, herbed olive oil for dipping, Sriracha and real shredded Parmesan. You and I know how to eat.

But about your request.

When I was about twelve, my parents took me by a funky little bookstore after a day of shopping. It was crammed to the ceiling with new and used graphic novels and irreverent small-press magazines. It was the seventies, so Mom and Dad were off finding computer manuals and self-help books. They left me to peruse a newsstand of the unfamiliar and strangely erotic.

I got an eyeful of comic-book heroine Vampirella in her painted-on bodysuit. I read a hippie treatise on throwing an orgy. I pored over a fetish photo collection featuring a woman on all fours buckling under the weight of a horse's saddle. And then, flipping open some obscure cult magazine, I saw Dr. Frank-N-Furter for the first time.

Clad in his trademark fishnets and heels, Tim Curry's mad scientist spanned the magazine's centerfold. Though I'd seen a Playmate before, I'd never seen a crossdresser—*The Rocky Horror Picture Show* was still relevant but I wasn't exactly its target demographic. I was old enough to know sex when I saw it, though. And I'd never seen it quite like this.

I'll never forget my first glimpse of that "sweet transvestite." He was statuesque. He was tattooed. His hip jutted obscenely and a cigarette hung from his crimson-painted lips. His shoulders were broad, his biceps pronounced and silky black briefs outlined his junk. His flat chest was laced into a corset, sexualizing a man in a world that usually sexualizes women. Dr. Frank-N-Furter—it's in the name—was hot because of his masculinity, enhanced by its juxtaposition to femininity.

Like a hard cock peeking out of tight lace panties.

I was mesmerized. I was titilated. I reached into my pocket—my allowance would cover the cost of the magazine—but my mom materialized. Shocked at my newfound interest, she held forth on the "abomination" I'd found—citing Deuteronomy—and took the magazine away.

So I get where you're coming from, Jamie. And I can find what you want.

You respond well to the photos I now curate for you: one of a young punk rocker in spiky leather, pants down, revealing a bulging pair of pink panties. Another of a flat-chested woman wearing a strap-on, reclining against her bent-over male lover. You also like a video called "Sissification" of a crossdressed man slithering on the floor.

I wonder what prompted your interest in sharing porn this evening. Had you already tried and failed to find what you wanted? Did you see me as the more experienced connoisseur? Because whenever *I* suggest looking at erotica, you balk. Even if we're drinking or already fooling around.

Do you remember my failed *Emmanuelle 2* experiment? It was our first year together. I'd brought up the subject of adult films once or twice, and though you were intrigued, the time was never right. You felt "silly" trying to choose a title. So I decided to get you watching before you knew what you were watching.

While you were away I slipped the French soft-core film into the VCR—remember the days when such equipment cluttered our console?—and queued it up past the title. When you got home, I flipped it on for a presumably innocent evening of television. I thought you'd be fooled by its feature-film look and the exposition preceding the smutty parts. But as our heroine weaved through a crowd of sailors in a flowing white dress, you became suspicious. You weren't fooled when she stopped to lend a friend her comb. You guessed the ruse. You laughed at me and left the room. We did not watch *Emmanuelle 2*, that night or any other.

But tonight you're on a mission. Your interest is new to me, but I'm game. Crossdressed men aren't really my bag, despite that youthful moment at the newsstand. But sex is my bag. And discovering and supporting the kinks of my lover is my bag. I enjoy any opportunity to make things interesting in the bedroom, and I have yet to be scared away by the fantasies of the men and women I've dated.

And you, you're very much my bag.

I'm not sure how far you want to go, but I'm willing to accommodate. "I could give you a makeover," I say in a playful tone I can blame on sarcasm. But your eyes light up.

I dig in the bathroom cabinet and dust off my makeup kit. It's old and disused. I'm an aging tomboy, not one of those ladies who drops half a paycheck at Sephora on her way home from work. I own a good-quality "corrective" foundation for job interviews, drugstore eyeliner, and eyeshadows in kohl and silver so I can glam it up for the occasional rock show. These choices reflect my age; I'm more comfortable channeling a world-weary Chrissie Hynde than a subtle and "dewy" Taylor Swift. But I rifle through dried-up nail polishes and dirty applicators and find what I need for your fairer complexion: eye color in sienna and pink, bought for our wedding day; brown mascara; a powder that'll minimize your freckles and a tinted gloss.

You submit placidly while I apply the products. Your eyes twitch and water when I get to the eyeliner—you've always had trouble using Visine or rescuing a stray lash—but you soldier through. You're relaxed, aroused. Positively transfixed.

It's kind of cool.

I'd planned to stop here but I'm inspired by your reaction. I plug in my curling iron and frame your face with delicate tendrils. Then we head to the bedroom to find you some clothes.

I don't have much that'll fit, but you stand by patiently as I go through my closet. At length I retrieve a stretchy skirt and a bell-sleeved blouse that'll wiggle past your shoulders. You're barefoot but it will have to do. You'll never fit in my shoes.

I kiss you once before leaning back to appraise my work. You bite your lower lip, tuck your chin and gaze up at me through sticky lashes.

12

It's a look I've seen on a porn star who's about to give a blow job. I'm surprised it turns me on.

And now, I'm in my element. You've always praised my "sexual aggressiveness," and while I don't see it that way, I suppose there's truth in it. I lead you to bed and take control because it's what you want. You go limp in my arms, relishing the experience of being ravaged.

Afterward, I watch you fall asleep in the blouse, illuminated by an aureole of fireflies that have gathered on the window behind you.

It's July. I don't know it yet, but I've got a long eighteen months ahead of me.

ONE | JULY
An UNCLOUDY Day

"Why get married?" your friend Theo asked me, all those years ago. I'd ditched the four-inch heels and settled into the warm dampness of my crocheted flats as I planted my feet in the grass. Cradling the flute of champagne against my tea-length dress, I raised my eyes to a clear, steel-gray sky. The clouds had lifted just before the ceremony, defying a forecast of scattered thunderstorms.

I knew what he meant. Some of our friends had taken a stand against marriage. "It's just a piece of paper," Darcy had said. "It isn't necessary for commitment."

Willow had been harsher. "Marriage is an economic arrangement," she'd said, "where men trade daughters like livestock." She doesn't wear makeup or shave her legs, either, in protest of the patriarchy. Her longtime partner Red is on the same page. He eschews bathing for patchouli oil and so distrusts the "medical-industrial complex" that he's never seen a dentist about the front teeth he lost in a bicycle accident twenty years ago.

I appreciated Willow's point of view. But I knew early in our relationship I wanted to marry you. I'd never met anyone in my thirty-something years I connected with so completely. And to me, the concept of marriage had evolved and taken on new meaning.

"I think it's important," I said. "I want to give my partner the honor of standing beside him, publicly, and stating: 'I'm committed. I'm sure. I'm not waiting for a better offer.'"

"I think it's important too," Theo said, glancing toward his girlfriend, who browsed the buffet in a little black dress that showcased an extravagance of tattoos. He'd been playing devil's advocate.

It took you and me a while to marry—we waited until I finished my bachelor's so I wouldn't lose my financial aid. We lived frugally as we saved for the event. You even got into the planning. You wanted a genteel, Southern look for you and your best man, Lyle: Western-cut jackets, brocade vests and cowboy boots. You spoke with affection of the salesman who taught you the etiquette of suit ownership—the art of fastening only the top button of your jacket, of unfastening it with a single hand before sitting. The look fit our vision: an easy, outdoor gala with upscale picnic fare and unamplified music. Elegant, but casual. Sophisticated but a little bit country.

A friend with a mail-order ordination married us under the boughs of a weeping cherry overlooking a lake. Your mother set eyelet-covered tables with wildflowers and your oldest brother, a chef, provided cedar-plank salmon, wild greens, and a strawberry shortcake station straight from the pages of *Martha Stewart Living*. The air swelled with the harmonies of a local bluegrass quartet: Gillian Welch covers for us, gospel standards for our parents.

Your parents, I mean, and my surviving one. Though you and I had been together for years, they'd just met that morning. My mother rarely leaves Western Kentucky, where she lives among white-tailed deer on twenty goldenrod-covered acres. Socially anxious and visually impaired, she'd arrived frazzled after navigating a busy airport and summoning a taxi driver with a lead foot. But your mom, always the social butterfly, enlisted her help stringing lights on a gazebo. Then your dad pulled up a chair and asked her about the wild birds of Land Between the Lakes.

They'd taken to me just as quickly, though I'd appeared on the scene all too soon after your divorce. "We will always love Melanie," began the two-page note your mom slipped me early in our relationship, "but we love you, too. We can see you're good for James." Later your dad pulled me aside to thank me for "taking good care" of you.

Your parents, though from small-town beginnings, proved as tolerant and urbane as anyone I've known. This came by way of profound compassion, not political dogma. I credit them with guiding you, once the arrogant whippersnapper, onto a path of grace and maturity. Because of them you approach the world with an openness I've seldom seen, at home in a Moroccan tea house or a greasy-spoon diner, kind to the stranger who tried to sell you drugs in Memphis, patient while a single mom wrangled a bunch of kids into a hotel check-in line in front of us. You understood, as one of five yourself. It was easy to befriend Jake, Jeremy, Jill and Jessica when I met them, too.

As a first-generation college student with a history of drag racing, Hank Jr. concerts and felonious exes, I never thought I'd find someone like you. Someone who shared my tastes for Picasso, Nietzsche and picnics on the museum lawn—but wouldn't reject me for what I call, in the parlance of Ben Folds, my "redneck past." In fact, you not only tolerated, but *cherished* it, finding my Kentucky accent not uneducated-sounding, as I feared, but charming. "There's nothing wrong with having a regional dialect," you said, "and yours is lovely." You welcomed into our lives the best parts of my history—my grandpa's paintings, my aunt's handmade quilts, my recipe for burgoo—as I left behind the worst: meth-addled former friends, memories of my parents' drunken rampages and a scrubby hometown abandoned to graffiti and ruin.

Only a few people from my life attended our wedding. There was an early childhood friend, my favorite cousin, and my best friend from high school—who's since succumbed to a fatal illness. Even my maid of honor backed out to present research at a conference. I was never as blessed with friends as you are, having run from my hometown, postponed college and moved several times. My dad had passed away, my brother was estranged and my extended family lived far away. The rest of the guests belonged to your life: your family, your music scene buddies, your friends. But now they were my friends, too. I reflected on my good fortune as I watched you play at square dancing with them under the white canvas tent.

"You look happy," Theo remarked. I *was* happy. After six years, our love was well established and our public expression of it overdue. But it wasn't always obvious we'd get married. When we began our fling, I identified as a lesbian and you had a wife.

We met at the home of polyamorous triad Rory, Agnes and Sage during one of their famous parties, which attracted underemployed creatives with primary-colored hair and alternative sexualities. Rory served vegan snacks, distributed his socialist-anarchist zine and played John Waters movies on a loop. I'd met the trio through my ex-girlfriend Isabel, who'd found them on a poly message board. You knew them as employees of a used bookstore several of your friends had worked at in college. Those friends, who seldom went anywhere without one another, were with you. One was your best friend Lyle. One was your wife, Melanie.

You were thin with disheveled, shoulder-length hair and a two-week beard, and in a military jacket and ripped jeans, you exuded an understated sexiness that reminded me of Kurt Cobain. I liked the way you moved about the room like a ragdoll, slumping onto a sectional, sloshing your drink. This wasn't drunkenness but your natural manner: the muppetish, distracted quality of one who gives no fucks. I thought you were cute for a guy. I knew the occasional—if fleeting—attraction to men.

We talked only briefly that night, when someone brought up housework. "I hate cleaning," I said, stirring my Manhattan. "What I need is a wife." My thoughts wandered to Isabel. It had been a couple years since we'd parted ways.

"I'd rather do housework than have a job," you said. "Work sucks."

I'd reached the sort of tipsy that makes me want to touch people, and Melanie had left the room. "No way," I said, tapping your chest. "My job lets me learn and grow. Housework is repetitive and never-ending." I was flirting, sort of, but thought myself unlikely to follow through.

"The trick is to find the Zen in mundane tasks." You spoke on this vein, invoking The Tao of Pooh, then quoting the Dalai Lama: "If one's life is simple, contentment has to come."

I was impressed by your centeredness. And I was drawn to your impish smile, with those widely spaced teeth; your pale blue eyes; and the tangled hair I couldn't resist brushing from your cheek as you spoke. You reminded me of a jackrabbit—I'd say this later, when you asked me what animal you most resembled—scruffy but soft, wiry but cuddly, wild-eyed but wise. Sometimes you looked still on the surface, but underneath, ready to run.

You were still regaling me with your insights when Agnes grabbed my arm and dragged me away. "Body art time!" she said, giving me a handful of fluorescent highlighters and a knowing look. Rory fired up the black lights as we stripped to our panties and settled onto the living room floor. We drew swirls and whirls on each other's breasts, smearing wet light across gray skin with our fingers.

Isabel had invented the body art game, during our stint in a town where a throng of bohemians gathered. They were writers and artists, filmmakers and poets, their three a.m. philosophy debates fueled by Tom Waits and Johnny Walker Red. As a writer and third-generation artist, I'd felt at home there. I'd been looking for a similar vibe ever since. Rory and crew were fun, but not as literate, and too often substituted shock value for personality. *Your* friends, though, had promise.

They were liberal arts majors, bookworms, and studied connoisseurs of high and low art. Darcy was a scholar of Victorian death poetry and a sci-fi geek. Theo was a music fanatic with an encyclopedic knowledge of artists and genres. Paige was an art collector who rescued feral cats. Melanie was an English professor well-versed in the Western canon.

Your best friend Lyle was a Spanish major interested in legal protections for immigrants. Though his views largely aligned with those of the others, he kept everyone on their toes with his conservative stance on gun ownership, his fervor for starting debates with unwilling participants, and his tendency to argue points of view he disagreed with for the hell of it.

I had only an associate's degree at the time, but I yearned for better-educated friends. So I bragged about my love of Coltrane and Dostoevsky. I name-dropped important figures in art, architecture, and philosophy. I spoke of my erotica collection: lesbian rag *On Our Backs*, classic novels like *Fanny Hill*, Pat Califia's *Macho Sluts*. I was no stranger to affectation. But it wasn't so long ago that I'd left a hometown that never suited me. I craved intellectual stimulation. I was looking for my people. You and your friends were the sorts I longed to bring into my life, and I very much wanted to know you better. So that night I befriended Darcy and Lyle and Theo and got myself invited to their parties.

You and I really got to know each other then. Melanie posed no obstacle to our budding friendship; she often drove separately from you and went home early. Sometimes you and I found ourselves the last ones awake, carrying on about the relationship between Kafka and Brod or whether Lichtenstein was a plagiarist, as friends snored on couches and floors nearby. Over time we learned we both loved David Lynch and longed to homestead a small parcel of land. We were both backpackers and web developers. I was a music aficionado and you were a talented musician.

I remember the first time I heard you play. Your friends loved theme parties in those days. Having exhausted the obvious choices, like "The Eighties," as well as more creative ones like "The Great Gatsby," they'd settled on the decidedly punny "Communist Party." You wore a plaid shirt with a bowler hat and carried an old guitar, across which you'd scrawled "This Machine Kills Fascists." Woody Guthrie called himself a communist, you said, even if he never joined the party.

You flopped onto the floor and began playing. Lyle, dressed as Che Guevara in fatigues and a beret, placed his unlit cigar in a tumbler and joined you on harmonica. Friends gathered around, propped on sofa pillows and against walls. You delivered a selection of songs on train-hopping, cheating, and unmarked graves. You played covers by Bob Dylan and Leonard Cohen. You ad-libbed new stanzas for "In the Pines," constructing a tale of a recluse who'd murdered his wife and buried her in the forest. You belted out these tunes in the gravelly wail that was your trademark, inviting folks familiar with your repertoire to sing along. You played originals, too. A song about falling for a prostitute. Another about running from the law. One in which you wake up on the street, a homeless woman mopping your brow. Gritty blues themes were your thing.

Your friend Fuzzy arrived with his new girlfriend Claire in tow. He was a super-sized bass player and disciple of Prince, she a scenester who cinched herself into tight rockabilly dresses. They placed a bottle of Chivas and a couple of Solo cups next to you. Your banter grew ardent as the two of you poured and belted drinks between songs.

Later, on the balcony, you and Lyle continued to imbibe, pacing, cackling, and occasionally yelling over the railing at folks in the street below. You held forth on the merits of socialized medicine, the poetry of Bukowski, and which Led Zeppelin song was the greatest (Gallow's Pole, in your opinion, for its double entendre). A debate about the

Oxford comma digressed until Lyle screamed, as he often did when he was drunk, and chucked his beer bottle off the balcony. "I am a lion!" you shouted. It was a thing you said from time to time in those days. Something about feeling too fierce and powerful and important for the banality of your life. Then the two of you littered the street with bottles, half in jest, half from some unarticulated frustration. Melanie interrupted to tell you she was going home.

"My wife and I only have sex twice a month," you announced in the hallway later, pressing a finger into my chest. "Do you think that's enough?"

By this time, we'd played more than a few games of Never Have I Ever, so you knew how I'd respond. "It wouldn't be for me," I said on cue, and we lingered for a moment on the thought.

Our mischief was cut short by a band of carousers on their way to the kitchen. "Shannon wants me but she won't admit it!" you shouted, making a brisk exit. Lyle appeared in the expanding space between us.

"I'm a boy," I told him. It was a thing *I* said from time to time in those days. Something about feeling different from other girls.

"No, you're not," Lyle countered, dropping his eyes to the flesh heaving over my push-up bra.

"I like women and whiskey and camping," I informed him. "And I don't cry much." That last one often made me feel like a defective woman.

"I see," Lyle nodded. "Maybe you *are* a boy."

You and I picked up the risqué banter later on the deck. With each gathering we edged closer to our impending affair, always retreating to safety before night's end. It was a practical arrangement for a while. Then we found ourselves on that dance floor at Eden.

"I intend to crossdress," you announce now, a few weeks into July. You say it without smiling, all wide eyes and raised eyebrows. Then you lean against the couch and look at me, as if waiting for an objection.

"OK...?" I peer over the unwieldy book on front-end development I've lugged home from the office—my bonus depends on my acquisition of a new certification every quarter. The night of the makeover, you slept in my blouse. So I searched upscale thrift shops and surprised you with a free-size kimono. You were touched. You've slept in it ever since.

So your desire to crossdress has hardly escaped my notice.

But I put aside the book and give you my full attention. You want to crossdress in the daytime now, you say, and in public. That's significant for you, but honestly, it's not for me. Clothing rules are socially constructed, and "women's clothes" don't belong to women. As far as I'm concerned, anyone can wear whatever they want. We have no kids, so there's nothing to balance there. And while a bit of propriety is warranted when it comes to our careers, I won't yoke myself to a job that punishes petty "transgressions." Isabel, who found it shocking whenever I grabbed her hand in public, can attest.

In the personal taste department, I'm not your average woman, anyway. I'm attracted to few men, and those who catch my eye aren't classically masculine.

I'm not like my pageant-winning cousins. They married men who wear bespoke suits, run hunting lodges, and "summer" in Texas. By middle age, they'd been left for prettier, younger conquests. I've no use for alpha males, with their bland wardrobes and wandering eyes—I prefer your long hair and your pierced ears. Most of all, I prefer a self-actualized person, not a walking indicator of status or group membership. In you I have a real friend and a life partner, one I can't imagine losing to a midlife crisis.

Your fashion choices have always been enigmatic, anyway.

Before I met you, you went through what your friends call your "pirate phase." Darcy rolls her eyes when she speaks of the early Steven Tyler-inspired look: billowing poet shirts, lace-up vests and large hoop earrings. I think it sounds adorable; I'm sorry I missed it.

In the early days of our affair, you and Lyle wore mirrored aviator glasses and wrinkled Hawaiian shirts, signaling your affinity for Hunter S. Thompson. I thought it was fun, unaware it's an obligatory phase for pretentious young men of a certain demographic.

For several years you adopted a hobo look, no doubt inspired by family legends of the train-hopping, alcoholic grandfather you never knew. For this you wore a moth-eaten, floor-length wool jacket from the army surplus, a long scarf, and patched jeans. You wore this look proudly until Darcy, during a Twilight Zone marathon at her house, offhandedly called you "slovenly." You scoffed, but your friends agreed, indicating your loosening Willie Nelson braids and threadbare pants. Shortly afterward you changed your look again.

Next were the days of checkered shirts, dark blue Levis and the impressively large lumberjack beard. "It's not a good look," your youngest sister said. But she might have been the wrong age to appreciate the cachet it gave you with the Johnny Cash-loving hipsters that hung out at the Melody Inn on Punk Rock Night. You prided yourself, though, on not combing your beard or plying it with tea tree oil, carrying yourself like a regular blue-collar guy who was only accidentally in style. "I was raised in the country," you reminded me, when I assumed you'd curated the look for music scene cred. "This is authentically me."

And earlier this year, after we both lost a ton of weight, you shaved your face for the first time and switched to emo skinny jeans, high-top Chucks and long, tight tees from Urban Outfitters. The look accentuated your newly slim silhouette and went over well with the high school students you now teach Python programming to.

I've appreciated each of these looks and I'm game for whatever comes next. Crossdressing is sexy in its own way, and if I'm honest, I relish the thought of walking arm in arm with you as you flout the straight world's pointless rules.

Since we live in a small town and you work with kids, you've felt inhibited about crossdressing outside our home. But now you're longing for an outing in the city, away from the prying eyes of neighbors. I'd guessed as much. That's why I bought tickets to a Cincinnati showing of the *Rocky Horror Picture Show* for my turn at Date Night.

Our monthly Date Night has brought real variety to our entertainment routine. You know the rules: whoever's in charge chooses and pays for the evening's activities, which cannot be vetoed. Our arrangement staves off the rut that comes from always compromising. Seldom do we see the latest blockbuster; instead, we visit the butterfly show at the conservatory (your idea) or the demolition derby at the State Fair (mine). I get to see Ani Difranco when you would have saved your money for Wilco. And you get to eat at the Thai restaurant that's too sweet for my taste and take me to the Medical History Museum. For the third time this year.

Per the rules, I can do anything I please for Date Night. I could take you to the arts cinema to see one of the "gay foreign films" you accuse me of preferring. Or I could drag you to Wine & Pottery Night, one of those "chick activities" you're less than enthused about. But for ages I've wanted to revisit the *Rocky Horror Picture Show*, having enjoyed it in my younger days. And you can crossdress there. In the past you've complained that it's lame and starts too late. But that doesn't matter now. I'm invoking Date Night authority.

You love the idea.

"I like the word 'transvestite,'" you say, loudly enough to be heard over Avenged Sevenfold. You pull a plaid miniskirt from the rack and check its size. "It has a sort of old-school formality that I appreciate."

You need something to wear to the show, so I've brought you to Hot Topic, a teenage mall destination smelling of patent leather and lip gloss. A wall to the south is covered with corseted dresses, black and red and adorned with bows and skulls. Near the entrance a topless mannequin sports pleather hot shorts, ripped tights and over-the-knee boots. To the north, metal and hardcore t-shirts hang alongside fingerless gloves, seamed stockings and studded belts.

A high school girl with mermaid hair starts a fitting room with the dozen garments you've collected. I join you behind the thick black curtain, reading the band stickers plastering the walls while you try things on. "I'm an executive transvestite," you continue, squeezing into a babydoll dress.

We recently watched Eddie Izzard's "Dress to Kill." The comedian coined the term to distance himself from what he called "weirdo transvestites," like a Bronx man police found living in an underground lair amid guns, stolen goods and women's shoes. You admire the way Eddie integrates crossdressing into his life, refusing to let his clothes define him. That's what you want, you say. To wear what you please, even if it has some feminine flair, and to go about your business. If anyone accuses you of wearing women's clothes, you'll use Eddie's witty retort: "They're not women's clothes. They're my clothes."

An ultra-short skirt dangling with ripped tulle and garters meets with your approval. You become enamored with a pair of rainbow-colored thigh-highs, too. To complete the outfit we stop by a thrift store where you find a man-sized pair of chunky high-heel oxfords laced with fat ribbons.

When Date Night rolls around you rummage through your top drawer, lamenting that you forgot to buy underwear.

I'm intrigued. Are you worried your boxer briefs will peek out beneath your skirt? Or do you find the idea of wearing panties erotic? I'll ask when we can linger on the matter. For now, I cast about in my dresser and lend you a black boyshort trimmed with lace.

They're too small, but you love the look. You pull on your new skirt, thigh-highs and shoes, finishing with a Yoda t-shirt and an armful of leather wristbands. After shaving, you do your own makeup: a generous layer of foundation to hide the hint of stubble beneath your skin, black eyeliner and red lipstick. It's a bit much, but I assume that's what you want. I layer a sheer top over a cami, pull on jeans and combat boots, and twist my hair into two sloppy knots.

You hand me your phone so you can pose for photos: hands in front, hands in back, knock-kneed, head tilted. Eager to see, you grab the phone from my hand. But your face falls as you scroll through the gallery.

"I look garish," you say.

I shrug. "It's the *Rocky Horror Picture Show.*"

You grow quiet as you lock up the house and start your truck. I guess garish isn't the look you were going for.

The line to the theater spills into the street. You lower your eyes and fidget with your skirt as you fall in line behind me, conscious of your big legs and the clunky, ribboned shoes. We're the oldest people present. The punk kids waiting for the show greet us, but so do the senior citizens passing through on their way to dinner.

You scan for other crossdressers, smiling when a skinny twenty-something teeters past in a gold bustier and stilettos, raising laughs from the crowd with the punchline to a joke we've missed. With his plain boy's haircut and unadorned face, he looks like Perfume Genius. But when he grabs his girlfriend's hand, you assume he's an impostor. A pair dressed as Magenta and Columbia fail to make the cut, too—they're likely role-playing for the evening. You're convinced you're the only one present of your kind.

Taking a seat on a long pew in the sparse warehouse space, we examine the contents of the prop bag we purchased, trying to remember the purpose of the playing cards, the newspaper, the piece of toast. Meanwhile, the "virgins" in the house are identified and dragged front and center for their hazing. A man impersonating Brad in nerd glasses and tighty whities circles the cohort, threatening to rub his balls in the face of anyone who won't fake an orgasm while screaming her father's name. A woman of nineteen or twenty in a sailor dress grabs her fifteen minutes, filling the theater with screams and moans.

When the film rolls, we watch the crowd for cues, yelling "Asshole!" at Brad and "Slut!" at Janet, firing our water guns at the right time, littering the concrete with rice. The "Time Warp" turns into a conga line, sweeping us into a dance around the theater, hands on strangers' backs. Covered in confetti, our ears ringing, we turn onto Ludlow half-conscious in the small hours of the morning.

When we're snug in bed I dream I'm married to someone else. He's nice looking, intelligent, kind to me. But I'm distraught. *How did I get here?* I think. *This is not right.* I know, in the deepest part of my soul, that I've known true love. I labor to recall the specifics. I only know that my life with this other person is a grave mistake.

A moment before my eyelids drift upward, and I see the dull slant of moonlight stretch across the quilt, I remember you. I sense your heat and move toward it. Nestling my face into your back, I'm relieved to live in this world instead of that one. *This is the love that's meant to be,* I think.

It's a recurring dream. It casts ex-boyfriends and ex-girlfriends, kindly strangers and dark figures. But each dream partner is hopelessly wrong. And I can't recall you until the moment I awake and touch your skin, assured again that all is well with the world.

Sunlight floods your laptop as I part the curtains and raise the living room window to a cloudless sky. The air brims with the sounds of summer: the chitter of the young swallows, growing stronger in the nest. The low hum of distant cicadas. I settle onto the couch next to you with my textbook and a cup of tea, arranging index cards on the coffee table. I'd rather be cutting back the forsythia, but I have an exam to pass. I need to learn JavaScript prototype chaining.

You need to buy panties.

The boyshorts were all wrong, you tell me. They rode up and failed to keep things in place. Surely, you muse, a product exists to meet your needs. "Panties for crossdressers," you type into your search bar, articulating the words as you enter them. Muttering under your breath, you scroll and click as I hand-write programming terms onto the ruled lines of my cards.

"Whoa!" you cry out, spinning your laptop toward me. On your screen I spy a femme fatale with her back to the camera, platinum locks falling against bare skin, peering over her shoulder with full, parted lips.

"This is a dude," you say. There is reverence in your voice.

"No way." I squint to read the caption: "The androgynous Andrej Pejić—not afraid to be himself."

A succession of gender-bending fashionistas graces the "Inspiration" section of the crossdressers' bulletin board you've stumbled across. They hail from the street and the runway, each waify and weightless, with a sinewy masculinity underpinning an impossible body mass index. They peek through manes of tousled hair, draped in sheer scarves or unbuttoned men's shirts, splaying slender legs and baring hairless chests. You right-click and download a photo, wishing aloud for a way to preserve and organize the stash.

"You need Pinterest." I put away my flashcards and walk you through the creation of your first idea board, which you mark secret and name "Girly Boys." I'm all eyes as you pin Stav Strashko in a featherweight slip. Van Burnham in metal lacework. Seth Atwell in fur. They're smoking hot and I'm as smitten as you are. I want to help when I have the time, so you grant me contributor access.

Returning to the bulletin board, you find its members are two decades older than the girly boys who inspire them, with decidedly lower-brow tastes. They pose for a selfie thread in bodycon dresses or leopard-print heels, pursing lips, sticking out bottoms, channeling Bettie Page. You call it "off-putting," moving on to the thread that brought you to this site—a discussion of favorite products, starting with those panties you wanted.

Available in pastel shades of lace, they boast a "contour pouch" in front for accommodating their clients' anatomy. As you head to the foyer to fetch your wallet, an ad slides into the page's margin. It's for a "body shaper"—a pair of silicone shorts that look more like an off-brand pocket pussy than a garment. Mounted unnaturally high on the pubis, presumably for easy viewing, is a molded labia crudely etched in florid red lines. The ad slides left just as you return.

When you've ordered two pairs of panties, you read through the thread. Experienced crossdressers, you learn, prefer breast forms from suppliers that serve mastectomy patients. You find that troubling. "I'll never wear prostheses," you say, launching into your burgeoning philosophy on the matter. You want to be yourself, not impersonate someone else. You can't imagine "strapping on breasts or hips or a butt." You'll never "put on a girl suit."

I start to crack open my textbook but the post you click on next catches my eye. "Crossdressing has strained my marriage," it begins. Comments beneath number in the hundreds. "Mine too," they all seem to say. One contributor's wife worries he's gay. Another's claims that hormone treatments have wrecked their sex life. Couples clash over surgery, impotence, sexual demands and unchecked spending.

I look at you, perplexed. I hadn't worried about any of these things. Should I?

"The trick is to establish boundaries," says someone whose badge reads "charter member." "Let your partner set them. Respect them. It's the only way to stay together."

Another agrees. At his wife's request, he dresses only at home—never in public. Still another negotiated the opposite deal: dressing only at out-of-town events. Some wives limit their partner's dressing to once a week. Others draw the line at bringing it into the bedroom. "I feel lucky that my girlfriend puts up with this at all," one member says. "So I honor her wishes."

You close your laptop and swivel to face me. "Let's talk about boundaries," you say. You take my hand in yours, explore its contours with your fingers. "I'll abide by any rule. I'll give this up completely, if you want. It's one hundred percent up to you."

I love that you're checking in with me—it's so very *you*. I think for a second, though I know there's nothing to think about. The fact that you offered means the world to me. It shows your compassion, one of the things I appreciate about you.

Compassion is one of my three highest values.

"I don't need to make rules," I say.

I expect to see relief in your eyes; instead I see pleading. "I'm not gay. You know that, right? You're the sexiest thing in the world to me."

I do know. We've always had a sexually charged relationship, and our passion has not waned with time.

"What happened with Blaze was purely sexual. I can only fall in love with women."

You're referring to your one and only homosexual encounter; we've discussed it many times. It happened ages ago, when a friend from high school came to visit while Melanie was away. Blaze was an older guy you admired—he always seemed to have concert tickets or an album by an obscure band. The two of you smoked a joint together, then he pushed you onto your back and kissed you. One thing led to another until you were unbuckling his belt and giving him what he wanted. Then he had a crisis of conscience and bailed on reciprocation. Still, you thought of the incident fondly, if with a measure of shame. I've always felt honored that you trusted me enough to share it with me.

It shows your honesty. Honesty is another of my three highest values.

"I don't want surgery," you add. "I like my penis."

"I like it, *too*," I say, attempting a lecherous tone.

31

But you're in no mood to joke.

I don't need to be convinced—you like sex too much to go that route. And you were terrified when you got your gall bladder removed. "It's OK," I assured you for the third time, kissing your forehead as the anesthesiologist wheeled you away. In truth, I was worried too. Someone planned to open your flesh and remove a living, pulsating part of you. I couldn't take such a breach of your bodily integrity lightly.

"I'll always respect your wishes," you say, letting go of my hands and wrapping your arms around me. "You can change your mind at any time."

I press my cheek against your neck and allow myself the indulgence of gratitude—for you, for fearless intimacy, for *us*.

You lean back and look into my eyes, your own moist with emotion. "I won't let anything come between us," you say. "Least of all this."

But I have no doubt. With compassion and honesty, we'll make this work.

"Are you here?" you ask, quoting some Zen kōan you often refer to. I don't remember the story or its lesson. But I know how I'm supposed to respond.

"Yes," I say. "I am here."

"Then have a cup of tea," you say.

"The kettle is still hot. I'll pour us some."

I walk to the kitchen buoyed by a familiar feeling: that we are exceptionally resilient as a couple. More than steeled against whatever life may throw at us. That I am loved, supported, prioritized. I want more than ever to give you room to do what you want to do. It's clear you'll never take advantage of that.

I return with two steaming cups, placing one on the coffee table near you. But you're confounded by whatever's on your laptop screen. Your eyes narrow as you scan the text. Your forehead wrinkles.

"What's up?" I ask.

"I don't get this." You've found a joke on the bulletin board that's purportedly well-known in the queer community. "What's the difference between a crossdresser and a transgender person?"

"I don't know," I say. What is it?"

"Two years."

I'm baffled too. Is this a thing?

People say of certain jokes: "It's funny because it's true." This will be one of those.

But for you, it will take only months.

TWO | AUGUST
BETTER THAN GAY

That night in Yellowwood State Forest, in the early days of our affair, I lost the borders of my body. I forgot where mine ended and yours began, where the two of us stopped and the night air started. We fucked relentlessly, sliding into an uncanny realm where exertion was effortless, losing five or six hours. The stars breached our tent and circulated through us. You were on top. We flipped. I was on top. Then gravity failed and direction lost meaning and there was no such thing as top. I later said it was an out-of-body experience. You called it "tantric."

Tonight, in an August heat untamed by the open window, you lie on your back and I straddle you. My knees are on the bed outside your hips, my right hand on the headboard to steady me. The caress of repetition has blotted out conscious thought and left me in that same space of pure sensation. I'm satisfied with the generosity of the universe, your hand grazing my hip, your damp hair fanned on the pillow. I rock against your body in a rhythm that's not too fast and not too slow, like the drum track of *When the Levee Breaks*, climbing a steady rise. I'm oblivious to sweat and strain and for the moment I'm sure I could go on forever.

But now I'm losing my balance. You're struggling, shifting around. You seem to be up to something.

You splay your legs out like a bullfrog, jostling to position them outside mine. Their efforts prevail, knocking my knees together and causing me to fall forward. I now lie on my stomach on top of you, my legs between yours. You put your hands on my waist and wrap your ankles around my butt. I see where you're going with this: I'm now the man and you're now the woman. You want me to pretend I'm penetrating you.

It isn't what I had in mind, but I'll play. I try to move between your legs but it's hard to keep you inside me. The angle is all wrong. You need to be underneath, at the entrance, pushing upward. Instead you're angled to pass up the target, only a bend in your flesh allowing now shallow penetration. You're pressed too hard against me where I'm most sensitive. It chafes.

I want to give you this thing you want so I throw myself into the game, hoping to drive us toward its efficient conclusion. Cradling your neck with one arm, and bracing myself with the other, I move my body forward and backward, staying close so you won't slip out. "Are you able to imagine it?" I whisper. You nod.

I get in the headspace, too. The feeling of friction between us softens and blurs, becomes something it isn't. Your flesh is mine, mine is yours. I'm pitching. You're catching. It's remarkable how well we can conjure the illusion using only our imaginations. I exaggerate my thrusts in a display of dominance that meets with your approval, understanding intuitively that you want to be taken. Like a possession. Like a prize. I call you a little bitch, tell you I'm making you my wife. You melt. But it still takes longer than I would like. When I finally roll off you, my urethra feels bruised.

"I can't wait to become an old man," you said, spreading a comforter across the living room floor. Remember that evening? It was seven years ago, the day we took possession of this farmhouse. The place was unfurnished but we were eager to spend our first night here. We had a duffel bag of necessities, something to read and each other—what more did we need? The attic bedroom was stifling—we needed to install roof vents, the inspector had said. But the living room, with its windows open to a cooling purple twilight, felt perfect.

"What's so great about getting old?" I asked, failing to suppress a chuckle. I was in no hurry to get old. I didn't know *anyone* was. Together we spread out a sheet, then a worn quilt we'd found at an antique store, its squares comprising a pattern my aunt called "providence." Though it was simple and its edges were frayed with age, it was carefully hand-sewn from the soft, patterned gingham of old feed sacks.

"There's a grace in it," you said, as I switched off the overhead lights and turned on the sconce in the foyer. We'd need a bit of light for navigating the unfamiliar house at night.

Grace. There's a good word. It is perhaps one of my *favorite* words. Or at least one of my favorite concepts.

Plopping onto our pallet, I pulled my shoulder tote into my lap, rifling through the books inside. We'd long ago started a tradition of visiting the library once a week. Since we returned so often, I chose my titles on a whim and swapped them out frequently, choosing a how-to on tie dye as often as a classic novel. I packed the books into my tote and carried them everywhere, reading a bit when work was slow or I found myself standing in a long line. That night I had a selection of philosophy books—a perennial favorite—and a pocket-sized dictionary. You fluffed a pillow and reclined next to me as I found the first definition of "grace" and read it aloud, squinting in the dim light: *"Simple elegance."*

But that wasn't right at all.

The second definition came closer: "courteous goodwill." But neither carried the connotations *I* associate with the word. Aging gracefully, after all, does not mean staying stylish. And showing grace under fire is not the same as being amiable. Grace is something more important and more enduring. But how to define it? It's a constellation of traits making up a specific character. It's easier to describe than to define.

A Buddhist friend of yours calls "grasping" the source of all suffering. A person with grace doesn't grasp. She accepts reality in its imperfection. She watches and waits instead of trying to control. And she does so unflinchingly. Grace is an act of *courage*.

Courage is the third of my highest values.

Yes—there *is* a grace in growing old. It's shedding your youthful vanity because it doesn't serve you anymore. It's growing out of your physical beauty and into your wisdom.

"There's a reprieve from social expectations," you added, resting a hand on your expanding waistline. You stroked your whiskers with the other. "When I'm old, I'll be a mall Santa."

I thought of you in that red suit and smiled. Your unruly beard, naturally amber and already flecked with gray, would imbue your performance with a certain credibility.

You said you couldn't wait to spend your golden years puttering around this house. You declared you'd never move again. "They'll carry me out of here on a stretcher," you said.

We reiterated our plans. I'd found a developer position nearby. You'd make the long commute to your old job in Indianapolis for a while. Later you'd transition to full-time homemaker. "I'll be your wife," you said, alluding to my comment at Rory's party—which seemed like a feasible goal. I hated keeping house, after all, and you claimed to like it. A division of labor would facilitate our homesteading plans.

We'd get a pair of goats; we've loved them since we befriended the one at the apple orchard. A Nigerian Dwarf would provide milk for yogurt and farmer's cheese, which we could sell. An Angora could be sheared for mohair, which we'd spin and share with our friends who knit. The animals would browse our overgrown three-acre lawn, knocking back brush and berry-laden poison ivy.

You'd make pickles, kraut, and apple cider vinegar. You'd enlist your mom to teach you pressure canning. We'd cover our land with pecan and fruit trees for food and ground-covering sedums to reduce the area that needed mowing. We'd add solar panels, water our garden from a rain barrel and maybe even get a windmill. We'd barter—a neighbor had already agreed to exchange her hens' freshly laid eggs for computer maintenance. Eventually I'd start freelancing and drop out of the rat race, too. Leaving the city—with its gourmet restaurants and specialty stores—would be a challenge. But we yearned for the fresher air and slower pace of country living. It would feed our souls, we thought, to head eastward, leaving behind the stop-and-go traffic and the noise pollution. We didn't need so much stuff anyway. All we needed was each other. All we needed was love.

"This house is 'worlding,'" I said, retrieving *Being and Time* from my tote. Since I'd studied it for a class we returned to it often. Its message of fully "being" fueled our decision to move to the country.

"Yes," you agreed. "And the things in this room are 'thinging.'"

The world is not to be described in the soulless language of science, Heidegger thought, as interactions between disconnected objects. The world is to be understood through *poetry*. The world is a place to dwell, and to dwell is to *belong*. Therein lies "worlding." Nor are things discrete bits of matter. A carafe is not merely a cylinder some cubic inches in volume, some case study in physics. It's a vessel for sharing wine with friends in celebration. Therein lies "thinging."

We appreciated Heidegger's respect for divinity. And Nietzsche's, too: his famous cry that "God is dead" lamented the world's loss of wonder. We were atheists, then as now. But neither philosopher was concerned with literal deities. Each spoke of the void left in human hearts when belief in the enchanted is lost and only cold materialism remains. They, and others, warned that the conditions of modern life—urban living, individualism, technology, our war against nature—rob people of happiness and purpose. But we know too much to find comfort in premodern mysticism, so we struggle to create meaning in our lives. That's the *crisis of modernity*. It's a notion we'd become obsessed with.

I don't buy into the religious or the paranormal. I *know* everything is made of matter. But I do believe in the sacred. The sacred is another thing. It doesn't come from berobed men carrying flaming tablets etched with rules. But it does lie beyond the explanatory power of science.

I first knew the sacred as a small child, when I wandered outside at three a.m. and raised my eyes, for the first time, to a staggering number of stars against a crystal-clear sky, whirling into infinity.

I find the sacred in the bright little prism cast onto the grass by the spray of a garden hose when I water my roses under a scorching summer sun.

I find it when I can see for miles, when I have stared into the eyes of a wild animal, and when my dreams are dark voices from my subconscious, arising so vividly I'm sure I've been dropped into another time and place. I see it in the jagged channels of light carved into the night air by a metal sparkler on my birthday, the Fourth of July.

It is the sacred that makes life meaningful.

The sacred is what can't be reduced to reason or evolutionary function. It's what is more than the sum of its parts. Love belongs to this realm. Music, too. And sex, when it's transcendent. The alchemy of the sacred transforms the mundane into the profound.

"This *whole place* is worlding," you said. We had come to use the term as shorthand for the feeling that our surroundings were benevolent and familiar and imbued with meaning.

We talked about how to fight the crisis. We rejected postmodernism, with its call to "burn it all down." Renounce reason, it says. Distrust justice. Eliminate morality. Destroy truth. To throw away what's *good* about modernity, along with the bad, is to give in to what Michel Foucault called "the 'blackmail' of the enlightenment." My path was to seek out the sacred and hold onto it. Yours lay in Eastern philosophy: learning to be happy with less. Meditation. Self-control.

You dug in the duffel and pulled out *The Story of B*. "Then again," you said, "Daniel Quinn calls Eastern and Western philosophy two sides of the same coin."

"Like horseshoe theory."

"Before agriculture," you said, "we had a simpler way of life. Quinn calls our alienation from it 'The Great Forgetting.'"

Just then the power flickered and went out.

The darkness lay broken up by moonlight, but the silence was complete. No appliance beeped or hummed. No car engine whirred in the distance. The people of the town had settled in for the night and even their dogs were quiet.

"We will be OK," you said, laying your head on my shoulder. "Humans are meaning-makers." We lay motionless, watching the slow sway of elms in silhouette, until our eyelids faltered and we teetered along the precipice of sleep.

An otherworldly shriek woke us. A chorus of blood-curdling clamors joined, first in short bursts, then in long wails. The sounds became indistinguishable, a wall of witchy wailing that reached for the sky like Saturn Missiles.

We didn't speak, each nervous, I suspect, about the open window. Each paralyzed by indecision. I'd heard only one other sound in its league: the screech owl that haunted our campsite that night in

Yellowwood. But this was something else. A banshee. A grieving woman from the faerie realm, gray hair streaming as she foretold of death.

Coyotes were more likely, we decided, when the baying ended and we found our voices.

We dwelled there, that night, under the antique quilt, a thing thinging with its history of feed sacks and the seeds they once carried and the farmhouses and beds and floors it had seen. We beheld the worlding of the darkening sky and the swaying elms and the silence and the howl. This was the sacred, I thought. The wail of coyotes cutting through the night's stillness. The communion between us—the meeting of minds, of bodies. The comfort and constancy of your presence. Our journey through the city, through the country. The long ribbon of our future unfurling ahead, assured and safe.

The magic that dwelled there, with us, when science was done with its explaining.

The morning brings a familiar burning between my legs, and not the fun kind. It's a urinary tract infection, brought on by sustained irritation. The clinics are closed on Sunday and those antibiotics give me a yeast infection anyway, so I'll drink cranberry juice and wait until I pee blood before considering the emergency room. When you rise, I break the news to you—our sexual role-swap won't work for me. There will be no repeat performance. You're bummed but you don't complain, and soon your thoughts turn to what to wear. You browse my skirts, promising you'll get your own soon.

"I'm going to order a corset," you say, settling into the couch with your laptop open to the crossdressers' bulletin board. Though you complain about the site, it keeps drawing you back. You've even added it to your news aggregator.

"You can borrow mine," I say, raising the window to an empty nest. The fledglings are standing along the string of porch lights, their mother flitting in and out in a demonstration of flight.

You shake your head. It seems the little red number you got me one Valentine's Day isn't good enough. "I need a waist trainer," you say. Like Kim Kardashian's."

What's a waist trainer? And when did you start following the reality TV socialite? I'm about to ask when you draw my attention to an email from Paige, who's been campaigning to get us back to Indianapolis.

She's forwarded a job opening at Cuppajoe Media, the hippest new employer there. They're housed downtown in an open industrial space paneled with reclaimed barnwood and flooded with natural light. They run an online arts magazine, sponsor literary readings and coordinate an annual benefit for the poor. The startup was founded by friends of Paige, and she's vying for their poetry editor position. "One of you should apply," she writes.

It's an opportunity to work in a cool space with smart people doing artsy things—what's not to love? But the position—an easy mishmash of web design, communication and light IT skills—is better suited for a jack-of-all-trades like you. I work in a lucrative niche, and thanks to my recent certification, I'm being considered for team lead. We can't weather a cut in my pay.

You spend the afternoon sprucing up your resume and emailing Paige, the two of you embroidering tales of your future at Cuppajoe: brainstorming sessions in beanbag chairs, meetings with famous authors, walks to downtown hotspots for bánh mi and steak tartare. It's hard not to feel jealous.

On a spring afternoon during fifth grade recess, I sat on a far corner of the lawn. Grass stained my dress, but I didn't care—making chains of clover blossoms was more appealing than asking to join someone's game of tag. I was an introvert, and thanks to my parents' penchant for drinking, not particularly well-liked. I faced away from the schoolyard, looking through a chain-link fence. I was eleven.

Inside the fence was a field for playing sports, an activity I neither understood nor appreciated. On this particular day girls from a neighboring school used the lot for softball practice. I stared absent-mindedly in their direction, seeking only to look occupied. A girl named Wendy Thomas stepped up to the plate. I knew *of* her—she was a classmate's older sister—but I didn't *know* her. As a grade schooler, I had little occasion to interact with someone who went to middle school.

In retrospect, Wendy was a plain-looking girl. Her hair, feathered and shoulder-length, was a light reddish-brown that was neither here nor there. Her smile revealed front teeth just a bit too large for her mouth. She wore a t-shirt, running shorts and banded knee socks. But as I watched Wendy lift and swing her bat—which she seemed to do in slow motion, that day—I felt a dull ache in my lower belly I'd never before felt while looking at another human being.

Her hair blew back, as if she were a model doing a photo shoot, and its copper highlights caught the sun. Her muscles flexed as she swiveled through the swing, showing off strong arms and sturdy teenage legs. Focused on her task, she looked confident, capable—like an adult. I saw in her a beauty I hadn't seen before, least of all in the ladies with the plunging necklines gracing *Cosmo*, the ones I was told were beautiful. Wendy was three dimensional. She was powerful. She was a *person*.

Some things suddenly made sense to me. Like why, when the other girls asked who I liked, I settled on Ollie, a delicate, long-haired boy who was younger than me. Why, when I won a poster playing darts at the fair, I picked the one of Farrah in the crimson swimsuit—not the one of Shawn Cassidy. Why I couldn't quit looking at photos of Kristy McNichol in my *Tiger Beat* magazine.

"I think I'm gay," I announced to my mom after school. This was not OK with my Christian mother. But it also wasn't believable. She looked startled, then amused. Then she sat me down for a talk.

"Wendy's a couple years older than you," she said. "The perfect age for a role model." Maybe I was impressed by Wendy's athleticism.

Maybe I liked her fashion sense or wanted to copy her hairstyle. Maybe I was just looking forward to leaving the tween years and becoming a young woman. It was perfectly normal to admire other girls. So don't worry, she assured me; while being a homosexual was a crime against God, I was not one.

I believed her, sort of, in the way religious-indoctrinated youth believe such things. I repeated her theory like a mantra when I fell for Sandra Prewitt, then Julie Nicholson, then Karen Estes, all the while tormented by a hunger I came to believe haunts admiration. When I fantasized about women, I called it sin. When I found a guy mildly interesting, I built up its significance. I worked hard at being attracted to men even after I admitted to myself and others I was attracted to women. Sometimes I would almost succeed.

Over a decade after noticing Wendy, I found myself rolling around with her brother on the floor of his studio apartment. He was a catch— good looking and smart and a working artist. He knew I preferred women; perhaps he saw me as a challenge. When we made out, my passion would mount for a moment, then drop off abruptly. He noticed. I shrugged. There was someplace I'd rather be.

Wendy's brother didn't care for unrequited lust so he set me free. But other men tried harder. I found I could maintain arousal if I drilled deep into my own head, losing myself in fantasy. I was less successful at inventing love, though, so I came to think of myself as incapable of it. I dated men I couldn't commit to, enhancing the sex with my imagination. I pushed away the suspicion that this was unhealthy or sad. After all, it was better than being gay.

Anything, my world had taught me thus far, was better than being gay.

Your family gathers around the island in your brother's kitchen, seemingly oblivious to your patterned jeans and subtly flared blouse. Jake's wife Rosa, who has changed into scrubs and sent Nina and Lia to their rooms, scoops freshly ground coffee into the filter basket. She has to leave shortly; since finishing her residency she's at the hospital most evenings and weekends.

Your aunt is here—she never misses anything. Your sister Jill, a house painter who crashes at your dad's when she can't get work, is here. Your brother Jeremy and his long-time partner Tegan, both hermits who skip their share of family events, are present. Even your youngest sister Jessica, who works in retail and has little control over her schedule, has made it. It's unfortunate your mother's no longer with us; it's otherwise a perfect turnout. But it's not often you call a family meeting.

I bet people think I'm pregnant.

"I want to come out to my family!" you announced early this week. I still don't understand why. Does your family need to be apprised of your clothing choices? If I know them, they won't be fazed.

Maybe it's because we're moving back to Indy, so we'll see them more often. Your boss knocked on our door while you were dressed one day, provoking abject panic. "Tell him I'm in the shower," you said, darting about the room like a rabbit in the way of a car. I kept him occupied as you changed, but it was a close call. "I can't live this way," you said afterward. "Let's get serious about moving."

"I have something to say," you announce now, as the chatter dies down. "I am transgender!"

It's the first time you've used that word to describe yourself—and I wish I wasn't hearing it here first. It's confusing, to say the least. You've gone out of your way to call yourself a "crossdresser." You've said that identity is "valid" and not to be confused with a "female gender identity." You're a man, you've said repeatedly. A man with a feminine side.

Maybe you're reaching for language you think your family will understand. Maybe, like Eddie Izzard, you're distancing yourself from "weirdo transvestites," or even the ones from the bulletin board with their leopard-print heels. I'll ask you about it later. I'll make sure I understand what "transgender" means to you.

Scanning the faces in the room, I find your family looks unconcerned. But a moment passes while they wonder what to say.

"That's fine," Jessica says, at last.

"Sure," Jake echoes, shrugging.

Jill looks restless. For years, she's avoided her own "big reveal." Though she's introduced you and me to a couple of her girlfriends, she's never let the rest of the family know she's a lesbian. I suspect her secret propels her chronic depression and tendency to drink too much.

Your dad looks amused. I half expect him to deploy his favorite response to personal confessions—"this is none of my business." Your aunt looks conflicted, but folds her arms and nods. Tegan seems unperturbed, as does Jeremy, who now shakes a new role-playing card game from its package. As the usual family rumbling commences, there's a palpable sense that you're overthinking things. Jake brings chips and hummus to the dining room as Jeremy deals out the first hand.

You see your family as reticent. I see them as the closest-knit I've ever known. They are affectionate even if they don't gush. They are caring even if they don't meddle. It's clear, by the way they gather for every major and minor holiday, that they genuinely enjoy one another's company. Now they quibble over faeries and elves, form alliances and lob accusations of cheating; but they also banter and laugh and play again.

"Does this mean you'll have surgery?" your aunt asks, when we've packed up our stuff and started our goodbyes.

"My genitals are no one's business," you say.

She recoils. I feel bad for her—she's family, after all, and too old to know what's politically correct. I give her an extra-long squeeze as we part. You've told me you're averse to surgery, anyway. Why not just say so?

"How do you develop self-esteem?" you ask, as you start your truck.

It isn't the first time someone's noted my good self-esteem. But until now, you've never let on that yours is in peril. I knew it, though. After your divorce, you had your own place for a while. While looking for a misplaced sock one day, I found something under your bed. It was a poster board covered with statements in your handwriting.

"I hate myself," it said. And "I'm ugly." And "I'm worthless." And a hundred other things, covering every square inch of the thin white board. I put it back where I found it. I never mentioned it.

"I'm not sure I can explain," I say. And it's true.

Poor self-esteem, ironically, seems self-important to me.

I know a woman who refuses to be photographed. She throws her hand in front of her face when a camera is pointed her way. Others try to console her: She looks fine. They want a record of the moment, not a perfectly posed masterpiece. She thinks she's protecting them from her hideous looks. Instead, she's allowing her hangup to ruin their photo. Her flaws are utterly ordinary, just like everyone else's. Self-esteem isn't the conviction that you look amazing. It's the acceptance that you don't. Self-esteem is humility.

It's about integrity, too, of course. But you're compassionate and honest; your character is easily sufficient. I think you're ashamed of your bisexuality. But self-esteem, like grace, is an act of courage. Joan Didion called it "moral nerve."

I have good self-esteem because I'm ordinary and I know it. My shortcomings don't call for some great penance. We all suffer frailties and temptations. We all fail. I am as bad as anyone.

But I am as good as anyone, too.

THREE | SEPTEMBER
SWEET Transvestite

"I swear it's me," you say to the server checking your ID. Your mugshot's that of a chubby man with a sizable beard and a low-slung, dishwater ponytail. Tonight, you're thin and clean-shaven with your sun-bleached hair around your shoulders. You're wearing my denim miniskirt with your new knee-high boots and a long, flouncy scarf.

"Nah—you look great," he says, with a genuine smile. We seldom visit mall bars, but a martini sounds great after a day of shopping. You order a traditional one with gin. I go for the one with Godiva chocolate.

When the drinks arrive you propose a toast—to my promotion to team lead. It's thoughtful of you. I *am* proud, especially since I outcompeted a male colleague with more time on the job. With any luck, we'll be celebrating your success next. Though you were nervous about wearing a dress to the Cuppajoe interview, the hiring manager was unfazed and the staff loved you. You were slick at answering the questions and more than demonstrated the relevant skills.

You dig through your shopping bags, evaluating today's purchases. We've been coming to Newport on the Levee, a charming little shopping complex near downtown Cincinnati, nearly every weekend. It's enough off our beaten path that we won't run into people we know, and it's got a store you love—Kelley's Kloset. Everything there is under twenty dollars, so you can build your wardrobe without going broke. Today the young women who work there—who always seem thrilled to see you, and call you by name—helped you find a ladies' button-up blouse without darts, a coveted item you can sneak into your work wardrobe.

You enjoy walking the mall dressed, usually in a silky shirt, a necklace, and a pair of tight pants. Sometimes you completely shave your face, but often you wear the short, soft beard that looks so good on you. With your mostly androgynous wardrobe, you look more like a rock star than anything. Still, the response has been overwhelmingly positive, and that's a pleasant surprise.

Only once has someone been rude—and you weren't around. While trying on a blouse in the changing room of a coat store, I heard two employees chatting near the entrance.

"Did you see the fruitcake in the ladies' department with the short pants and the purse?" the man asked. You *were* wearing capri pants, but your bag was just a military canvas messenger. The woman roared as her colleague mocked your clothing, doubted your prowess in bed and questioned your sexual orientation. He got a little vicious, and it shook me up. I considered stepping out to defend you—maybe telling him you're my husband, and you're sexing me up quite well, thank you very much. But I wasn't sure you'd approve.

I kept it to myself for a while, fearing you'd be devastated. When I finally got it off my chest, you laughed it off. "People will talk," you said.

You stuff your acquisitions back into the bag and stir your martini. "'Transvestite' is a poetic word," you say, continuing a monologue you've been polishing for weeks.

"Is that how you identify?" I'm still curious about the words you chose on coming out day at your family's.

"It sure is," you say. "I'm a crossdresser—a kind of trans man. We're the least understood of the transgender spectrum."

It's good to have a bit of clarification.

"I'm a man who enjoys fashion," you continue. "And that's OK. Why should beautiful clothing be reserved for women?" You're in good company, you point out—crossdressing is practically the norm for musicians. You love Ziggy Stardust's space-age jumpsuit and the glam of eighties hair metal artists. "Even Kurt Cobain," you say, dropping your credit card on the bill that materializes, "has performed in a floral dress."

"And how about the lead singer of the Black Crowes?" I say. "In that video for 'Remedy.'" As I recall, he wore velvet pants and chandelier earrings. I thought he looked sexy throwing himself around, flashing his toned belly. His retro style reminded me of my brother's friends in the seventies. They wore slinky, half-buttoned shirts and low-rise jeans and they tamed their billowing hair with headbands. I came of age admiring young men who asserted their softer side as elders sneered, calling them "draft dodgers" and "queers."

"I need to visit the facilities," I say, as we exit back into the mall.

"Me too." You hesitate, then turn your attention to the single-occupancy family restrooms positioned outside the men's and women's. "I'll be over there."

I nod. But you launch a defense: you feel silly going into the men's room in a skirt. At the same time, you don't want to creep out the women. I smile at your thoughtfulness, but your tone grows serious. "I'll always respect women's boundaries," you say, as if the choice is obvious.

"Can we make another stop?" you ask, when we reconvene. "I need a bra."

I'm amused at your use of the word "need." But a self-conscious panic washes over your face, so I wipe the smile from mine.

"I need your help," you say, with gravity. "I don't know how to navigate a bra department."

"Of course," I say. "But I didn't think you wanted breasts?"

"I'm not going to stuff it."

That's interesting. I'm not exactly sure what to look for, then.

"What is it you want from a bra?"

"I'm not ready to examine that too closely," you say.

I guess your interest is erotic. You blushed and deflected when I asked about the panties, too. For the first time in our lives, you're keeping your thoughts in a closely guarded Black Box. I trust it's temporary; that you'll let me in once I prove I'm more than willing to cherish this side of you.

We can't find your size, because bras aren't made for your build— flat in the chest but wide in the rib cage. I show you a lace cami that will look sexy but fit you better—but you shake your head. You want a "real bra."

As you drive us home, I put my mind to the task. A lace leisure bra without structured cups might work. I'll shop online and surprise you with one.

Back home, a backache and a migraine forewarn of my impending period. Pain killers aren't making a dent—maybe I can find that missing heating pad. Dragging a chair to the bathroom cabinet, I strain to reach a plastic bin in the back of a deep shelf. I try to inch it forward, instead sending it crashing to the floor. You arrive to investigate, helping me collect an Ace bandage, some out-of-date contact lenses and a long-neglected electric toothbrush.

"What's this?" you ask. You hold up a white wand with wire coils and a carefully bundled power cord.

"It's an epilator." I retrieve the heating pad from a corner of the room. "That thing's been around for twenty years. I should throw it out."

"What's an epilator?"

"An alternative to shaving. It pulls out hair by the roots."

You turn it over in your hand with interest. "I want to shave my legs with it," you say. "And my arms."

"Give it a try before you say that. It's widely considered a torture device."

You unroll the cord and plug it in, gently touching the whirring coils.

"And don't shave your arms," I suggest. "It won't look right and it will make them itch."

You run the device lightly across the back of your forearm; it tangles up the hair and savagely rips out a patch. "Holy shit," you scream, letting go. "That hurts like hell!"

"I told you." I watch the appliance twist and turn like a snake as it dangles a few inches from the floor. You pull it up carefully by its cord and turn off the power. Cradling it in your hands, you examine the controls.

I explain the speed settings: the right one, unfortunately, is the one that hurts. Dial it up too fast, and you'll break off the hairs instead of pulling them out, which will leave you with worse stubble than if you'd shaved. Taking a hot bath first will open your pores. And if you use it every day, there'll be less hairs to pull and less pain. "It takes skill and endurance," I warn you. If you're going to use the god-forsaken thing, you're going to need these tips.

Undaunted, you place the epilator in your shaving drawer.

"Waist training works," you say, for the third time since your corset arrived. You pull the nude-colored contraption around your waist as I tighten the laces on my sneakers. We're preparing for our Sunday walk.

The garment, heavy-duty and lined with twenty-four rigid steel bones, is more sculpture than article of clothing. I am reminded of so many feminine cages of yore: Catherine de' Medici's iron girdle, a medieval scold's bridle for hushing a nagging wife, a Victorian crinoline of whalebone and horsehair. The Spanx I wore under my wedding dress is leisurewear in comparison.

"From what I've read, that's far from settled."

But I'm being polite—there's no evidence that thing works. Regular use, the myth goes, will permanently alter your body into an hourglass shape—something about fat redistribution or floating ribs. I can't believe you've bought into the idea, considering how mercilessly you and Lyle chide others about their unproven "woo." I watch you grab the edges of the tiny bodice in a death grip, your hands shaking as you struggle to make them meet.

"That looks about three sizes too small," I say as you bring the edges ever closer, still failing to close a single hook and eye.

"It's supposed to be that way."

In fact, you tell me, you've been wearing it for twenty minutes a day on the loosest row of closures and now it's time to tighten it. You pull it up toward your chest, suck in your gut and thrust your hands together, your biceps flexing as you finally get a closure fastened. The next two close more easily. You pull the corset down into place and fasten the remaining sixteen.

"What about the fainting?" I picture Pittypat in *Gone with the Wind* collapsing into the arms of her friends.

You smooth the garment and straighten your back.

"And the organ damage and the cracked ribs?" I've done some research into your new hobby and I'm not impressed with the cost/benefit analysis.

"I'm careful," you say.

But I doubt there's a careful way to compress your organs into a rigid cylinder several inches smaller than your natural waist.

You layer your t-shirt over the corset as I grab some carrots from the fridge for the painted horses down the road. It's a two-mile round trip to their barn and back, perfect for keeping off the weight we've lost.

"I can't wait to start working at Cuppajoe Media," you say as we turn onto the gravel road. You haven't heard from them yet, but you felt great about the interview. So you've gone ahead and notified your boss that you won't be renewing your teaching contract after spring.

Though Labor Day's around the corner, summer lingers on, dotting the landscape with prickly seed pods and little brown grasshoppers. The horses come running as we near the split-log fence. The friendly one gobbles a carrot from my hand as you try to coax the shy one closer. Reaching into the bag, you notice the outline of your corset pressing through your t-shirt.

"What if someone we know stops to talk to us?" you ask, pulling nervously at the hem of your shirt.

It's true; that could happen. You've stopped dressing only at home and you've started removing the hair from your arms and legs. With that comes the risk of getting caught—a risk you've chosen. You could easily wear the corset only at home, forgo the bra you don't need, even skip making appearances at the mall. Haven't you deemed whatever you get from dressing worth the risk?

"If you're worried on my account," I say, "don't be."

But there's something strange in your expression, a sort of shock—as though you've met with this danger through no fault of your own. As though your clothes are not something you put on, but something that springs from your body, like a stigmata, destined to give you away. You seem to simultaneously need, and yet resent, the risk of exposure.

Homesteading never really worked out for us, anyway. That's what I remind myself when I'm sad about our decision to move back to the city.

We never really made friends here.

When you started working at the school we acquired a bit of a social network. We can count on your boss to drag us out of a ditch on a snowy day. We can bum a jump start off the farmer across the street.

But these people aren't actual *friends*. We'll never hang out with them on a Saturday night.

A friendly couple kept their horses in a nearby lot for a while, and we enjoyed talking to them. But then they ended their lease. Then we developed a rapport with the bartender and the chef at a craft brewery that opened in a neighboring town. But they were young and busy and too hip to hang out with a couple of old people who live in the sticks.

Once we met a couple I regret not keeping in contact with. We were seated next to them at the hibachi at a Japanese steakhouse in that same town. They shared our taste in music and they'd just moved to the area so they were looking for new friends. We jotted our numbers on slips of paper, promising to keep in touch.

When I suggested meeting up with them later, you groused, saying you weren't that impressed. You had no specific complaint. You just didn't think they were as cool as your other friends. You just didn't feel the need to bring them, or anyone else, into our lives.

I did. I was feeling isolated. I wanted a friend I could meet for a latte without driving all day. I didn't care if they were the coolest people ever, and besides, how can you tell after one encounter? I begged you to join me for dinner with them, but you refused. In retrospect, I should have pursued the friendship without you. But that was several years ago and that ship has sailed.

And we haven't succeeded at getting off the grid. Or even keeping the place under control, really. You stopped working for a while but you never really became my "wife." Despite your assertions at Rory's party, housework neither came naturally to you nor fulfilled you.

You spent most of your time making big plans. You sketched out a daily chore schedule with rotations for deep-cleaning tasks like washing windows. You went online and priced fermentation kits and hydroponic systems. You dumped your tools onto your workshop floor, planning to buy specialized bins to sort them into. The bins never materialized and the tools never left the floor. Meanwhile, mold grew in the toilet and dishes piled in the sink.

A mountain of laundry took over the unfinished basement floor. My clothes got chewed by insects and stained by rust. I asked you to keep them off the concrete, but you said there wasn't enough room in the hamper. So I spent hundreds of dollars on a twenty-bushel industrial cart. It was a crazy purchase, but it was big enough to hold every article of clothing we own, so I was sure it would solve the problem.

It didn't. You continued to pile laundry on the floor and leave it there, claiming you needed room for sorting. We'd agreed on a laundry arrangement years ago, when we first lived together: you'd wash and dry the clothes, I'd fold and hang them. You bragged you'd scored the easy job. In practice, you couldn't keep up with it.

You enjoyed cooking dinner, often tying up an entire day infusing oils with tarragon or grinding dried anchos with a mortar and pestle. But you weren't as much a fan of wiping out the fridge and throwing away the spoiled milk.

Before you became a full-time homemaker, I used to joke that I wanted you home, where you belonged, "making me pies."

"My pies will win ribbons at the State Fair," you'd say.

I think you romanticized housework. I think you thought it really *was* about inventing award-winning desserts. Or designing custom labels for homemade preserves. Or rescuing a tarnished silver platter from the Goodwill and polishing it up for the Thanksgiving table.

But housework is about collecting those coffee cups in the living room. It's about going through the avalanching pile of mail and figuring out what to toss and what to file. It's about sweeping away the dirt that's accumulated in the foyer. It's unglamorous and it starts over every day. No one wins any prizes. No one even gets any credit.

At least that's how it's been for me.

You tackled a few interesting projects, like making kimchi. But we couldn't live on kimchi.

Financing your ventures became prohibitively difficult, and no return on the investment seemed forthcoming. So when our neighbor offered you the teaching position at his school, I encouraged you to take it. I think you were offended. But I couldn't afford to have you as a wife. After an exhausting day at work, I needed some sort of help from you. If you couldn't manage the housework, perhaps you could contribute to the finances.

You enjoy teaching programming to high school kids, but it isn't your dream job. And neither of us feels at home in this town.

"Who wants to see the beefcake!" I yelled into the mic, as four men in gold lamé thongs rushed in and began gyrating around me. I strutted across the stage in a skin-tight silver dress and shiny slides, the sort of nineties mall fare I had yet to learn was attracting more gay men than lesbians. I was in my twenties, blissfully unaware of the responsibilities of adulthood. It was the first time I'd ever used the word "beefcake." It wasn't something I'd planned to say, either—it just came out. A crowd of sweaty men cheered and waved dollar bills, so I guess it worked.

"No dead air," Hammer told me when he offered me the gig. "That's the only rule. Say anything that comes into your head, no matter how silly, but don't stop talking." The freelance male dance revue had lost their emcee at the last minute, and they desperately needed someone to advance the tracks and rustle up the crowd's enthusiasm.

"I have no experience," I said. "But I'm not shy."

"Let's try it once and see how it works out," Hammer said. It worked out fine. I traveled with them for six months.

We gathered backstage after the show. Hammer gathered tips from each of the men and sat down to count the take. "How ironic," said the troupe's only straight man. He dropped his thong as I settled into a chair. "She's the only one who gets to see us 'take it all off' and the only one who doesn't care to."

Six drag queens filed into the dressing room. They hung formals in dry-cleaners' bags on doors, draped scarves and boas over chairs and plopped massive bags onto vanity tables. "Shannon darling!" Wisteria said when she saw me, grabbing my hands and kissing the air near my cheeks as if she were French. She had thrown on a coat and t-shirt over stockinged legs in above-the-knee boots but was bare of makeup with her buzzed head exposed.

Wisteria was the program coordinator as well as a performer. We'd been friends since I first came out. "Please come to a gay bar with me," I'd begged a straight friend, choosing the only one in town I knew about. There we found Wisteria and Jaqquee and Pandora sipping cocktails in full drag on a Tuesday afternoon, thrilled to regale a couple of neophytes with the secrets of their world. When I placed in a lip-syncing contest that Halloween, I was dubbed an Honorary Drag Queen and invited to participate in shows.

Wisteria removed her coat. "Shannon!" she called, backing into a chair and spreading her legs wide, draping them over the arms. "Can you see my dick?"

I moved in and took a look at the crotch of her lollipop brief; the days in which I found such dialogue strange had long passed. I assured her she was fine. She had layered nylons over opaque nude tights over padded shapewear, and her tucking job was actually quite impressive. I had only a vague idea how it was done.

"Thank you darling." She took off the t-shirt and examined her chest, using tweezers to remove a couple of stray hairs. Then she bent forward, pressed the flesh on each side of her chest together as tightly as she could, and stretched a piece of duct tape from one nipple to the other, constructing a bit of cleavage. After a few more wraps she pulled on a white merry widow with black boning and stuffed the space under the shelf of flesh. Then she sat down at the marquee mirror.

To stand up to stage lighting, a performer's makeup must be truly frightening in the stark light of the dressing room. Wisteria was an expert in this art. She painted her eyebrows high and arched, added fuchsia and red to her eyeshadow, and drew on cheekbones with a contour pencil, only barely shading. It was a spectacle incongruous with her bare head until she pulled an auburn wig from its foam stand and adjusted it into place.

Jaqquee appeared and delivered a pair of gloves to Pandora, who was in the show. Jaqquee was always in drag, even when she wasn't. Her natural hair was long and thick and fell to the small of her back, and she wore it in a simple barrette. Even without makeup, the residents of the nursing home where she worked assumed she was a woman.

"Oh Mary," she said to me, fanning herself with her clutch. "It is *hot* back here." She looked around for an empty chair, and failing to find one, took a seat on my lap.

Hammer handed me a handful of bills. "Your percentage."

"That reminds me!" Wisteria retrieved a roll of drink coupons from a drawer and distributed four to me and four to Hammer.

"Girrrl," Jaqquee moaned, in the affected nasal tone of her namesake and current obsession, Jackee Harry from *Sister Sister*—a hot sitcom of the time. "What about me?"

"Hit up your wife," Wisteria said, glancing toward Pandora. "Or get your ass onto the stage."

I patted Jaqquee's hip to get her off my lap, took my cash and coupons and spent the remaining hours until closing time in the bar, ineffectually hitting on women who assumed I was straight.

At Max's diner afterward, Jaqquee slid up next to Bubbles, one of the dancers from the nearby gentlemen's club who'd started joining us after their shift. "Your eyeshadow is to die for," Jaqquee said, taking a bite of cherry pie. Outside, an old-school neon sign flashed, periodically lighting up the circle of Formica between us. Next to Jaqquee were Pandora, Wisteria, and eight young men who'd been going out for years with fake IDs.

Swinging a high, sleek ponytail with a toss of her head, Bubbles offered to show Jaqquee her technique. She lowered the heavily gilded eyelids. They were, indeed, like a well-executed oil painting: dark in the corners, lighter in the middle, luminescent toward the brow line. The enormous breasts for which she was named grazed the table as she grabbed her pink leather satchel. She'd chosen saline implants instead of silicone, she once told us, because they were available in a larger size. But she regretted the decision because they caused her pain.

"Mary, please," Jaqquee said.

Bubbles narrowed her eyes in confusion. But she opened her purse, depositing its contents onto the table in handfuls: baby wipes, nail polish, tampons, cinnamon gum, scented body spray, a bottle of aspirin. Finally she located the eyeshadow palette.

"Oh Mary," Jaqquee said. "I love these shades."

"My name is Bubbles," the dancer said, brushing primer onto Jaqquee's eyelids. She was growing annoyed.

"Bubbles," I said, leaning across the table. But my voice was lost amid a cacophony of laughter from the younger men—they were gay in every sense of the word. I hoped to tell her Jaqquee had not forgotten her name, but called *everyone* Mary.

FOUR | OCTOBER
THE DEATH CARD

From high above the Garden, atop the stone wall, she sees the Paradise she once knew.

I find the scrap of paper tucked into a greeting card emblazoned with an apple, on the top shelf in my craft room, while looking for some lace to sew onto a hat for your Halloween costume. I wondered where I'd put it. It's penned neatly in your handwriting on a page ripped from the Yin and Yang journal you used to carry. You gave it to me on my birthday, a few months into our affair.

My latest library finds cover world religions; I know more about Lilith now than I did then. She's even mentioned in my book of Dante Gabriel Rossetti's paintings. She was the first woman—the artist called her "the witch Adam loved before the gift of Eve." God made her not from Adam's flesh but from the earth, so they were equals. She was a seductress. A woman who would not "lie below" Adam, the Alphabet of Ben Sirach says, but preferred to climb on top. She gave up her children and would not bow before God.

No wonder you saw her in me.

In the original story, she fights with Adam, who thinks himself superior to her. But she will not be controlled. Instead, "she pronounces the Ineffable" and takes flight. God then makes Adam a proper wife, one formed from his rib, who knows her place, who'll submit to his will.

In your story, you are Adam, I am Lilith, and Melanie is Eve. But Lilith hasn't fled the Garden of her own accord; she's been cast out by God for sexual impropriety. She lives in exile, where she can only watch her former helpmate with his new wife. Both she and Adam pine for reunion. It's only an unfair, moralistic world that keeps them apart.

Where the pair dwells, bushes sag with fat roses and bluebirds fleck the lilac-scented air. Wild vines burst with berries near the waterfall that empties to the stream. They eat, they make love, they sing His praises. But beyond the wall where the angels dragged her asunder, the earth is scorched and nothing lives. She climbs the wall. She catches his gaze.

You said I looked lonely, back in those days. That's because I *was*. I'd been single a while and my liaisons with you were brief and duplicitous. We'd meet for lunch, bringing a book on Python we could pretend to discuss if we ran into friends. We'd leave parties separately and meet up afterward. You'd tell Melanie you were working late and stop by my apartment for a kiss. Forbidden fruit was part of our origin myth; our relationship lay outside moral law. It was even kindled at a nightclub called Eden.

Remember that night? I'd assembled a group of your friends and mine for an evening of dancing. Melanie was too tired to come and Lyle bailed at the last minute. Only a few showed, and they dispersed early to chat in lounges at the club's periphery. You and I stayed on the dance floor, propelled by pounding techno, adrift in a strobing sea of bodies. It was easy to play drunk. Easy to get close, then closer. We moved in sync. Your hand grazed mine. I leaned in, let you feel my breath on your neck. We didn't give in that night, though. We knew we'd roused a beast that could leave us both in ruin.

We'd gotten together by the time my birthday rolled around. But I was surprised when you arranged an alibi and arrived at my door with gifts. All were Eden-themed: the story, the card, a candle the scent of a tart McIntosh, an apple-red silk scarf.

The story was more than a parable. It was a tribute. It acknowledged my sex appeal, but also my assertiveness and strength of will. It revealed, for the first time, the gravity of your feelings. You thought of me as your rightful partner, the one you preferred to the one you had. My banishment from your life was tragic, and your union with Eve—with Melanie—was a mistake. I wasn't simply a fun diversion. I was a soul mate arriving at the wrong time to consummate our destiny.

In your story, ours was *the love that was meant to be.* I cherished it. On some level, I believed it.

I felt bad for Melanie, though, and I didn't want your divorce on my conscience. My feelings would likely prove fickle, as they had with other men. I told you, not for the first time, that you should not leave your wife for me.

But I was falling for you anyway.

"Your party's in the back," the hostess says, pulling menus the size of street signs from a slot in the wall. She leads us across a swath of laminate, behind a superfluous, raisin-colored partition, and onto a carpet that off-gasses as we step, releasing the soured bouquet of meatloaf and shrimp.

It's the kind of restaurant you call a fern bar: a place that does everything—steak, tacos, pasta—and none of it well. But this is where the Dayton crossdressers meet. The establishment is gay-owned and serves alcohol—compromises were made. Tonight they host a joint social with a local transgender group, and partners are invited.

When paneling gives way to a mauve fleur-de-lis that clashes with the orange pendant lights, I spot our destination: a table seating thirty, recognizable by its density of heavily styled wigs. My first impression is that everyone is wearing *a lot*. A lot of makeup, a lot of hair spray, a lot of accessories. Already large bodies are adorned in ways that make them look larger: draped with furs and billowing scarves, clad in statement necklaces and boots. The group looks larger than life.

In a tunic and leggings, with minimal makeup and natural hair, you stand out from the others. You seem more natural, more at ease. Smaller, even. You've found an undergarment that's boosting your confidence, too—it's called a "gaff." High-waisted and super tight, it flattens and smooths the crotch, someone from the crossdressers' bulletin board informed you.

As we near the table I detect a familiar scent. It's the waxy alloy of perfumes layered over synthetics—stockings, spandex, acrylic hair extensions. It takes me back to Wisteria's dressing table, strewn with atomizers and Lee press-on nails. I look to you to find our seats, as I can't distinguish your new crossdresser friends from those you now call "trans women."

"Wait," I said, when you used the phrase on the drive over. "What's a 'trans woman?'"

"A male-born person who identifies as a woman."

"But I thought you said those were trans *men*."

"That makes more sense to me," you said—adding that this is not your first clash with the community. As it turns out, you've been chatting with some of the Dayton trans women online—and growing annoyed. They're older and they lean conservative. They manage a website for these events but aren't tech-savvy enough to keep it updated. They're prudes, you said, who won't admit that "this thing is tied up with sexuality."

For you, it certainly is. The makeover that first night really got you going. And you've only gotten bolder with your requests to be treated "like a woman" in the bedroom. You want to be dominated. You want to be bent over and manhandled. You want to be called a bitch.

Your friend Lotus waves. Thin and of Asian descent, she's reportedly envied for how well she passes—and her minidress does belie her forty-something years. Only when we draw near do I notice the funereal texture of her pancake makeup and a seam at her hairline. "Wives don't usually come," she says when she shakes my hand, her voice much deeper than I expected.

"It's great to see another partner here," agrees Alex, the only female-born person present besides myself. She puts aside a pair of knitting needles to greet me, then introduces her spouse, Rhiannon—whose flaxen hairpiece and fringed shawl betray a more-than-casual interest in Stevie Nicks. We've barely taken our seats when the server appears, so I quickly choose a cod on rice pilaf that looks inoffensive enough.

Rhiannon introduces Krystal, who looks toward Alex when she shakes my hand. "*My* wife is supportive," Krystal says. "But she couldn't be here tonight." Clad in a black dress that matches her thinning hair, Krystal is in her late sixties with drawn-on eyebrows and a smile that takes over her whole face. "She has stood by me, even though this cost us my job and our faith community!"

"Krystal is Catholic," Lotus announces, with a sidelong glance that suggests something short of sympathy.

"That's right!" Krystal says, eager to share. She served on the Board of Trustees at a prominent university out East, and was a respected catechist of her parish—until she announced her desire to transition. When the priest and his inner circle couldn't rein in her plans, they removed her from parish activities. The school was no more impressed, and she lost that position, too. She found a more tolerant community in Dayton, but now works as an adjunct at a secular school. "I lost it all," she says, still sporting an ear-to-ear smile.

Without prompting, she takes us through the journey that brought her here. Only a year in, she's undergone breast augmentation, facial feminization, and an operation to minimize her Adam's apple. I look her over, searching for the feminine edges of her clearly male body.

"This is a physical condition," Krystal adds. "Not some lifestyle choice!" She tells us her mother took a drug while pregnant that "feminized" her in the womb. Then she pauses, her smile fading. "Well, I don't know that *for sure*," she admits. "But it was a popular drug at the time!" In any case, she says, she *needs* the procedures to alleviate her "gender dysphoria."

Gender dysphoria. I've heard this phrase before. I think back to the way you explained it, just recently: it's a "mismatch" some people experience between their internal sense of gender and their physical body.

"I don't have gender dysphoria!" Rhiannon jumps in, as if waiting for this term to come up. "I have gender *euphoria.* I'm comfortable with my body and able to live happily as a man. But living as a woman makes me *feel good.* So why not? What's wrong with feeling good?"

"There's nothing wrong with it!" confirms Alex, now furiously knitting a beanie. "People need to *relax* about gender roles."

"What's *your* story, Cameron?" Lotus addresses someone in ankle pants and crocodile loafers.

"I'm just a gay man," Cameron says. "As a hairdresser, I like pretty things." His ballet-pink eyeshadow attests to that. You smile; he returns an appreciative glance.

"Isn't your church anti-gay?" Lotus asks Krystal, pointedly.

"We believe gay people are born that way," Krystal says, the huge grin returning to her face. "But—"

She's interrupted by the server, who deposits a burger piled high with limp shredded lettuce in front of her. Next comes my fish, your Hawaiian chicken, a leathery sirloin and a taco salad glistening with a runny salsa. I'm curious about Krystal's stance, but condiment and drink requests monopolize the conversation. I sample a rubbery mélange of vegetables bathing in pearl onion-flavored water, and wait.

"It's not a sin to *be* gay," Krystal interjects, when the commotion dies down. "But it *is* a sin to *act upon* gay feelings."

The Protestant church of my childhood shared this view. Its tragic flaw is that it reduces homosexuality to lust. Only a straight person, blissfully spared the experience of falling in love with someone of their sex, so easily dismisses "acting upon" those feelings. Rhiannon is unimpressed. Cameron looks poised to respond. You turn over a chunk of pineapple with your fork, breaking the skin on a gelatinous sauce.

"But look," Krystal says. "God loves everyone! We're all tempted, whether by sexual sin or alcoholism or something else." This doesn't help Krystal's case, but she's granted a reprieve when someone addresses the table.

"I'm just starting hormone therapy! What can I expect?"

The jumble of responses is enlightening. No one present passes. But those who come closest—like Lotus—are not taking hormones. Others have used them for years but have reaped little benefit. A few volunteer they've had sex reassignment surgery, and these aren't the ones I expect, either. It seems the current standard of transgender care is hit or miss, at best. It seems the accident of smooth skin and a slim build does more for these folks than a whole slew of expensive interventions.

Those who've undergone the most procedures rely the most on sartorial cues. Mostly senior citizens, they wear sweater sets and knotted pearls, false eyelashes and pantyhose. Girdles compress waistlines and low heels bear the weight of swollen ankles. One of them, introducing herself as Nell, now stands.

She's well over six feet tall and immense—a former firefighter, whispers Lotus. In a black swing dress and Naturalizers, Nell's less dolled up than some. But her choices are likely constrained by what's available in her size.

"Hormone therapy interferes with your driving," she announces.

"It affects your concentration?" someone asks.

"No," Nell says. "It's made me into a woman driver."

A few laugh, but Nell doesn't appear to be joking.

"I hope I never hate myself that much," you say, as we cross the parking lot. "Krystal's mom never took that drug. She's grasping for a biological explanation for her predicament, because of religious guilt."

"It *does* sound that way." I button up my cardigan. The evening air, descending ever earlier into the day, is crisp but not yet cold.

"The evidence for that theory is weak, anyway," you say.

I haven't read the studies. But I do know Krystal's struggle. As a teen, my same-sex attraction persisted despite my effort to "pray it away." When I couldn't reconcile my reality with the teachings of my church, the cognitive dissonance became unbearable. I lost my religion to avoid losing my soul.

"It takes a strong mind to tolerate the truth," I say, paraphrasing Nietzsche, whose *Beyond Good and Evil* knocks around in my tote. "I've never liked the 'born-this-way' argument, anyway. Being gay or trans isn't a crime, so we don't have to care how people get that way."

"I'd hate to think of myself as a chemical accident," you say, as we climb into your truck. "I'm a human with agency. I *choose* to wear women's clothes, just as a punk chooses to wear a mohawk." You want to flatter the body you have, you add, not "build a new one from fake parts and padding."

"To be fair," I counter, "Krystal's trying to pass as a woman. You're not."

"Passing is a bullshit goal," you say. "People rarely achieve it. And if they manage to, it *hides* gender nonconformity—when we should be normalizing it."

In the heyday of your friends' Halloween parties, hundreds crowded into Theo's apartment. Many were friends, some strangers. They wandered in off the street, curious about the bounce house or the billowing plumes spilling from the smoke machine. They found their way to the basement, where people smoked weed, played spin the bottle or thrashed to death metal. Or upstairs, where Paige sat cross-legged on the hardwood floor across from Fuzzy, arranging tarot cards into a pattern she called the Celtic cross. Folks dressed as pregnant trailer trash and a giant foam penis and Mia from *Pulp Fiction*, syringe wedged in breast. Once, you made out with Darcy's boyfriend. Another time I convinced a woman to pose for a nude photo shoot. These were celebrations of youth and debauchery, as All Hallows' Eve is meant to be.

But that was over a decade ago. Your friends have abandoned such revelry for childcare and grownup jobs. And I could never get you to the gay masquerade ball in town, which I hear is a riot. "I'd feel like a tourist," you'd say. Nowadays, we stay home and watch *Invasion of the Body Snatchers* or hand out candy with Rosa while Jake takes the girls trick-or-treating.

This year we settle for a suburban affair in a McMansion on the marina, hosted by friends of our former neighbors Brent and Sheila. The hostess has adorned every surface with bric a brac from her part-time gig at the craft store: luminarias, linen pumpkins, apothecary bottles filled with Black Widow Eggs and Ogre Breath. Clad in a bodysuit and a cat-ear headband that won't spoil her makeup, she fusses over the buffalo wings while her husband slumps in a recliner, swigging a holiday ale.

It's a bit basic. Still, I'm glad to get you out of the house. You've been moping around since you got a rejection letter from Cuppajoe Media. "I don't get it," you said. "I did everything right."

You were worried about your costume, too. You longed to debut a vintage dress you found at the thrift store, but wondered what Brent and Sheila would think. "It's Halloween," I assured you. "No one will bat an eye." You were apprehensive until I offered to crossdress with you. I became freelance bio-exorcist Beetlejuice and transformed you into the "strange and unusual" Lydia Deetz.

Now I leave you with the Jasons and the sexy nurses, watching your dress twirl as you dance to Monster Mash. With a white wine in one hand and a fistful of gold doubloons in the other, I stumble down the hallway toward the softly lit room where Madame Violet has set up shop. Eyes fixed on greige carpet, I careen into the wall, pausing when I reach the doorway. I have made a big decision.

"Tarot is about intuition," Paige said at one of those parties back in the day. She was trying to quell my fears. As an ex-Christian, I've never had a reading. I once regarded the practice as witchcraft and it still strikes in me an irrational fear. "It's not about fortune telling," she insisted.

Someone should tell that to Madame Violet. Strung over the doorway of her lair is a paper banner that reads "Let Me Predict Your Future."

But I won gold doubloons at Halloween Trivia that I need to spend, and a visit to Madame Violet is the best prize in the house. I'm sure it'll be the sort of cold reading so often debunked by James Randi: insights gleaned from my body language, platitudes meant to appeal to everyone. Madame Violet isn't practicing magick; Madame Violet is another party trick. Maybe it's the wine, but I'm ready to shake off the chains of religious superstition. Wiping a moss-covered cheek with the back of my hand, I take a breath and part the sheer red curtains.

She looks the part: a robust woman in a peasant dress with wavy black hair, a large mole dotting her cheek. The odor of burning wax singes my nostrils as I pull up the purple bench in front of her card table. "For you," she says without smiling, "a special pattern." She lays five cards in a straight line, face down, moving her hand over them. "Rungs on the ladder of your story line. Some nearer than others."

I'm unnerved by her omission of the usual pleasantries.

"Two of Pentacles," she says, turning over the first card. On its face a snake curls around two coins, its tail in its mouth. An ouroboros! I recognize the creature from the encyclopedia of ancient religions in my tote. It represents life, death, and fertility. And, ironically, self-renewal—to eat oneself seems pretty *self-destructive* to me. "Light and dark," she says. "Male and female. In balance, for now." As she speaks the edges of her voice, like the edges of her body, begin to blur. I touch the card. He "fertilizes himself and gives birth to himself," writes Carl Jung, referring to the dual-sexed god in the masculine. A creation myth of a familiar tradition. The earliest gods were female, as Merlin Stone explains in *When God Was a Woman.* But with the arrival of agriculture men appropriated creation, sanitizing the messy business of childbirth.

I guess that's why Zeus pulled Dionysus from his thigh and Athena from his head, and Jehovah forged humans from dust and breath. But even the ancient ouroboros frames creator as male—indeed, as the disembodied phallus itself. My mind drifts to the sheer physics of the thing. Suppose its walls have no thickness and it moves without friction. What happens when it reaches the back of its own head? Does it coil inside itself, eternally? Yes—this is why it represents introspection.

"The Chariot," Madame Violet says, turning up the next card. "It foretells a journey." Maybe we'll finally get to Europe! We could schedule a break between our old and new jobs and spend a *whole month* there. As she speaks, my eyes adjust to the darkness, bringing into focus a pair of massive windows: the heavy upholstery of the drapes, the tiebacks, the double rods with crystal finials. Expensive and soulless decor.

"Death," Madame Violet says, turning up the next card. She gasps.

I gasp, too. Maybe dabbling in the occult tonight was a bad idea, after all.

She apologizes. "The Death card rarely foretells a literal death. Instead, it means the loss of something big. A home, a job, a marriage, a family. A definite and final end."

But none of that seems likely to me.

"Two of Cups." The card is upside-down, calling for a "reverse reading." It's a communion between close companions, but the relationship's in peril.

But it is you with whom I share communion. And with compassion, honesty and courage, we can't fail. Maybe this reading was meant for my hosts. Are people who spend good money on finials capable of love? If the reading has merit—but of course it doesn't, what am I thinking—does that mean you will soon die? The Death card lodges itself in my imagination.

Madame Violet flips the final card: "The Tower." On its face lightning strikes, people fall. "Everything will change," she says, with sorrow. What I rebuild will rest on "stronger foundations."

But I don't want anything to change.

In the beginning, we had an affair—a reckless and foolish endeavor. But we turned it into a partnership built on mutual respect and tenderness. We served time in tiny apartments so we could save for a house. We worked hard and acquired the means to live well. When I survey our homestead, I feel gratitude. The garden fragrant with oregano and fat tomatoes. The spacious country kitchen. Evenings on the deck with homemade lemonade, watching the cattle graze. And the love that has not faded in fourteen years, but seems to grow stronger every day.

FIVE | NOVEMBER
WHAT IS LOVE?

You're lying on your back in bed with your legs splayed in the air, your hands in your pulled-down underwear. You've abandoned the boyshorts, the briefs with the "contour pouch" and the gaff—you now prefer a pair of tight women's panties. You're struggling, brow knitted in concentration. This is what I see as I approach the bedroom, a basket of freshly folded laundry in hand.

I know what you're doing. You're wrestling your testicles into the "inguinal canals" from which they descended at puberty—a part of your body I wasn't aware existed until last week. Once you've gotten them as far back as they can go—they never fully recede—you'll spread your legs wide, raise your hips, and tuck your penis into your butt crack. Then you'll pull up the panties so their snugness will keep it all in place. You'll finish with tight jeans, examining yourself in the mirror for signs of the unwanted bulge. Over time your genitals will wriggle free; the look only lasts an hour or two. You'll forgo drinking water because peeing will undo your work.

"It doesn't seem worth it," I said, when you first explained the procedure. And, "Why do it at home, when you have no place to be?" And, "What happened to flattering the body you have?"

But you deflected these questions with a self-conscious shrug. The answers lie in the Black Box, that impenetrable capsule that now holds so many of your thoughts.

So I pretend not to see you and walk past quickly, as though there's some other place I need to take the laundry.

Your mom died suddenly at a relatively young age. I remember when your dad broke the news. You picked up the phone to the sound of a blood-curdling scream. He spoke so loudly, so frantically, his words were unintelligible. It was the most obvious, though not the first, sign of a deficit in coping skills that appears to run in your family.

"Your mom is dead," he finally spit out, and though the phone was pressed tightly to your ear, I heard it from across the room.

"Nooo!" you screamed, drawing out the word until you'd emptied your lungs of air.

"Mom is sick or something," you said as you hung up. "He's saying she's dead, but he's confused."

I'd heard of denial—experienced it, even. But I didn't know it could be so *literal*. It seemed to me that denial, for adults at least, was an act of holding unpleasant thoughts at bay—that you'd never taste her famous sugar cream pie again, that Christmas wouldn't be the same. Not an actual *disbelief* that the death had occurred. If things hadn't turned so hectic, I'd have caught a curious peek into your psyche. The way you process—or fail to process—stress. Your ability to lock yourself safely away from reality when it suits you.

But you grabbed your keys and ran for the door. I raided the downstairs closet where we kept some of our formal clothes, grabbing a skirt for myself and pants for you. I was looking for shirts when you ran back into the room. "What are you doing?" you screamed. "We've got to get on the road."

I tried to find words. Your dad's house was two hours away—we wouldn't be coming back. But it was easier to give in than to tear down your wall of defense. I supposed we could afford to buy clothes in town.

You insisted on driving though you were in no shape for it, presumably so you could go as fast as possible. "Dad is wrong," you said as you peeled out of the driveway, and again five miles down the road, and again when we stopped for gas.

I called my mom with the news when you went inside to pay. I was dialing Lyle when you climbed back into the truck.

"Jamie's mom may have died," I heard myself say, trying to relay the information while protecting you from a truth you hadn't yet faced.

"What do you mean?" Lyle asked. "Is she dead?"

"Yes."

Lyle was perplexed, but I'd accomplished the delicate mission.

As you drove, I oscillated. Being honest was the right thing to do. But allowing you the comfort of your error seemed compassionate. I finally settled on a compromise. I wouldn't volunteer anything, but I'd speak freely if pressed.

"Maybe she's unconscious," you said, as you pulled out of the station. You asked me to call your dad, having convinced yourself she was at a hospital. I dialed the phone in a show of support.

"Jamie wants to know where we should meet you," I said.

"At the house," he said. Your siblings were there, he added, as was the coroner.

"At the house," I repeated, sparing you the additional information. You looked at me, your eyes narrowing. Then you expelled the unwanted thought.

"Mom can't be dead," you said as we neared your dad's house, but there was uncertainty in your eyes. "So why aren't they at the hospital?"

You weaved through town erratically, taking twists and turns too quickly for safety.

"Oh my god," you said as you pulled up to a stoplight, looking directly at me. "Do you think she's dead?"

"Yes," I said quietly.

A look of desperation crossed your face. Then you looked skeptical. Finally, your face relaxed. Perhaps you returned to the comfort of denial.

When we arrived, they'd taken your mom away. Jill met us at the door, her hand wrapped tightly in a dish towel. She was smoking outside a bar when she heard the news, and reacted by putting her fist into a brick wall.

"Come outside with me," Jeremy said, after you'd hugged everyone and taken in the news. Out on the back deck, he pulled out a joint, lit it, and offered you a hit. You weren't much of a smoker, but perhaps it was a good time.

Inspired by news of a favorite cartoonist's hiatus, I recline on the couch, browsing the archives of *Achewood*. You introduced me to the webcomic years ago—a poetic chronicle of stuffed cats living amid robots and drug-addled squirrels. I'm cozy in my warmest sweatpants; November's begun seeping through the cracks of our little farmhouse.

In a discussion forum for its fans, I find that the contributors—who skew young in light of the comic's vintage—rarely discuss the strip itself. Instead, they talk relationships, mental health, and gender. Several prominent contributors are trans women—attractive, if their profile photos are any indication. "My wife and I are both femme," one writes, "so people think we're roommates. They can't wrap their mind around the fact that we're dykes."

I cringe, instinctively, at the casual use of that word; it was too often hurled in anger from car windows at my older lesbian friends as they walked to the bar. Language evolves and times change, and I know some have reclaimed the word. But this young person doesn't know its sting.

It isn't the only term the *Achewood* crowd has repurposed. Many identify as queer despite strong heterosexual leanings. Some call themselves "nonbinary" while dressing conventionally for their sex. Only a woman named Julia bows out of these discussions, calling herself "strictly an ally." With a strong, brooding face—certainly a masculine one, in some respects—she reminds me of one of Rossetti's subjects. I flip through the book on the coffee table—perhaps *Proserpine*. She's grateful to have a boyfriend, she posts, as her looks make men nervous. I think she's gorgeous, but I'm not surprised.

You join me on the couch, launching a search for Thanksgiving recipes. You want to take something to your dad's that's traditional, with a twist. "What would be good on sweet potatoes?" you ask.

"Bacon." I say. "And a drizzle of maple syrup." I tell you about Biddy, the female-born *Achewood* fan who uses male pronouns but loves short dresses and red lipstick.

"That's brilliant," you say. "The toppings, I mean. I'd feel silly calling someone like Biddy 'he.'" You log into your news aggregator and add the *Achewood* discussion forum so you can catch up later.

"Check this out," I say. A young woman named Britney, who started a family at the tender age of eighteen, has posted a full-length photo of herself. She's wearing a women's-cut jersey, jeans and tennis shoes. Her long hair is pulled into a ponytail. On a given day, she writes, she might wear a cardigan, a Henley, a pair of flip flops. Maybe a little foundation. In light of this, she wants the group's opinion. Should she identify as queer?

"This obsession with identity is out of hand," you say. "Why does everyone need a special label?"

I have to agree. Britney, like countless other women, prioritizes comfort. If she's queer, then everyone who shops at Old Navy is queer.

I doubt the webcomic community will entertain this navel-gazing. But when I scroll to the comments, I find I'm wrong.

They've launched a detailed analysis of the problem. Which side of the aisle are her jeans from? Has she ever used neon hair dye? An inquiry into her sex life—largely unremarkable, as she's had little experience outside her marriage—follows. Is she into bondage? Swinging? In the end, the questions are redundant. Everyone assures Britney that she is, in fact, queer. She's cool, they seem to say. She *belongs.*

I wonder why Achewood attracts a queer fan base. But then we find a similar trend in a Facebook group for curating playlists, and a Tumblr for photos of pets. It isn't the topic—it's the age of the participants. Everyone under thirty loves the queer kids. Everyone wants to *be* a queer kid. And everyone can. No experience is necessary, and no inclination or style of dress—however conventional—is a barrier to entry.

What is love? In my Christian days I'd parrot a line I heard in church: "Love is a verb, not a noun!" Then I'd launch, authoritatively, into a rant. Love is not some warm fuzzy feeling, I'd say, for someone who looks good and tickles your fancy. That sort of "love" is illusory and will fade. Love is *decision* you make. It lasts because you *choose* it. Love can be generated, then, between any two people making the appropriate effort.

I said those things before I knew love. I didn't know what I was talking about.

And isn't that a cold kind of love? A love without passion? One in which even admiring your partner is optional? One in which dreams of the future aren't shared, but may be shelved in the service of fulfilling a contract? And certainly, one that requires a God to stitch it together, since nothing else does. A God I no longer believe in.

In my twenties I fell in love for the first time. Her name was Paris, and she was the strongest and most compassionate person I'd ever met. I fell utterly against my will. My love was inconvenient, to say the least: I was closeted and she was straight. I told her how I felt because I *could not* do otherwise. The warm and fuzzy feeling was real and it drowned me. It did not release me when she said she was straight, but flattered, and would still be my friend. It did not release me when she left to teach English in Africa. It did not release me for years.

Still, my Christian friends had a point. Love is not, as the less enlightened might imagine, some lightning bolt of passion, some brainless "chemistry." That's just lust. Nor is it, as the romance film implies, pursuing some object of loveliness as the spoils of a well-played game. That's just acquisition. Youth and beauty fade—as my cousins know. A relationship built solely on desire cannot last.

In time I grew to believe that love was about compatibility. And I still think that's a component. But love isn't a business deal, either, procured for its utility. What is it, then? Love must be something more enduring than lust and better than a matching game.

Here's what I propose. Love arises when you recognize the good in another with an awe you can't suppress or deny. It's a *genuine* appreciation for who they are. Real love isn't random; it's targeted. It isn't charity—it's something deserved. I love you for the way you embody the values I hold dear: you're compassionate, you're honest, you're brave.

With real love, the commitment my Christian friends advocated for is not only possible, but irresistible—because one is not inclined to separate oneself from goodness. Longevity follows because you know your loved one acts in good faith. It's easy to offer the benefit of the doubt in conflict.

Love isn't acquired by the will, as my church imagined. It isn't *acquired*, at all. It's a *reality* you occupy when you truly apprehend another person's worth.

"I'm getting a divorce," you said. It was the eighth month of our affair. You were in my bed, bathed in the morning sun, fiddling with a strand of my hair.

I sat up. You followed suit. You faced me, placed your hands on my knees. I don't know why I was surprised. I knew things had changed.

If I'm honest, I knew just a few months in.

A few months in, we broke up for a while. Not because we wanted to—but because we felt we should. You needed to save your marriage, we told ourselves, and I needed to move on, to find a woman I could share my life with. And Melanie was a nice person—she didn't deserve this. We came together on a Wednesday in June, pressed our bodies together in a sort of grief, tore ourselves away and wished each other well.

At work the next morning, sorrow gathered in my throat, a lump I couldn't swallow. Support tickets piled up, unable to compete with the urgency of my pain. I walked outside, followed the sidewalk through the office park, landed on a bench where geese foraged at the edge of the lake, and lost several hours.

"*Must have been love*," belted eighties duo Roxette over my car radio as I drove home. "*But it's over now.*" It was a stupid song that never made sense to me until that moment. If it was love, why would it end? Now I knew.

Friday was no better; Saturday I slept all day.

You spent the days slipping out of the office to cry, the nights finding solace in your guitar. By Saturday you'd written a song. You wrote of lying prostrate, the walls around you crumbling, the floor buckling with the weight of your grief.

But when two people break up who don't want to, it doesn't stick. We reunited on Sunday after an email exchange. We didn't solve our problem. We didn't discuss its resolution.

You met me in the park with a picnic basket. You brought Nalgene bottles filled with homemade lemonade, a pair of wine glasses, and a locally made blackberry merlot. You'd assembled a salad, found a ripe brie and some concord grapes, and warmed a baguette. We found a spot in the grass in dappled sunlight to spread the serape from the trunk of your car.

A drop of rain kissed the back of my hand as we unwrapped the cheese. You glanced nervously at the sky.

We could skip it, you said. We could go to a café. But I was game if you were. And you were always game. It was one of the things I loved about you: you could roll, no matter what lay ahead. Rain or shine, you were in. That's grace.

Another drop fell. Maybe it would just sprinkle, we said. It wouldn't kill us to get a little damp. We arranged plates and napkins, split apart the grapes, tore off a chunk of the baguette. Rain began to fall. The bread got wet. Our hair got wet.

The picnic wasn't going to happen.

We packed up too late, shoving the waterlogged blanket and soggy food into your trunk, huddling in your car to regroup. We were soaked and undone and no longer fit to dine in public.

"Want to walk in the woods?" you asked. "Maybe the tree canopy will give us some cover."

It didn't. Rain fell at a clip as we followed the trail, streaming into our eyes, rendering our clothes heavy and slick. We forged ahead, undaunted. We walked in quiet reverence, in step with the pulse of rain strumming upon leaves, a rain that diffused the light, deepened the lush greens of the forest.

Thunder roared throughout the sky; the rain fell in buckets, deafening other sound. You grabbed my hand. We tried to speak, to laugh, but our voices were drowned in the deluge. So we stopped talking. We became pure reception, touching the rain, touching each other.

Then we stopped walking.

We embraced, pressed wet lips against wet flesh, ravenously, sorry we'd parted, the violence of our grip wringing torrents from our clothes. We stood in that rain for hours.

I knew things had changed, that day.

I knew things had changed when you said, a few months later, "there are things I want to say to you, but can't."

I knew things had changed when you said, "I had sex with Melanie, and it felt like I was cheating on you."

So I knew, somewhere deep inside, you'd get a divorce someday. But I didn't *really* know it.

"I know what you're thinking," you said, that day in my bed. "But this is what's best for me, whether or not you stick around."

You were giving me the gift of a clear conscience.

"Melanie wants to start a family, and I'm terrified at the thought of being a dad. I thought my feelings would change as I aged, but they haven't. And it isn't fair to her, either."

"OK," I said, failing to find better words. I didn't want to be responsible for altering the course of your life, perhaps for the worse. You claimed I wasn't the reason for your divorce. But we both knew I was the reason for your divorce.

Then again, it *was* an irreconcilable difference.

I understood how you felt about parenthood. I've often imagined myself a single mother of the Middle Ages, leaving my child on the foundling wheel of a monastery. Raising children isn't something I can do. It would destroy me. No reluctant person should sign up for it.

The truth is, I felt optimistic. I wanted to leap and shout. I wanted to clear a closet and ask you to move in with me. But I felt cautious too. I'd grown used to playing the game we were playing. I stared at you in disbelief, watched you squirm in the heavy silence I wrapped around the moment.

"Will you keep dating me?" you asked.

"Of course."

"And someday, after we've dated a while, will you consider the other thing? The thing that arises out of dating?" You searched my eyes.

I understood that the other thing was marriage.

"Yes," I said, surprising myself—not for my willingness to marry you, but for my willingness to say so. Even though I hadn't exactly said it.

"I love you," you said, for the first time ever.

I wanted to say the same, but I didn't. I was terrified of what I'd done.

SIX

DECEMBER
YOU DON'T HAVE TO CALL ME DARLIN'

"*I was drunk... the day my mom... got out of prison!*" Dakota screeches on the empty dance floor, raising a Jack and Coke to the sky. She swivels to extend a muscular, bare leg, sending the strained hem of a painted-on sheath dress toward the jingling coin belt at her waist. A telltale bulge betrays that she doesn't know how to tuck.

You weave around the wooden corral surrounding the tables, leaving me and Lotus and Rhiannon behind, and join her. "*And I went to pick her up in the rainnn!*" Arm in arm, the two of you sway in commiseration with David Allan Coe. Glancing down from a twinkling, tinsel-draped window, a chubby young DJ rubs his beard with tempered amusement.

You've been meeting the crossdressers at a dive bar near Dayton for a couple of months. But some wanted a change of pace, so tonight we try a country-Western gay bar in Cincinnati. It's dead here, but the group seems to enjoy the irony. That's what you like about the crossdressers. They're young at heart and always game for a good time.

You especially like Dakota, though she's not the type you usually befriend. You're college-educated; she's a construction worker. You dress to flatter your features; she goes for winged eyeliner and costume jewelry. You've been dressing year-round since July, but Dakota saves it for the winter months. She doesn't want to shave her legs in summer, when she takes her two boys to the community pool. Dakota isn't out to her wife and kids.

"Does Jamie take hormones?" Lotus asks when Rhiannon gets up to fetch another round. "He looks good."

You duck under a beam adorned with a red ribbon and sidle up to the table.

"I mean 'she,'" Lotus corrects herself.

"I don't care about pronouns," you say.

"At least you have a normal name." Lotus eyes Dakota, who now drags up a chair. "You're forty-three—your name didn't exist when you were born. You need one that's age-appropriate."

"Nah," Dakota says, in her unaltered bass voice. As it turns out, she's test-driving her fourth name, each more youthful than the last. "I'm going to stick with this one," she says, sitting forward with her legs apart and an elbow perched on her knee. She can't hide her blue-collar roots.

"It's a teenager's name," Lotus says. "No wonder the trans women think we're perverts."

"They don't all think that," you say with a smirk. "Some think we're closeted trans women."

"Wow, that doesn't hurt your feet?" Belinda asked. I had taken off my shoes and was strolling briskly along a gravel path at the Bean Blossom Blues Festival. You lagged behind, examining the ragged bloom of a purple thistle. It was the first summer of our affair and we were still sneaking around.

"Not really," I said. "I was raised in the country. I've done this all my life."

Belinda, a city girl through and through, dropped her jaw in amazement. She had just started dating Lyle, who rounded the corner ahead of us, lugging a small cooler and a bundle of blankets past the Pavilion Bar Stage.

In truth, it hurt a little. But an endless stretch of sultry days had culminated in an impossibly perfect morning. Moths and butterflies flitted amid wild sunflowers and fleabane. A clear, still sunlight warmed my shoulders and permeated the earth. I longed to sink my toes into the warm grass.

"I'm going barefoot, too," you said. The group maintained its pace as you hopped along behind, unlacing your hiking boots.

"Wow! Belinda said, walking backward. "You can walk on gravel, too?"

"Of course. It's no big deal." But I sensed a friendly competition brewing. When your boots were off, you rushed to catch up with me and walked by my side, flashing a shy smile.

We had planned to be discreet. We had pitched separate tents and promised ourselves we'd behave. But as the weekend wore on we'd tired of hiding and had relaxed our efforts. Perhaps secrecy wasn't even necessary—you had confided in Lyle about our affair, and Belinda probably suspected. In any case, she wouldn't report back to Melanie, who had rebuffed her offer of friendship.

It was a solidarity thing. Melanie's best friend Darcy had dated Lyle until a few months prior. And though it was Darcy who broke it off, she was offended by his prompt re-entry into the dating scene. As if that weren't infuriating enough, he'd chosen Belinda—the first woman who'd paid attention to him—and *not* Darcy's kind of person.

Belinda was a single mom with a high-school education and a job in sales. She couldn't comment on Emily Dickinson's use of slant rhyme or the influence of Victorian fairy tales on the work of Neil Gaiman. But Lyle adored her. She was tall and busty with a cascade of caramel-highlighted hair and the requisite vanity to care for it. She wore push-up bras and stacked heels and moonlighted as a cigarette girl. Her big doe eyes drooped languidly when she drank—which was often. The rift had worked to our advantage, keeping Melanie and Darcy home that year. Still, we cloaked our affection in combative banter. If we were World War II era classmates, you later joked, you would have dipped my pigtails in an inkwell.

A little brown duskywing alit on my wrist. "Look!" I said. "A butterfly!"

You grabbed my arm to investigate, but it flew away. "It might have been a moth," you said, with an air of authority. "It can be difficult to distinguish between the two." Your right knee buckled as a rock stabbed the ball of your foot, but you grimaced only slightly and limped along, continuing your lecture. "If you look at the antennae—"

"I know the difference," I said, giving you a shove. "It was a butterfly."

You met my eyes and smiled sweetly. "It might have been a moth," you repeated. Then you weaved sharply toward the grass.

"The trick is to walk evenly and confidently," I said, seizing upon your weakness. "Roll your feet from back to front to spread the impact. This is how they walk on hot coals, too."

I might have been making up that last part.

"I know. I'm just looking at a clover."

A nut casing the size and pea-green hue of a tennis ball appeared in my path and I bent down to pick it up. Digging my thumbnail into its firm, bumpy flesh, I wrestled a chunk of it away.

"What's that?" Belinda asked.

"It's a walnut." I rubbed the scarred fruit on my wrist, staining my skin yellow-brown, and brought my hand to my nose to take in the floral scent of furniture polish and hinterland. "Doesn't it smell amazing?" I asked, distributing bits for sniffing.

"How is *that* a walnut?" Belinda was incredulous as I chipped away the last of the hull, revealing the sturdy brown nut inside, and handed it to her.

"Is it ready to eat?" she asked. "I'm afraid to eat things from outside."

"Everything you eat is from outside," Lyle said. You glanced my way, tight-lipped.

"I know I'm weird," Belinda said. "But I prefer food that's been handled by professionals."

"You mean Mexican immigrants?" Lyle snarked, unfolding the event program. "Up next: Catfish Keith."

The relentless jab of stone against heel got to me and I joined you in the grass.

"Do your feet hurt?" you asked.

"No. I'm just looking at a clover."

"Maybe I'll take my shoes off, too!" Belinda announced.

"This grudge-fest is between me and Shannon," you said, exposing our bravado. "You needn't hurt yourself, too."

An acoustic twang pierced the morning as we drew near the Hippy Hill Stage. Spreading our blankets, we were treated to the improvisations of a slight, sharply dressed hepcat wielding a steel guitar. "*Love my cherry ball,*" he sang, in a falsetto that sounded almost facetious. A fringe of sideswept bangs peeked under his fedora as he bobbed his head, slapped his guitar and tightened his lips into a self-satisfied snarl.

I settled in and rested my head on your knee. You tied clover blossoms end-to-end and draped them in my hair. "You guys would make a cute couple," Belinda said, relishing the thought of you betraying Melanie.

"In defense of crossdressers!" you announce when I arrive home, pointing your open laptop in my direction. It's your Christmas break, so you've been home all day. I knock the snow off my boots, drop my bags and pull off damp gloves.

"Cool," I say. "I'd love to read it."

You've purchased a domain name, you say, following me to the thermostat in the hall. You've installed blogging software. You've written your first post.

"Do we have to keep it so cold in here?" I bump up the heat.

You've customized a theme, you add, following me into the kitchen. You're calling the blog "Outside the Binary."

"I'd love to read it," I repeat, popping a mug of water into the microwave. I sift rooibos into the infuser as you explain the impetus for your first post, "Open Letter to a Trans Woman."

It's to someone named Shesha you chatted with online. Your interest in crossdressing, she suggested, means you're really trans. Perhaps you're afraid to face that right now. But you should take a hard look at yourself. Maybe you're not a crossdresser at all. Maybe you're a woman.

Now I understand your comment at the country-Western bar.

I settle on the couch and pull a wool throw across my lap. Outside, a sprinkling of snowflakes stains a vista of brown: dead zebra grass, dried echinops, a lone maple leaf fluttering on a branch. Shesha's remarks got under your skin, you say, handing over your laptop. You were motivated to respond.

The post is a familiar synopsis of a philosophy you've honed over the last several months.

You're a crossdressing man, you write. A *man*, not a woman. You have male privilege, and you want to acknowledge that.

Crossdressers are the most closeted of the LGBTQ spectrum, you explain. You're called weirdos or perverts. You're made the butt of jokes. But there's no shame in crossdressing. You want to *own* it. You want to destigmatize the word "transvestite"—it's a beautiful word. You like women's clothes: the fine fabrics, the lovely patterns, the flattering fit. Why shouldn't a man enjoy fashion? You're proud of your sense of style.

You want to be yourself, not impersonate someone else. So you refuse to wear fake hips. You'll never "Spackle on makeup like a clown." You don't even want to stuff a bra. Women must sometimes work around a flat chest or a thick waist, so why shouldn't you? You reiterate a favorite line: "I wear women's clothes for self-expression, as a punk might wear a mohawk."

Folks like Shesha want you to say you were "born this way." You weren't much of a baseball player, to your dad's chagrin—but you were otherwise a typical boy. You wrestled with your brothers and hammered on odd bits of wood. You never favored girls' toys or played dress-up or got bullied for running weird. You're not "wired" to enjoy feminine things. You're a human with agency, not a medical anomaly.

Maybe you're not a typical man. But you're not a woman, either. You're fine the way you are! You have no desire to grow breasts or lose your penis. When it comes to gender, you fall "outside the binary" and you like it there. We need to *challenge* the gender binary, you say, not shove people into one or the other of its poles.

"There's no such thing as a sexed brain," you write in closing. You're still annoyed about Krystal's drug theory, you tell me, and now some of the *Achewood* folks are claiming "female brain structures." Lyle, the first guest to your blog, backs you up in the comments: "The science isn't there."

But you're swimming against a tide. Andreja Pejić, your first model crush, has gone under the knife, along with half the other models from your Pinterest board. Eddie Izzard now says she's trans. The world of gender benders you once admired is growing small. The trans world is growing larger—and skewing younger.

Discussion on the *Achewood* forum has turned to the costs of penile inversion vaginoplasty. With nerve injury and sexual dysfunction among its risks, the procedure was once pretty rare. But another crop of comic fans have just come out as trans, and for them, it's all the rage. Even Julia, the "ally" who looks like a Rossetti model, has become Jules.

You want me to contribute my perspective, so you set me up with a guest account. In the weeks that follow, I write a couple of posts. One defending trans teen Leelah Alcorn against a detractor. Another about open and honest communication, and how it's guiding us across this frontier.

Eggnog chai bubbles in the saucepan. Bing Crosby sings of Christmas in Hawaii. I unpack a bin of scrapbook embellishments while you dump the contents of a manila envelope onto the kitchen table. Ticket stubs, fliers and boarding passes come to rest between us. It's time to make our annual keepsake Christmas ornament—a tradition we've observed since our first year together.

It's a time to reflect upon our year. It's a way to pare down the bulky brochures and mementos we amass, while keeping the important bits. And it catalogs our life together, a record of everything significant we've been through, contained and complete and displayed on the tree.

We each grab scissors and start clipping. The logo from a Festival of Lights ticket. A blurb from the burlesque show in Denver. A selfie in front of the Ferris wheel at the State Fair. Bits and pieces commemorating Oktoberfest, a week at Myrtle Beach, a visit to a wild bird sanctuary.

This year, we'll include a photo of your tattoo. Though I designed it early in our relationship, it came to fruition only recently. It's the tree from the Garden of Eden. Its foliage covers your back and spills over your shoulders, and at its base, the Serpent sinks its teeth into the apple—the forbidden fruit that symbolizes our love, conceived in adultery, and the knowledge it brought—carnal and otherwise.

We should acknowledge your crossdressing, too, I say, ripping a page from a fashion magazine. You'd wanted to but were afraid to ask.

When the scraps are pasted onto the flat bell shape, we surround them with glittery trim and finish with a coat of clear glaze. As it dries, we hang previous years' ornaments on the tree, musing on the events they record.

King's Island. The Dali Museum. My graduation. Your record release party. The deaths of my dad, your mom, my friend from high school and your favorite dog. Covered in Modge-Podge, each jagged remembrance competes for space, overlapping, wrinkling, running off the edge.

We relive the Valentine's Day you got me tickets to the Vagina Monologues. We remember Memphis: Graceland, Sun Studios, a walk along Beale. We laugh at the photo of Sandi Patty. We'd gone to the Philharmonic on a whim one Christmas Eve, thinking we'd be treated to holiday music. Instead, we suffered a glitzy variety show hosted by the Christian vocalist. Little music was on offer between costume changes, religious commentary and bad jokes.

There's even a patterned napkin from a party at Belinda's—the year you made her daughter cry. Showing off for her mom's friends, the child had produced her Happy Holidays Barbie for the crowd's approval. "Great," you said. "Now you can fall short of impossible beauty standards." The crack went over her head, but she sensed she'd been insulted, and she started to scream. Then your friends began yelling—at you. With this I learned your competence with children was no better than mine.

We reminisce about Browngrass, the music festival in Rabbit Hash, where folk musicians played on rickety porches and guests shook paws with Lucy, the collie that served as town mayor. We were leaving the General Store with cold drinks when you got what you call "The Nod."

It's a secret signal men with huge beards exchange, you say—a sign of respect. Best of all, you got it from a weathered old-timer in a Dickies work shirt, banjo slung across his back—not some upstart who'd just discovered Bonnie Prince Billy.

This Christmas, we'll make the trip to my mom's, as we do every even-numbered year. She'll roast a duck and we'll exchange stockings stuffed with our famous homemade gifts. You've made fruitcake and pecan brittle. I've crafted bergamot-vanilla lotion and lip balm. We'll leave on Christmas Eve, right after "Usmas."

That's when you and I sip hot chocolate in our pajamas and present our gifts for each other. For you I needle-felted a Creeper, the monster from your latest video game obsession; sewed a laptop sleeve and made bookmarks featuring quotes by your favorite authors. I confess I bought you some things, too. My favorite is a pink and white plaid shirtdress. You're going to love it.

SEVEN | JANUARY
THE GHOSTS OF BYRON

You take off your Mary Janes and place them in the plastic tub alongside your phone, a ring of keys and your messenger bag. Your dusty-pink sleeveless top gapes to reveal freshly tanned skin as you shuffle in line behind me.

We've spent the week in Key Largo, courtesy of the consulting firm I work for. They kept me in conferences all week but made up for it with a swanky hotel room, lavish meals and evening parties on the beach. And the last day was free, so I was able to take you out for your birthday.

"What would you be comfortable with me wearing this week?" you asked as we were packing.

It was kind of you to ask. You'd be meeting my boss, and while I didn't intend to hide your crossdressing in the long run, I wasn't quite ready for disclosure. "Maybe stop short of wearing a dress or skirt," I suggested. In pants, however strangely styled, you'd seem eccentric— and I could deal with that for now.

"I can wear makeup?" you asked. "And women's shirts and blingy jeans?" You called my request more than generous.

You arrived at dinner in a boat-neck blouse and a glittery manicure from the resort spa. If my colleagues thought it was odd, they never let on. They passed their queso our way, drawing you into nerdy conversations on home music servers and how "Linux" is pronounced.

At the security guard's signal, I enter the airport scanner, stepping onto the foot-shaped spots and raising my arms as indicated by the diagram. After a few seconds a hefty officer waves me through, where I wait for you on the other side. His indifferent-looking colleague stands nearby, arms folded across his chest.

You step into the scanner next and assume the position, but you trip an alarm. The metal pin from your ankle surgery has never been an issue, so we're not sure what's wrong.

"Step out here, please," the officer says. His eyes flit from the Alice band in your hair to the silk top to the stitching on your jeans. He tilts his head slightly and performs some mental calculation.

You don't pass as a woman—you're not even trying—but he gets what you're about. "We need to do a manual scan," he says, with a knowing glance to his colleague. "Would you prefer a female officer?"

"Yes," you say, beaming.

"Hold tight." He shows you where to wait and walks away. His colleague, arms still folded, gives you a nod.

A uniformed woman appears with a wand. She waves it up and down near your body but detects nothing. Shrugging, she lets you pass.

"Did you see that?" you ask, smiling broadly. "They're trained to respect gender diversity!" You stroll confidently toward our gate, head held high. As we settle into our seats, you go on about how well you've been treated this week. By my coworkers, by the resort staff, by the Miami TSA. A smile brightens your face for the duration of our flight.

"You are *wrong!*" you screamed, your voice growing hoarse. Rolling across a bedspread pocked with burn holes, you topped off my plastic cup with bourbon. The polyester, printed with purple and brown maple leaves, reminded me of the upholstery in my grandpa's camper. But here, the mothball smell was tempered with sweat and cigarette smoke.

"There are *many* ways to rock! "

It was Saturday, the sixth of June, about twelve years ago. We lounged on a sagging mattress in a dirty motel off the interstate near Byron, Georgia, where we awoke in our clothes, surrounded by beer bottles, playing cards, a pack of cigarettes and crumpled paper bags. We were angry, homesick, and tired.

"Listen, " I implored you, with equal intensity. The delirium of being trapped at a rest stop for four days had fully settled upon us. "I know what you're thinking. " I rolled onto one hip, smashing an empty Popeye's box and a jack of spades, and took a swig. "There's the metal way to rock, and the Southern way to rock, and the punk way to rock. But—"

"It's about attitude!" you said. "Not genre." You weren't prepared to accept Hagar's claim, no matter how eloquently I defended it.

"Rocking *is* the attitude," I countered. I hauled myself off the bed, crossed the room and glanced through the blinds. Looking across the empty motel parking lot, I could see my car on the lift behind the slim, dirty garage window of the auto repair shop next door.

"I can't believe you're siding with Sammy."

"What ways are there to rock, then?" I picked up the terry-cloth bunny we'd snagged from the top of a trash can at Sarasota Jungle Gardens and held it close.

"There's the partying having fun way to rock," you said, shoving your cup forward to illustrate. "And the angry kicking ass way to rock." Bourbon sloshed on the bunny and pooled on the bed. We'd lost our head start, our savings and our morale. It was only fitting this small symbol of innocence should also be sullied.

"I think Sammy would say there's a core element to each," I said, "that qualifies as the rocking part. You know, the energy. The..." I shook my fist in the air to signify a concept for which I had no name except "rocking."

Tuesday night we'd left an idyllic camping spot on the beach in Siesta Key near pelicans, peach trees and pineapple groves. It was twelve hours earlier than our scheduled departure but we were feeling antsy, so why not gain an extra day of rest before returning to the grind? We broke camp in the dark, did a load of laundry and got on our way.

Six hours into our sixteen-hour drive the old clunker sputtered and coughed a cloud of rancid smoke into our path. We pulled over and added oil. After another a mile or two it jerked, lost power and slowed to a crawl. We called a tow truck.

We climbed into the AAA truck's expansive front seat and directed the driver to the only mechanic nearby. It was well after midnight but a cheap motel was a stone's throw from the shop. We'd get the car fixed and be on our way Wednesday, more or less as originally planned. We checked the car in, walked next door and got some sleep.

Wednesday brought the first wave of bad news: the engine was blown. It would cost a few grand but could be fixed within a day. We were over a barrel—far from home and too broke to buy a new car.

We called our bosses and extended our vacation time. We called our credit card company to report our unusual spending pattern. Before we knew it, the car was in the air and we were separated from our worldly possessions, including the books in my tote—a selection of Romantic poets.

Still, we'd make the most of it. We took off on foot to get lunch. We found waffle joints, diners and burger chains. There were no whole foods on that stretch of road, no greens, barely a vegetable. Indeed, most of the food was white. There were potatoes and biscuits, grits and gravies. Even the meats were breaded in a grayish husk. We choked down something scattered and smothered before exploring the town. There was little to see amid the desert of banks and real estate offices.

Back at the motel, you began an epic game of Minesweeper on your Palm Pilot. I flipped through cable channels and watched *Three's Company*. The day grew long. We called the mechanic for an update; the engine delivery would take an extra day. We took a nap, went for another walk, and got fried chicken for dinner. We trudged back to the motel and began a marathon-length evening of sex.

By Thursday we were on a mission. Malnourishment had us daydreaming about salad, broccoli, and carrots. Instead we found pancakes, hash browns and sweet tea. We walked across expanses of asphalt, sticky with sweat. We stopped by a phone booth to check in with the auto shop.

The engine was repaired, but the car battery was dead. "The mechanic forgot to hook up the alternator," the receptionist said, as though this were at all OK. "Also, the air conditioner needs recharged." All this would take another day.

We browsed the convenience store for Maker's Mark, trashy magazines and cigarettes. We drowned our sorrows in these vices along with more hanky panky and bad TV. We didn't even need to keep it quiet; the hotel was empty. We cranked up the radio and sang at the top of our lungs. We lost ourselves in screaming sex.

We slept poorly on the collapsing mattress. On Friday morning you called the auto shop, rubbing the aching arm you'd slept on wrong. The repairs were done, you learned, but the engine was leaking oil. They'd need a few hours to look into it. A few hours turned into another day.

"Adversity is the first path to truth," I said, quoting Lord Byron.

Saturday was day four of bad news, bland food, endless stretches of black tar and the musty air of our motel room. Stir crazy, our thoughts turned to the important questions of life, like How Many Ways There Are To Rock.

Unable to counter the "core element" argument, you took my drink, placed it on the nightstand and kissed me. I laid back, pulling you on top of me. We both jumped when the phone rang.

We needed a replacement seal. It couldn't be ordered until Monday.

We walked outside.

"This town is fucking with us," you said.

I agreed. "It breaks people's cars and traps them here."

"Let's pee on the *Welcome to Byron* sign."

Instead, we took stock. We couldn't miss another day of work. The Monday delivery wasn't even guaranteed. Could we drive the car home while it was leaking oil? We called our dads.

"Drive home slow and easy," yours advised.

"Check your oil every hundred miles," mine added. We settled up with the shop, drove our still-broken car across the empty lot and parked it outside our room.

"Hand me the vacation journal," you said, reclining on the bed. I tossed the small wire-bound notebook in your direction. It contained a day-by-day log of our lovely in time in Siesta Key alongside entries from two other vacations. You retrieved a ball-point pen branded with an insurance logo from the nightstand drawer and began to write.

Oh, what fresh hell is this? Why must I be stranded here with nothing but cigarettes, gin rummy, sex, and an alcoholic bunny to comfort me? Have I done something so unforgivable that this is my punishment?

We slept fitfully, waking at four a.m. to some clunking sound. Taking a peek out the window, we found the parking lot filled with cars.

"There must be a festival or event in town," you said. We returned to bed for a last bit of sleep.

Eager to get on the road, we rose to our wake up call, showered quickly, gathered our stuff and closed the hotel room door for the last time. But something seemed weird as we stepped outside. Something I couldn't put my finger on.

"There were a hundred cars in this parking lot a few hours ago," you said. "Remember? Now there are none."

We looked at each other with wide eyes.

"It was the ghosts of those who've been trapped here," you said. "The ghosts of Byron."

"What hell indeed," I said, as we climbed into the car.

"Wait til you meet Twyla and Raven," you say, helping me step down out of your truck. We cross the courtyard to the apartment complex where they live. "You're going to love them." They are intellectuals, you say, who love literature, art, and indie films. While chatting with Twyla online, you learned they live in Indianapolis, not far from Paige. So you met them for coffee while I was out of town for training last week. You knock on the door, eager to introduce me.

I'm surprised when Twyla appears in the doorway. I'm not sure what I expected a crossdressed intellectual to look like, but this is not it. She wears a hot pink wig from a Halloween store, its ribboned pigtails falling across the pinafore of a tightly cinched Alice-in-Wonderland dress. On her feet, lace-trimmed white socks—the likes of which I haven't seen since my mom dressed me for Easter—peek beneath patent leather pumps. She seems outfitted for a fairy tale-themed live action role play. The look is jarring against her athletic build, angular face, and dark eyebrows.

She greets us, tilting her head and curving her fingers nearly backward while stepping sideways in a curtsy. "Jamie!" she says, giving you a side hug. "And this must be Shannon." She offers a supple wrist, as though I might kiss her hand. Then she gestures toward Raven, who gives us a wave. Like Twyla, Raven is in her forties. She's an unassuming woman with unstyled hair, her long-sleeved graphic tee paired with plus-sized jeans and canvas sneakers.

The plan is to walk to dinner, but it's a bit early, so they invite us in. Glancing along the walls on my way to a chair, I see a wedding photo in a personalized frame that confirms what I suspect. Twyla, whose given name is Edgar, is classically handsome in a suit and tie, like a young Hugh Jackman. Raven, a woman of plainer countenance, married up.

The apartment is scattered with piles of unfinished projects and university textbooks. One or both of the pair are heavily into geek culture. Tall stacks of comic books teeter alongside fantasy novels and the complete *Twilight* series on DVD. The bookshelves are dotted with superhero figurines, a bendable Grey alien and a Starship Enterprise model. Under the large-screen TV a Playstation sits wedged between an old-school Atari, a *Dr. Who* Lego game and a Magic: The Gathering card deck.

Covering the walls are original paintings of stylized nudes leaning on cars. They remind me of the work of Patrick Nagel, that meticulous chronicler of eighties hairstyles and necklines. These are brightly colored, with a pair of lime-green lips here, a perfectly round orange nipple there. Twyla sees me looking and tells me she's the artist. She has a degree in fine art but currently works as a bartender.

"Cool," I say. "I have artists in my family. I do some painting myself."

Twyla misses my attempt to connect, launching into a defense of her career choice. Years ago, she informs us, she was a well-known mixologist in Miami. She wasn't crossdressing yet; in fact she was quite the bodybuilder. My eyes move to her arms, still ripped and sinewy from those days. She tells us she started out as a bouncer in one of the roughest clubs in Liberty City.

"Cool," I say. "And what about you, Raven? You teach, right?"

"I'm a history professor."

"Nice. What are you teaching?"

"The Frankfurt school of critical theory. Marxism and the Situationist movement. *Society of the Spectacle* by Guy Debord."

I perk up. I'm not well versed in European history, but *Society of the Spectacle* was on my reading list when I was studying the crisis of modernity with fervor. I started but never finished it; other reading took priority.

"That's about modernity's preference for artifice over authenticity, isn't it?"

"It's a critique of advanced capitalism," she says. "It argues that the modern era is no longer about 'living,' but about 'having'—with 'having' degenerating into 'appearing to have.' This takes a toll on the quality of our lives."

Now I remember why the book intrigued me. I pull a notepad from my tote and jot a reminder to pick it up again.

"One of my bouncer jobs was near a strip bar," Twyla continues, taking advantage of the pause in conversation. Raven gives me a glance that suggests we'll continue later.

"I walked some of the dancers home in exchange for cash. They needed protection and I liked the company of strippers, so it was a win-win." Twyla giggles and shrugs, pressing her chin into her shoulder.

"So this led to the bartender job?" I ask.

"Not right away. Some of the girls were turning tricks on the side. I organized an escort service for them."

I'm bored by Twyla's adventures in illicit employment—I'd rather talk about Raven's curriculum—but I try to stay attentive.

"I guess you could say I was a pimp!" Twyla says, giggling.

A wearied look suggests Raven's heard these stories one too many times. "Does anyone want a drink?" she asks, stepping into the kitchen and opening the fridge. She offers bottled water or beer. We accept a water.

Twyla doesn't answer, still absorbed in her monologue. Through twists and turns we learn that the escort gig led to connections of distinction in the Miami bar scene, then to a stint selling drugs, then to a couple of nights in jail. Finally, somehow—I space on the details—she met the entrepreneur who offered the bartender job.

When we're settled in at the restaurant, Twyla suggests an appetizer platter—but Raven, concerned about the cost, nixes the idea. So I order a sizzling paneer to share. You and I settle on the restaurant's specialty—lamb biryani, while Twyla and Raven choose a lentil dahl. When our orders are in, Twyla solicits your attention, so I'm able to pick up with Raven where we left off.

"It's easy to see how 'having' has replaced 'living'," I say. "But the replacement of 'having' with 'appearing to have' is interesting. It reminds me of social media—all curated selfies and bragging and signaling social affiliations."

"The book's from 1968," Raven says. "So social media wasn't a thing. But yes, I think it's a progression of the inauthentic culture the author critiques. 'Images have replaced human interaction,' he says."

As Raven and I talk, Twyla regales you with her exploits, her voice rising steadily in volume and speed, the words coming now as if fired from a machine gun. "Some say I make my boobs too big," she announces, tearing my attention from Raven. "But small boobs don't look right on my big frame." Seeing that I've heard, she cups the overstuffed bullet bra with her hands and giggles.

"Come visit us sometime," I say as we settle up, passing my contact info to Raven.

"We'd love to, when we can afford it." She agrees to keep in touch by email.

"Don't you love them?" you ask, when we're back on the road.

"Raven is great. But I don't get what you see in Twyla."

"I love Twyla!" you protest. "She's so creative!"

"That art is mediocre and Twyla is a bore. New friends are never good enough for you. Yet Twyla makes the cut? What's the appeal?"

You shrug. "When we move back to Indianapolis, we'll be close to them."

DETACHABLE PENIS

You campaign hard for the strap-on nowadays. More and more you want to "feel like a woman" in the bedroom.

We played around with it once or twice, many years ago, and I'm happy to don it again. But anal sex is not an act that favors spontaneity. You must be relaxed and clean, inside and out. We need several free hours ahead of us. And you want me to initiate because you "feel weird" asking for it. That complicates things—I don't always know whether you've had a shower or eaten something spicy. So I must find a way to inquire, with all delicacy, whether conditions are favorable. Then I have to get the harness in place and adjusted before self-consciousness breaks your mood. The stars seldom align.

I promise I'm doing my best. You like it, these days, when I look tough—so I ordered a black leather bra and shorts that coordinate nicely with the gear. I planned to surprise you with them on Valentine's Day. But you ordered the prosecco and the diavolo shrimp. We danced until late. By the time we hit the sheets, your belly was upset and we were spent.

I can't figure out how to overcome these obstacles. And yet, you seem to blame me. From time to time you ask, a note of desperation rising in your voice, whether we can make it happen soon. I'm trying, I tell you—but you want me to try harder. You list some days that would have worked for you. One Saturday, after I spent the afternoon in the office troubleshooting an outage. The other night, when I went to the library for books by lesbian poets. That Sunday morning when I just slept in.

In the meantime, I sometimes pursue sex with you, the old-fashioned kind. The kind that fits readily into our schedules, that requires no equipment and no game plan. I miss the days when I did not have to petition for that kind of sex.

Don't get me wrong; toys and props and role play are great. But for me a good sex life is *enhanced* by these things, not replaced by them. For me, the best sex is spontaneous, arising naturally from the rhythm of our lives. Remember the days when we'd wash the car or hike in the woods, and find ourselves physically and spiritually exhilarated, eager to shed our clothes and consummate our desire? That's when I feel most aroused, most loving, most loved. For years, you had your unusual requests and I had mine, and we indulged them for each other on the odd weekend. The rest of the time we simply made love.

Now, every day we spend with ordinary sex, the kind in which we use our bodies for pleasure without imagining they look or work differently than they do, is a day in which I deny you the sex you've come to prefer. You start to perceive a pattern in which, night after night, I fail to fulfill your request. But I'm not getting what I want, either. It's become so complicated that we rarely touch at all.

But now, huddled together under the wool blanket with a bowl of oil-popped popcorn in front of TV, you let your hand come to rest on my thigh. Snow falls at a clip, heavy and wet, battering the window and blanketing the rolling acres beyond. A winter storm warning's in its eleventh hour. You flip through our recommendations: a nature documentary, a Werner Herzog film, something in French. What do I think? But I can think only of the warmth of your touch. I lay my hand on yours, close my eyes, close my fingers over yours.

"Forget TV," you say, clicking off the remote and pulling me in for a kiss.

Yes. Putting my hands on your elbows, I lean in until our lips touch and our forearms meet, skin on skin.

Skin on poorly epilated skin.

Your arms are like sandpaper, bristly from wrist to shoulder. I try to hold still, to bring my attention to the kiss. But you move, dragging a prickly heat like nettles across my flesh. You try to maintain contact as I move my hands to your wrists, then to your knees, throwing us into an awkward dance. Finally, I cradle your face in my hands. There's no stubble here. But here, I expect it. You've worn beard of some style or length nearly every day of our lives together.

Now you shave twice a day, priming your face for makeup. But it's missing that downy hair that covers all human skin, so it's not like a woman's. Catching and stopping my caress at intervals, it evokes something else—racecar tires in the sun, silicone, the tacky skin of a tree frog. Razor-burned, bumpy, like my bikini line at the beach. Scabby, here, along the jawline, a manifestation of your zeal.

Back to the kissing, though. Focus on the kiss. My attention on your mouth, on your lips, not on your foundation, its chalky residue, its creamy smell. A smell that reminds me of childhood, of my aunt's handbag. Fake leather, drugstore salve, a stick of spearmint gum retrieved just for me. The cloying scent of a matronly babysitter, the Rolaids she kept on hand, the artificially-flavored lemon cake she brought to the potluck at the church annex. My passion starts to wane and I can't save it. I pull away and go in for a hug.

Nestling my nose into your hair, I find you've borrowed one of my perfumes. Not one of the trendy ones I found at the boutique in Denver. My oldest one, a keepsake, handed down by my mother. She kept it on her vanity table when I was a teen, nestled between loose powders, hat boxes decoupaged with flowers from a seed catalog, and collectible tins arranged on a mirrored filigree tray. It smells like her: rose and gardenia, Dove soap, a vinyl shower cap, an overnight cold cream.

Stay in the moment, Shannon.

Your hair is long and plain and familiar, the way you've worn it for years. So I run my fingers through it, focus on it. My hands follow the strands, across the strap of the new bralette I found for you, over the rough lace back of a high-low top from Kelley's Kloset. *But the hair.* I fixate on it like a fetish. Not even a sexual one—a religious one, a talisman imbued with the power of you, the unadorned you, the old you. I can't help it. Mary Oliver understands: *the soft animal of my body loves what it loves.*

You sense something's wrong.

You deploy the aggressive kiss. It's a maneuver that's really gotten me going in the past. But right now, it feels mechanical.

I know what to do—I've been here before. I'll fantasize the problem away. I replay the early days of our affair, when we couldn't keep our hands off each other. Our first kiss, stolen behind a garage. Sexy private messages. The pent-up desire of weeks spent apart, because you were married. Sex on my apartment floor, on the futon, against the wall. I move my hand up your thigh but it finds nothing interesting; you are tucked.

You don't feel masculine. You've succeeded on that front. But you don't feel feminine, either.

Freud called a woman a person in want of a penis. Shakespeare—in Elizabethan slang—called the flesh between her legs "nothing." They see woman as emasculated man. But that's wrong. Femininity is not generated by subtracting masculinity. Femininity is *its own thing*.

It's not a barren place. It's a *fruitful* place. Not the wasteland left when the loggers clear the forest; the meadow sown with wild daisies. "Feed me on flowers." Suniti Namjoshi. Femininity is juicy: Audre Lorde's "honey flowed from the split cup." It's soft and ripe and round. The "generous thighs" of Adrienne Rich's lover. "The half-curled frond of the fiddlehead fern."

The bulldozer destroys but it doesn't create. So it is with your corset, your razor, your gaff. They whittle away your waist, your beard, the bulge between your legs. They make you *less* of who you are. But they can't make you *more*. You're all too aware of this, yourself: "I refuse to build a body out of padding," you blog. "That body would never be mine." You can only move toward neutrality.

I think you're seeking the youth of your "Girly Boys." But you've aged yourself instead. Shaving has laid bare your timeworn skin, not made it tighter nor brought back its flush. Tucking and compressing has squashed what makes you vibrant. You're polished like a doll, now, veiled like a widow, perfumed like a corpse. The quest for immortality has always been futile; mummification leaves salt and resins where blood once flowed.

I move my hand away from your groin, toward your knees, toward knees knocked together tight, legs tilted to one side, toes pointed, a dishy pose. The pose of a pinup girl painted on a World War II fighter jet. The pose of a silver-screen vixen seducing her boss. It's an act. And worse, I don't know who it's for. You know I'm not attracted to prissiness, even in women. I need your carnality, your muscle, your sweat. You offer sterility, artifice, restraint. I need a rhythm. I need a heartbeat. I need to reach inside and touch your soul. You need performance art. A flawless finish. A filter.

I wish you'd be here for me, instead of wherever it is you are— wherever it is you need to be for yourself. I resent this affectation, the self-absorption behind it, the toll it's taking on our intimacy. I'll never build to any sort of crescendo as long as we play this game. My thighs are as dry as the desert you've made of your sexuality.

You pull away, look at me. "What's going on?" you ask.

"Honestly? I'm not getting wet."

I want you to do something with this information. Instead, you retreat.

"I'm lucky," you write in your blog.

I've opened the living room drapes and settled in by the window with my laptop and a cup of tea. The sun, finally out of hiding, glints off the icicled awning and floods the room. Today I interview for a lucrative short-term contract position that could ease our transition back to Indianapolis. But I've got a minute and I'm eager to see your latest post.

Many crossdressers have relationship problems, you write. You get why—partners have a lot to process. They may fear for their safety. They may worry their loved one is gay or pursuing transition. They shouldn't be blamed, you write, if they just can't hang in there. This isn't something they signed up for.

But you are fortunate.

"Introducing my partner, Shannon!" you write. "She's beautiful, intelligent, adventurous, and queer. She hasn't placed boundaries on who I am."

I appreciate the homage.

I have a history of dating women, you write, and a little "gender bending" is part of our dynamic. Maybe I saw this in you before you saw it in yourself. Because of my openness, you came out to me easily, through honest conversation and "deep sharing."

I ponder the post as I pull my Calvin Klein sheath dress from its dry-cleaning bag. It's a tad small, but it's my best option, so I suck in my gut and shimmy it on, squishing my body into the desired hourglass shape and tugging up the straining zipper. You never had to hide your feelings from me, you write, "as if they were some dirty secret." I'm glad you trusted me enough to share them.

Dabbing foundation in a slow, circular motion, I build up the opaque finish needed to cover my splotchy skin, my appreciation for your tribute yielding to thoughts of the interview. I ponder my salary requirements as I blend, careful to avoid the mask-like look that comes from stopping too abruptly at the chin. I rehearse a spiel about a time I led a team under adverse conditions. My middle-aged skin calls for a minimalist approach, so I finish with a hint of eyeliner and a tinted gloss. My lip line's too craggy for cream lipstick.

Fixing my long, thick hair is the most time-consuming part of my routine. Unless I straighten it, its wishy-washy natural wave makes me look as if I've just rolled out of bed. Pulling sections into clips, I consider the question of my start date. I'd love to leave time between jobs for a trip to Europe, but I don't see that happening now. Your contract ends soon, and you haven't saved a dime. I just can't swing the fare for both of us. Pulling each lock of hair through the ceramic plates of my flat iron is hot, sweaty work, and my makeup threatens to run.

The occasion calls for my "power pumps," a masterpiece of shoe couture in shimmering patent leather with statuesque, four-inch pillars for heels—and the most expensive part of my ensemble. I gave up pantyhose in the nineties; I'm no fan of the way they slash a painful groove into my belly. But as I squish my feet into the rigid toe box, I know forsaking that layer of nylon will mean blisters and bleeding before the day's end. I slip a couple of Band-Aids into the side pocket of my portfolio and grab a pair of flats for when my feet refuse further abuse. This sacrifice of bodily integrity for beauty is ridiculous, I know—but the shoes are damn stunning.

I pull on the blazer, its acetate liner clammy against my bare arms. Picking a cat hair off a lapel, I check myself in the mirror. I look sharp, if you're into this sort of thing. The last time I wore this outfit, a little girl appeared, blurted out "I like your high heels," and scampered away. But despite the endorsement of children and hiring managers, I'll wear the getup only as long as I have to. I long to wash my face, throw my hair into a bun and get into some drawstring pants. Looking like a sexy stockbroker is a social obligation, not a personal interest.

I'm ready early, so I return to my window seat. I've just opened my laptop when I hear your truck tooling up the driveway. The kids were sent to a career fair, you tell me, hanging your coat by the door. School's ended early. I check my email one last time as you bang around in the kitchen. At length, you set two jars of homemade lemonade on the coffee table and take the seat across from me.

"I've decided to get laser surgery," you announce. "To remove my facial hair!"

I look up from my laptop and promptly close the lid.

"Why?"

This decision is unexpected, to say the least. Only recently have you begun shaving, and you still go for spells without doing so—you have a week of beard growth right now. Never seeing you with a beard again? Ever? The thought bums me out. Facial hair isn't something I'm drawn to, in general. But when I think about what you look like, I see a man with a beard. It suits you. Casual. Unwittingly cute. It's soft and it feels nice against my face.

"Do you know how many razors I go through?" you ask. "Do you know how much foundation I use?" You scoot up in your seat, and sniff, and touch your nose, wiping at some speck that isn't there. It's a behavior I've seen in my dad. "It means he feels defensive," my mom once said.

I want to say something. I want to say I'm not OK with this. But my tongue feels thick, my brain unable to access words.

I pick up my phone. Soft clouds diffuse the light, and the gold in your hair picks up the lightest strands of your beard. I take a photo. There's something grounding about your facial hair. It brings a touch of mystery to your face, softens the goofiness of your smile, makes you look serious and smart. I think about never seeing it again, and I take a dozen more.

"I don't want you to do this," I say at last. "I love your beard."

Your face falls. "I never want a beard again. You better get used to that!" You frown, and look down, but in an instant you're chipper again. "Straight men do this all the time," you say, as if your sexuality is in question. It'll save time, you add. And money.

I remain unenthused.

"I'm doing this," you vow, in a tone I can only read as accusatory. Your eyes dart to the left, then to the right. "You can't stop me."

"I'm just telling you how I feel, Jamie. When have I ever tried to stop you from anything?"

But your eyes narrow, and you search my face as if for some unsavory motivation.

"I don't care if you shave most of the time," I say. "But couldn't you have a beard occasionally, just for me?" It's one thing to abide a particular look now and then, I think. It's another to live with it forever.

You shake your head. "My beard is not attractive."

"Not *attractive*? To who?" It's an odd assertion, as though you're reporting on something objective, like a measurement or hue. "*I* find it attractive."

And who else do you need to be attractive for?

"This isn't about you," you say. "I can't stand to look at myself in the mirror."

I try to wrap my mind around this. Isn't attractiveness for attracting? Isn't it like the tree that falls in the forest, meaningless without an observer? Why would you need to attract *yourself*?

I look down at the costume I've assembled for the day: unyielding footwear; man-made fabrics that bind and reshape. It's for an audience, not for me. The demands society makes upon me are trouble enough. Since you love me as I am, why would I add the pressure of trying to fancy my own reflection? Age has ravaged me—less than some, but more

117

than others—and it isn't finished with me yet. Gone is the toned body I carried around in my twenties, resilient to binges on milkshakes and buttery fried potatoes. Gone are the days when my skin was bright and taut and a perfect canvas for trendy makeup techniques. I've had my day, and so have you. Beauty is ephemeral, not ours to keep. Aging gracefully means growing into better versions of ourselves. Shedding youthful vanity. Eating well, staying fit. Finding ways to make the world a better place.

Primping is a way to get along in society. To impress a hiring manager, a lover, even the hostess of a party. I wouldn't primp on a desert island, after all. Would you? Why take on a grooming chore imposed by no one at all? Why care that your face looks like your face?

I don't ask these questions—but you sense my confusion.

"I'm trying to look feminine," you say.

But I don't understand when—or why—that became important. You said you want to flatter the body you *have*. And though it sounds weird, you look more feminine *with* facial hair than without. It softens your square jaw, hides your jowls and your middle-aged pores. It's shiny and healthy-looking. It's youthful and stylish.

"You'll get used to it," you say.

"And if I don't?"

You ignore my question, rambling instead about shaving clubs and lotions and salves. I'm afraid this will put a significant damper on my attraction to you. I'm trying to say so, but I can't find the words, and you keep interrupting.

The last time we made out, we couldn't seal the deal. I don't want our sex life further compromised. I need to say so. Explicitly. But that will hurt your feelings, and I don't have the stomach for that right now. I also don't have the time. I've got to get to my interview.

The end of February brings a stretch of sunny days that thaw the ground and usher in crocus and snowdrop. Driving home from work, I long to ditch my career slacks for some ankle pants and canvas shoes. I pull into the strip mall with my windows down, drive crosswise across the lot, and glide into a parking spot. As I'm collecting my phone and wallet, a pickup truck peels into place next to me, its driver's side window facing mine. A husky woman in a ball cap lowers her window and leans out.

"Are you fucking crazy?"

I glance around nervously.

"You almost t-boned me back there!" she screams, loudly enough to wake the dead. She leans out further, her hulking figure dwarfing the small window, and I feel the heat of her rage. Did I almost hit her? I look around at an empty parking lot. I didn't see her or anyone else.

But I've got no defense. I *did* disregard the lane markings.

She tears into me, straining her voice. I'm a crazy bitch. I'm a fucking idiot. She hopes I kill myself with my own stupidity. She carries on for three solid minutes.

My hand cradles my phone, now damp with sweat. I consider raising it to my ear. Will that make her angrier? Can I get my window up before she pulls me out of my car and kicks my ass? I sit, mute with fear, until at last she raises her window and drives away.

I'm trembling. I want to lay my head on the dash and bawl. Instead, I start my car and drive uneasily out of the shopping center, tormented by a jumble of contradictory thoughts.

It was my fault. I wasn't paying attention.

It was not my fault. Crossing a parking lot diagonally is an utterly common offense. I was going too slow to put anyone at risk. She was looking for someone to abuse.

I'm a doormat. I should have quipped: "Are you quite done?"

I should have dialed the police.

I did the right thing. She was unhinged. She could have pulled a weapon.

I'm still shaking when I pull into our driveway. I want nothing more than to rest my head on your shoulder and cry my eyes out. But you aren't here. I wonder why—your commute is short and you're usually home hours before me. After starting a pot of tea, I take a seat by the window and breathe, trying to get centered. My phone rings.

"I've signed up for laser treatments!" you announce.

You're at the salon. You went in for a consultation but ended up signing a contract, and they want to start your first session. It will take a couple hours. You'll get home late.

"I just wanted to make sure that's OK!" you say.

I swallow hard. I'm not ready for this. Not now, while I'm decompressing from a crazy woman's road rage. I hoped we'd have another conversation about this—you know it makes me sad. I don't want you to do it, ever. I especially don't want you to do it now.

"I've had the world's shittiest day," I choke out. "Could you not do this, right now, with no warning?"

"Sure," you say. "Of course." You tell me you're on your way. But you've signed a contract; what I dread will come to pass. It's just a matter of time.

For the first time, I realize I need support. But I have few friends and you're still in the closet. Climbing into bed with my laptop, I launch a search. There are no support groups for people like me in Ohio. None in Kentucky or Indiana. None anywhere, in real life.

There's an email distribution list, though. It's called "Regenderate," and it's for the partners of crossdressers and transgender people.

When my membership is approved, I see that the group serves several hundred members. About twenty post regularly. Almost all are straight women. Many want to stay with their partners, but they're struggling. Only two are veterans at this. One is Margot, an author who writes books on trans rights. She shares a sneak peak of her upcoming book with the group. The other is a free spirit named Viv. Her partner identified as a crossdresser, but is now transitioning.

Your friends in Dayton say this never happens. The webcomic community says it, too. Crossdressers are sexually motivated, they claim. Trans women express a deep-seated identity. But more than a few women on Regenderate have watched their partners morph from one to the other. Then there was that joke—the one you found on the bulletin board. Maybe the two groups aren't so different, after all.

There's only one man on Regenderate; he's partnered with a woman who identifies as a man. "I've learned to give up on heterosexual sex," Perry writes, "and adapt to gay sex." At first I can't imagine what he means. But as I read through his posts, I begin to understand. His partner probably forbids vaginal contact. Many men, I imagine, would be thrilled to find more blow jobs and anal in their future. But the tone of Perry's posts is sad.

I fall asleep before you make it home, laptop still in hand. I dream you and I own an artisan bakery. We make a cake shaped like the rotund man from the board game *Operation*. His penis, made of fondant, is attached to a ring pop and inserted into a slot at his crotch. News of the cake has spread. Folks come from far and wide to watch us detach the appendage, then put it back. It's a sensation.

"It's configurable," I brag, when our friends stop by the shop one afternoon. Eager to demonstrate, I unbox the cake, humming alternative nineties tune "Detachable Penis."

But the famed organ is missing.

"It's gone out with the trash," you say. "I threw it away."

I'm disappointed. I'm angry. I thought the cake belonged to both of us, something we shared. You could have put the penis aside, for however long you liked, instead of disposing of it forever.

The cake was something special. Now it's just another cake.

PART II

REVERING GENDER

SEXUAL SELECTION

"You look like Brad Pitt!"

The gray-haired gentleman delivers the compliment with an air of good humor. He's been glancing our way across Moon Garden, our favorite little mom-and-pop Korean restaurant, since we arrived to celebrate my new contract position. He now pauses at our booth as he winds his way back from the restroom. "I've been trying for the life of me to figure out who you look like, and it just occurred to me. It's Brad Pitt! You're a dead ringer!"

It isn't the first time someone's made the comparison. You share the actor's stormy eyebrows, his piercing blue eyes and his strong jaw. Last year a cashier, seemingly interested in more than your patronage, gave you the same compliment. "I doubt that, but thank you," you said, beaming. Afterward I teased you for carrying on with another woman in front of me.

This time, you aren't pleased. Bewilderment crosses your face, anguish close at its heels. Tears well in your eyes. You open your mouth but you don't know what to say. Failing to notice your distress, the fellow gives you a pat on the shoulder and returns to his table, where his wife awaits.

"What's going on?" I ask, grabbing your hand. Whatever's happening seems to require damage control.

"Are you kidding me?" you ask, pushing aside plates of bulgogi and house-made kimchi. Lowering your head, you glance upward at me through a knitted brow, your expression suggesting I'm supposed to understand.

"Brad Pitt is... attractive," I say, feeling silly for stating the obvious. Hell, Brad Pitt is a *cliché* for attractiveness. "It was a compliment?" I add, with the upward inflection that suggests a question, though it's not really a question.

You look at your blouse, finger its keyhole neckline. "Don't I look like a girl?"

A girl?

I've been called a girl a time or two. Once by a client who assumed I was the secretary instead of the software engineer, and asked me to take a memo. Once by a gang of construction workers in a strange city who bored holes with their eyes as I passed their site to get lunch. The word "girl," unless it's used for someone like Nina or Lia, rubs me the wrong way.

But you asked a question—a confusing one—and I should answer.

The truth, of course, is *no*. You look like you. Strong, wiry, disheveled, with a puckish smile and a guitar player's hands. You're makeup-free at the moment, and while your hair is long, you've worn it that way for years. What sorcery would have transformed your face into a female's? Did you think placing it near silk had fundamentally altered it? You said yourself crossdressers rarely pass, and you haven't been trying. So no, you don't look like a "girl"—or even a woman. Your high-top sneakers came from the men's department, and even your jeans, a bit whimsical with a floral print, are obscured behind the table.

You're wounded by my hesitation.

"Maybe I don't look like a girl," you admit. "But clearly I am *presenting* as one. That man insulted me."

"That man is old," I offer. "He didn't know."

Actually, *I* didn't know.

My mind races. Have you given me any indication of this? For the past eight months, and as late as last week, you've claimed—ranted even—that you're a man. You've said it aloud and you've written it on your blog. You've reiterated, to me and to your online friends, that you reject the "gender binary" and that trying to look like the opposite sex is a "bullshit goal."

"You're presenting as a girl?"

"Well, *yeah*." You lower your head into your hands, and your shoulders twitch as you hold back sobs.

This is a surprise. I've been taking your claims at face value.

"Don't you think of yourself as 'Outside the Binary?'"

"I guess I don't," you say, slowly raising your head. It seems you're just now learning this about yourself.

"And you care about passing, now?" I ask, squeezing your hand.

"I guess I do care about that," you admit.

So you've developed an interest in passing. That's new. But something *else* is happening, too.

You thought, until this moment, that you *already* passed. You were shocked, after all, by the man's comment. As if your face—so often compared to Brad Pitt's in the past—couldn't possibly look like Brad Pitt's today. Even though you've done nothing to change your appearance.

Something else is weird, too. You were just compared to one of the most attractive actors on the planet. Instead of hearing a compliment—as it was clearly intended—or even a neutral statement, you heard an *insult*.

When did your feelings change? What changed them? Why was there no corresponding change in your identity, or even your manner of dress? Your inner world is a mystery to me right now. I suppose there's more in the Black Box than I'd guessed.

When it's clear we won't be finishing dinner, I pay the bill and ask for carry-out containers. We make our way toward the door, passing the gentleman, who now chuckles softly. "I love it!" he says, with a thumbs up. You give him a wry smile.

"At least he called me pretty," you say, pulling your seat belt across your lap.

"When did he do that?"

"As we were leaving. He said, 'I love your pretty face.'"

"That's not what he said."

"Yes, it is. He said, 'I love your pretty face.' He was trying to make up for upsetting me."

But this is not what I heard. And why would a man dining with his wife say such a thing? He didn't see someone presenting female—he saw someone who looks like Brad Pitt. He doesn't even know he's hurt your feelings.

I love your pretty face?

Something—wishful thinking, perhaps—is messing with your head. You think you look more feminine than you do. You're reading too much into innocent comments. You might even be hearing things.

And it seems you no longer identify as a man.

The delivery driver flings the parcel onto our porch just as we step outside. We're on our way to Indianapolis to grab sushi, then to attend a live storytelling event sponsored by Cuppajoe Media. It's a chance to see some friends and to schmooze with the company's elite—you still hope to work there someday.

You pick up the package and examine its label. It's a dress from Modcloth you've been anxiously awaiting. You want to wear it to the annual plant swap at Darcy's. Every spring we drive to her house, surplus plants from our yard in tow, to drink wine, eat cake and trade seedlings with friends.

"We have a minute," I say, as we step back inside. "Why don't you try it on?"

"Nah." You rip open the package then shake out the garment, a yellow and navy sundress. "It's adorable!" you announce.

Indeed. "Try it on real quick," I suggest.

"I don't need to," you say, holding the dress in front of your body. "I can tell it fits."

Maybe it does, but I wonder if you know how often a dress fails to flatter, squishing you in one place and gaping in another. But I can't change your mind; you slip the dress back in its bag and toss it in the stairwell to deal with later.

I organize my tote as you drive, pulling out Camille Paglia's *Sexual Personae.* Lately I've focused my library acquisitions on the ways thinkers, old and new, conceptualize "masculine" and "feminine."

Paglia's known to be controversial. But her views on gender come from Nietzsche's *The Birth of Tragedy.* She refers to his "Apollonian" realm, a masculine domain of "reason and logic," control over nature, "thing-making" and science. And his "Dionysian" realm, which she renames "chthonian"—an "enchanted," feminine realm of nature, sex, procreation, and the fat, blood and "albumen" of the fertile female body.

Such dichotomies abound in the hive mind, I'm learning. The Chinese have Yin and Yang, the symbiosis of active male and passive female energy. Freud has his egoistic death drive, associated with men and violence, and his creative pleasure principle, associated with women and reproduction. Psychologist Erich Fromm posits a "biophilia" that loves sex, joy, and growth, and a "necrophilia" focused on "death, war and destruction." Do these realms truly map to the sexes? Perhaps, perhaps not—but they certainly resonate across cultures.

As we enter the outskirts of Indianapolis we realize we're thirsty. I hoist up my tote as you pull into a mega-sized truck stop. After stopping by the restroom—you use the women's, now—we head toward the floor-to-ceiling coolers to find something cold to drink.

I can tell we're back in the city—seventeen kinds of lemonade offer themselves. Organic lemonade, sparkling lemonade, pink lemonade, sugar-free lemonade. Lemonade squeezed from Meyer lemons, sweetened with honey, mixed with green tea, scented with rose. There's even a green variety for St. Patrick's Day. It's what Paglia calls a "teeming multiplicity" of consumer products. I reach for a familiar brand, but is that the right strategy? Should I support a small startup, instead? One brand offers a two-for deal—but do I need two? I settle on something whose font suggests healthy, sustainable, small batch. But I haven't researched this company. Lemonade is the simplest of concoctions, reputedly for even those whom life hands little. Who knew it could be coaxed into so many variations?

I feel something like guilt as I bring my dubious choice to the register. What's my priority? My budget? My health? Is this bottle recyclable? Focusing on something means neglecting something else. Choice is good, but it's subject to diminishing returns. What happens to the human psyche when these little doubts pile up? This too-muchness of capitalism, this fetishization of choice—it is a crisis of modernity. Paglia calls it "decadence."

I pull out my dictionary as I wait in line. "Moral or cultural decline." Decline! Advertising frames decadence as a well-deserved morsel of rich chocolate. How did we get from luxury to decline?

I begin to understand. It's about taking things for granted—a prerogative of the affluent. It's not about enjoying that piece of chocolate. It's about losing it in the cabinet behind the kale chips and the turmeric tea. Yes, decadence is porn and foie gras and cocaine, thrills underpinned with slavery and violence. But decadence is also advanced capitalism's keto-friendly and stevia-sweetened glut of options.

It's modern. It's Apollonian. It's Britney and Biddy's fifty shades of queer.

Abundance is another thing.

It's Heidegger's jug of wine, that "essences in the gift of the pour." It's Epicurus's "single good piece of cheese." It belongs to the sacred, chthonian realm, where dreams haunt and sex performs its sublime magic.

I place the drink on the conveyor belt and swipe my card. Seventeen kinds of lemonade have not brought me joy. One kind, hand-squeezed from real lemons and shared with you on the front porch, has.

"It's a good thing everyone calls me Jamie," you say, flashing a wide-eyed smile. You pour yourself a glass of plum wine from the carafe as I choose a tiny pencil from the cup next to the low sodium soy sauce. "Since it's already a feminine-sounding name, I won't have to change it!"

"Yes," I agree, unrolling my chopsticks and placing the napkin in my lap. "That's fortunate." After fourteen years, I'm glad I don't have to get used to another name.

Though it's mid-March, and still quite chilly outside, I could swear Sakura has their air conditioning on. Maybe the place is just drafty. I pull on the cardigan I've draped over my chair and wrap my hands around my mug of green tea. You're faring better in an ankle-length skirt adorned with paisleys in autumn colors. It's a bit dowdy for spring but at least you're warm.

"Do you want the Arizona roll?" I ask, my pencil hovering over the relevant column.

"Oh, no," you say. But not in response to my question—you're looking at your phone. I don't know what's on the screen, but your eyes convey sheer panic.

"What?"

"Paige's birthday is the same day as my first laser appointment. How did I mess that up?"

Paige struggles with depression and one of her cats is dying of pancreatitis. "You guys are my first choice," she said, when she asked us over to celebrate. "But I know you have a long drive so if you can't make it, I understand." We really want to come through for her. Still, there's no reason to panic. It's over a month away.

"Can you move your session?"

"Yes," you say. "I have six months to schedule all my visits, and it doesn't matter when I take them." But you frown and start to fidget with the hem of your blouse. Some trouble is brewing behind your eyes.

"So... postpone it?"

"Why should I *have* to postpone it?" you blurt out, loud enough to raise the eyebrow of a neighboring diner. You look no less outraged than if I'd suggested postponing a funeral. I'm taken by surprise—you normally avoid drawing attention to yourself in public, even when I'm straining to hear.

"You *don't* have to," I say. "Do what you want." I'm confused by this implication that you're under some sort of duress. I think rescheduling your appointment is a trivial matter, but you're free to skip Paige's birthday if you want.

"I plan to go," I add. "But I can go without you."

You look past me toward the rice-paper blinds, seemingly through them, into some offensive distant scene. You set your teeth together, breathing through them, and say: "I've already spent *forever* finding a date."

This is news to me; you haven't mentioned any scheduling difficulties. Besides, school will end soon, leaving your calendar wide open. There's simply no drawback to postponing your appointment. You can take it any time, while Paige's birthday can't be moved. But whatever. I'm not your mom and I don't intend to goad you into going.

"So don't go." I become aware, too late, of a dismissiveness in my tone that's sure to rub you the wrong way.

You look relieved. "I'm not going!" you say, waving your arm widely. "It can't be helped!"

"Fine."

A moment passes in silence while I study a plastic-encased table card listing the day's specials.

"What?" You're indignant. It seems backing off is not enough. You want me to sympathize. You want me to concede that your laser appointment is more important than Paige's birthday.

I don't get it. Your decision is patently absurd. At the same time, I've done nothing to interfere with it. Can't we just agree to disagree? Frankly, I'm little annoyed at the prospect of defending your absence to Paige. With considerable effort I suppress the urge to roll my eyes.

You come to your senses. "I guess I'm going," you say, dropping your shoulders in resignation. "It's Paige's birthday. We don't make enough time for her."

I know better than to show relief. "It will be fun," I say, keeping my tone light.

I hand the table card to you, suggesting the octopus salad. You look at it without acknowledgment, still wallowing in your private anguish. You knit your brows and scowl. Tears fill your eyes.

"It isn't *fair*," you say, placing an odd emphasis on the word "fair." "I shouldn't *have* to cancel."

Now I'm concerned. My attention shifts from trying to duck your anger to wondering if you're thinking clearly. This is a minor dilemma, not a cosmic injustice. It's a simple matter of managing your calendar.

Who do you imagine is being unfair? Is it Paige, because she requested your company? Me, because I plan to go? I watch you seethe, your eyes shifting subtly from side to side. It makes no sense, but you seem to suspect sabotage.

"Why can't I have this?" you demand, slapping the table. "Why can't I have this *one thing*?"

I don't know what things you've been denied, or why the timing of this appointment ranks as an important one. I hoped to rescue the evening; now I want only to escape this conversation.

It occurs to me I can simply postpone it.

"Why don't you decide later," I say, placing a mark next to the Arizona roll.

TEN | APRIL
THE CRYING GAME

You've cried every night for the past three weeks.

I ponder this as I walk through the garden, finding contributions for tomorrow's plant swap. Perhaps these yellow irises, growing too dense for their circle of plastic edging; chunks from the prolific catnip patch; astilbes and coral bells that prefer more shade than our yard can provide.

It started after your revelation in Moon Garden. That night, you dreamt you were a pair of fraternal twins. James was a little bruiser with a military buzz cut. Jamie was a girl with bows in her hair. James grabbed Jamie, pulled her behind a tree and beat the shit out of her.

I was awakened by your sobbing. I held you until you were ready to sleep again.

You often cry over your appearance, now. You tell me you've developed "gender dysphoria"—a mismatch between your "gender identity" and your body. When you look in the mirror, you expect to see a woman, but find only a stubbly face, a shapeless body and big hands. You cry because you're "not pretty enough." I've held you through these crises, assuring you you're beautiful, telling you every woman feels this way.

When we gathered at your dad's for Easter, you told your family you wished your mother were alive so you could come out to her.

"That wouldn't have gone over well," Jill said.

"That's not true," you countered. "Mom was very tolerant."

"Jill's right though," Jeremy chimed in. "It's good she was spared the heartache." You were appalled, but your siblings only reiterated their certainty.

When I think about your mother, I know they're right. She was tolerant, yes. She was also a no-nonsense woman.

As an orphan raised in foster homes, she'd spent her childhood in forced farm labor: hauling wood, cleaning rabbit cages, wringing the necks of chickens that thrashed about, resisting death. She'd lived with lots of people, she once said, but never knew family until she started her own. With tremendous gratitude for the five of you, she tackled homemaking with a passion, cooking from scratch, sewing curtains and tablecloths, setting a Sunday dinner table with candles. She was generous to the community, too, reading to kids at the library and teaching craft classes at the nursing home. She cared deeply for the downtrodden, but her troubled past brought her a kind of perspective. She spared little time for first world problems, and her way of curtly dismissing them sometimes hurt feelings. Just ask Jill, who once failed to exact her sympathy with a temper tantrum over a misplaced cell phone.

I can easily imagine your mother's reaction, had you come out to her:

"Jamie. You are *not* a woman."

She would have stated it simply, with no malice, and an unceremonious return to whatever gravy she was stirring.

You'd have been offended. You'd have asked her to respect your identity.

She'd have assumed you were joking. Upon learning you weren't, she'd have put down her slotted spoon with measured impatience. "Jamie. Seriously," she would have intoned, shaking her head with an incredulous half-smile, as though she really had no time for this, and anyway you knew better. And then she would have asked you to fetch her the milk. No amount of discussion, over dinner or board games, would have changed her mind. The more you explained, the more she'd have suggested you find something productive to do. "An idle mind is the devil's playground," she would have said.

I didn't share this, of course. But I watched you struggle to reconcile her response, however hypothetical in the family's posthumous assessment, with your craving for her approval.

That night you cried for the heart-to-heart you and your mother never had. You cried about the things she might have said, the things she might have failed to say. I held you again, this time for many hours, and told you everything would be alright. It was after midnight before we got to sleep.

Sometimes you cry over something I say. I admitted I felt cute after getting a haircut. That turned into a discussion of whether you, too, were cute, and whether you could muster the confidence to presume so. Another time, I asked you to open a jar, and the reminder of your strength was triggering. I second-guess myself before speaking now. I never know what innocuous comment will cause you pain.

Your crying jags last until two or three in the morning. I talk you through them for as long as I can, but eventually I roll away from you, apologize, and surrender to sleep. I wish I could stay up, but I've started my contract job in Indianapolis and my commute is nearly two hours. Every morning I'm sleepier than the morning before. The road stretches ahead of me, a blur of muted blues and grays, an ever-lengthening demand. I lower the window and turn up the radio, cruising on a lapse of memory.

Your blog takes a dark turn. "This thing will take all of me," you say in your latest post. "It will leave me with nothing."

When we first dated, you once asked: "Do you ever enjoy being sad?"

I hadn't. Never, for a moment, have I wanted sadness in my life.

"I enjoy it sometimes," you said.

I found this as troubling as the poster board. I didn't understand, and I still don't.

Now I walk back to the porch and take a seat, noticing the Grecian windflowers have started to bloom. I could stand to edge around them. Maybe someone will share sedums or creeping phlox tomorrow.

You emerge from the front door and hand me a homemade lemonade. You don't seem to enjoy this sadness, I think, as you take the seat next to me. And I don't want it for you. I hope you'll soon come to peace with who you are.

"I'm so glad you're into our new life," you say, grinning broadly.

I hesitate. "You mean the fact that you're transgender?" I'm OK, of course, but I wouldn't say I'm "into" it. Have I given off that vibe?

"Yes! Isn't it fun, now that I'm a woman?"

"You're... a woman?"

I wasn't sure how you identify, exactly. That's been locked in the Black Box—along with why you wear panties and bras, who you're dressing for, and when laser appointments became more important than friends' birthdays.

"Obviously I'm not *literally* a woman," you say, exhaling. "I mean I'm going to be *living* as one."

"Right."

That's a good way to frame it, I think. I can't help but wonder if a little cognitive dissonance led to your shock and distress at Moon Garden.

And a person who lives as a woman is a woman, of sorts. So says queer theorist Judith Butler. Womanhood shouldn't be judged by a chromosome test, or, as your Tumblr friends are fond of scoffing, a "panty check." It shouldn't mean commitment to some stereotype or medical intervention. It's appropriate to believe, based on your word alone, that you're a woman. It's not a new concept, actually. It's called a "performative utterance."

A statement can be at once word and deed, linguist J.L. Austin proposed. When you say "I promise," you make a promise. When you say "I bet," you place a bet. By identifying as a woman, you make yourself one. And if, through some change of heart, you declare yourself a man, you will be a man. No evidence is needed; your word is law. Because the construct doesn't *describe* reality. It *creates* reality from the raw material of language.

"Isn't it exciting?"

"I mean..." You're so often on edge now that speaking my mind feels like asking for a fight. But I'm not sure what excitement you expect living as a woman to bring into our lives. Shouldn't it be a neutral state, at best? I'm put off by this implication that it's all a big game. The endless crying hasn't been exciting for me. It hasn't even been exciting for you.

"I wouldn't have chosen this," I say, after carefully considering my words.

Your face goes white, as though this is unexpected and terrible news.

"This is something *you* want," I say, surprised at your surprise. "I like you fine the way you are."

You look into the distance, scan the horizon. "Your last guest post on my blog was so supportive," you say.

"Well sure, I *support* you. But I'm not *excited*. What do you think is in this for me?"

I wrote that post when you called yourself a crossdresser. You were different then. You were happy. We were growing stronger as a couple, I wrote, because we were talking it through. Now, our communication is eroding. So many of your feelings are locked in the Black Box. So many of mine are held back in the interest of sparing yours.

That's apparently left you more in the dark than I realized.

It would be easy to blame this on you—you've become averse to frank discussion. And when I *do* speak up, there's a disconnect between what I say and what you hear. But it takes two. I need to tell you how I feel, plainly, even when it's hard.

I need to talk to you about your laser surgery. In a way, it's too late—you've signed a contract. Maybe you even did that to sidestep conversation. But it's important, and I can't keep biting my tongue. Our future depends on it.

"Have you forgotten I don't want you to remove your beard?"

"I have no choice about that!" you say, looking down. "It's what I *need.*"

It is this *need* of yours—the way it's replaced your personality, the way we've reorganized our lives to accommodate it—that has made it hard for me to tell you how I feel.

But it's my fault, too. When you told me your plans, I was confused by my own reaction. After all, I'm hardly an enthusiast of masculinity. I rarely find men attractive, and when I do, they're effeminate, sensitive types. I like your long hair, your gentle eyes and your pacifism. If asked, I never would have named your beard among the things that turn me on.

But your beard is a part of you, and it's a good part. It reminds me of the first time we kissed, at a party at Belinda's. We'd been exchanging racy texts when we found ourselves alone behind her garage. Awash in sexual tension, we couldn't resist the long-awaited kiss. You put your arms around my waist; I cradled your face in my hands. Your beard was short and soft and I enjoyed the way it brushed my cheek.

If I couldn't explain my feelings to myself, I certainly couldn't explain them to you. And I didn't want to hurt your feelings. You were blindly optimistic; I tried to be, too. But the last time we got frisky, I was forced to realize the limits of optimism. That was over a month ago and we haven't tried again. Our relationship began with a strong mutual interest in sex. In nearly fifteen years, it's scarcely flagged. This change to your face is permanent, and its effect on our sex life could be, too. I may be middle-aged, but I have a strong libido and we've chosen to be monogamous. I don't want to face a life of frustration.

"Your laser surgery is going to be bad for our marriage," I choke out.

"What do you mean?" you ask. Your eyes widen in the fight-or-flight response one has to an emergency.

I take a deep breath. "It's going to interfere with my attraction to you."

"It will not!" you say. "You will find a way!"

"Jamie. I need for you to hear me. Remember the last time we made out? This is not rhetorical."

"It's going to be OK," you declare, waving your hand to dismiss my concerns.

But it might not be OK.

It really *might not.*

I have an idea. I browse to the photo gallery on my phone and scroll to February, choosing a photo from that series I took of you, when you had a short beard. Then I find my most recent photo of you, and place the two side by side. You're vibrant in the first one: smiling, flushed, your hair glistening, your natural charm shining through. And you're... *still* in the second. Washed out, your expression pained, your features traced starkly in black and red.

I hand my phone to you. "Which photo do you look better in?"

You point to the newer one.

It's hard to wrap my mind around that choice. To be frank, no one else would make it. I think of Caitlin Moran's take on some socialites who wore their fear of aging on their surgically altered faces. They looked "literally and figuratively petrified," she wrote. You're wearing that look in this second photo. And right here, right now, in real life.

"I need to be my true, authentic self," you say, but your eyes are faraway and your voice sounds mechanical.

"I want you to understand what's at stake."

"This is going to happen," you say, shaking your head vigorously, as though flinging unwanted thoughts to its perimeter.

This laser surgery bothers me. And it isn't just that I prefer your face unshaven, though it turns out I do. Something else bothers me more. I don't want you to favor your own gaze and your own touch, when *I* am your lover. I don't want you to value this cosmetic change more than you value *us*.

I want you to *want* to attract me. Because you want me that much, because it's *that important*. That's how *I* feel. I don't need to turn other people on. I certainly don't need to turn *myself* on. Our intimacy is sacred. It brings us together. I can't imagine sabotaging it.

Why don't you feel the same way?

"I'm worried about our future," I say.

And I keep it to myself, but I'm worried about the way you aren't worried.

I want to tell you this part, too. But there's an intensity in your eyes that stops me in my tracks. You're angry. You're hurt. I look for the words that will reach you. I can't find them.

I back down.

"This is the beginning of the end," says a voice in my head. But I squash it down. I tell myself we'll revisit the topic later. We'll talk again. We'll talk about everything, like we once did.

In the evening I see you standing in the foyer, examining yourself in the mirror. You stroke your jawline and frown. You look at your hands. You're not happy with your body anymore. A few months ago, that wasn't the case. What happened between then and now?

"I'm drawn to mirrors," you write in your blog. "But I want a reassurance they refuse to provide. Sometimes I can't tell if I'm really a girl."

When Isabel and I went poly, I would have told you it was a mutual decision. It was, kind of. I certainly didn't go in kicking and screaming. As I browse my phone in bed on the morning of the plant swap, I ponder my foray into the world of open relationships. They're a hot topic on Regenderate. You're sleeping beside me, though you've begun to stir.

I was, after all, the one who first stumbled into the polyamory chat room on AOL and asked what it was about. "Loving non-monogamy," I was told. It sounded so enlightened. Indeed, if you truly care about someone, why shouldn't you want her to experience *all* the good in the world, even if that good is love or sex or both with someone else?

We were four years into our relationship. Cuddling up to Isabel at night was the most natural thing I'd ever done, and I needed it to last forever. Same-sex marriage wasn't legal, but one day, I thought, we'd go to P-Town and say our vows.

The day came when polyamory ceased to be a philosophical exercise and became a reality. I could have lived without it. She latched onto it with great interest. I was sure we were rock-solid; nothing as noble as loving someone else would threaten our relationship. But just because we could do it, did that mean we *should?* What of protecting *us* at all costs, because it's that important? What of forsaking others, because we are enough? I sensed that polyamory would be our undoing. But it was the right thing to do, I told myself. To prove how progressive I was. To prove my love. Then I let my eyes wander, let the thrill of something new distract me from the sadness.

Isabel found a girlfriend first. Then the jealousy came, but not in the way I expected. I accepted that she was with someone else. But I was surprised by her choice of partner. And a little insulted.

Dixie carried a keychain that read "Zero to bitch in 60 seconds." She was nice enough, but she was hardly special. Her personality fell somewhere between redneck and "basic bitch." She wore her jeans too tight and flirted with everyone. She was addicted to television and didn't get our jokes. Was I not special? Was I comparable to Dixie?

But then I did the same thing. With Isabel at home, I didn't have to be picky. I messed around with whoever, like the crass barfly whose arrogance kind of turned me on. Or the woman whose sunny smile could turn to rage on a dime.

Polyamory was supposed to be about *loving* more than one person. But Rory, Agnes and Sage imploded when they sexed up each other's siblings and then those siblings' spouses. And a poly convention we attended proved a thinly veiled orgy in a two-story Victorian. Guests mingled in a lukewarm hot tub floating with clumpy bodily fluids. Men lined up in damp towels to sign a "dance card" that gave them a turn with the hostess. Isabel and I volunteered for a beer run and never returned.

Jealousy, shifting boundaries, and the never-ending party that became our life did us in. There was a lesson to be learned, but I struggled to pinpoint it. Surely the philosophy itself was sound. Maybe we'd drawn up the wrong guidelines. Maybe we'd failed to check in. Or maybe what we had done, and what Rory and company had done, and what we had witnessed at the convention, wasn't polyamory at all. Maybe it was decadence. A glut of unappreciated options.

"I'm hard-wired for monogamy," Margot—the author who writes on trans rights—once told the Regenderate list. Maybe that was my problem. Maybe polyamory wasn't part of my orientation.

You rise and start to browse your closet. I should get ready, too. I put my phone down and pull on the sleeveless blouse I set aside for today—a fancy one I seldom find occasion to wear. It's flared and longer on the sides, made of softly draping rayon and scattered with watercolor violets. I layer it over cutoff shorts and lace up a pair of gladiator sandals. Checking myself in the floor-length mirror, I find the ensemble's surprisingly flattering. The gathered neckline emphasizes my bust, the cropped hem shows off my newly trim belly, and the glimpse of my thighs between short shorts and tall sandals looks sexy. You've always loved my bare legs, and this look would have driven you mad only months ago. But when you look up, your eyes land on my blouse and stay there. You walk over to me, finger the hem, and examine the length of fabric between the arm holes.

"This looks like it would fit me," you say. "Can I try it sometime?"

Sadness washes over me. But I suppose I don't deserve your flattery at every turn. And why should I, alone, enjoy the clothing I bought for myself? Before I can answer, you become preoccupied with your new Modcloth dress, removing the tags, setting aside the spare buttons.

I leave you to it and head outside. I dig up the plants we're bringing and arrange them into trays, then raid the shed for old flowerpots.

You're standing in the kitchen in your new dress when I come back inside, waiting for my help. I zip it up effortlessly; you've chosen the right size. You run to the full-length mirror in the hallway, giddy. I follow.

But you don't like what you see.

"This is no good," you say. "This is no good at all!"

It's actually a really cute dress. "What's wrong?" I ask.

"I didn't know my shoulders were so broad," you say, touching the area where the strap meets the bodice. "I didn't know my hips were so small."

It's true. You're shaped as you've always been shaped: like a man. When did you lose sight of this? "I'll never strap on breasts or hips," you blogged, not so long ago. Surely you're aware those serve to make the male body look female? Didn't you make a conscious decision to accept yourself as you are?

You turn and look at yourself from different angles. "Unzip me," you demand, turning your backside to me.

I oblige.

"What am I going to wear now?" you ask, panic rising in your voice. "Can I borrow something?"

"Of course. But the dress is fine." There is no clothing, in my closet or anywhere else, that will transform your shape into something it isn't.

I follow you upstairs. Rifling through my things, you produce a black skirt with an elastic waistband and pull it on. It's heavy polyester, too hot for the season, and it's a little shiny for casual wear. You dig in a drawer and pull on a t-shirt for a local band. The ensemble's no improvement over the dress, and it's a bit cheerless for a summer party.

"This doesn't look right, does it?"

I shrug. It doesn't, but I'm afraid to say so. I'm also worried about the time. It takes nearly two hours to get to Darcy's, and if we're late, we'll miss out on the best offerings. I wish you'd figured out your outfit in advance.

"Why not?" You twist and stare at your silhouette in the mirror. "You wear t-shirts with skirts all the time!"

I have to think about the answer; I toss outfits together without thinking. "I guess I wear them with cotton skirts. That one's too dressy."

"You're right," you say, examining the skirt's textured surface. You flop down on the bed. "How will I ever learn the rules?" You cover your face with your hands. You start to cry.

If the past month is any indication, we're about to lose the day to your inconsolable sadness. I head downstairs to the kitchen and browse the fridge. Finding a bottled iced tea there, I take it with me to the couch and sit down. I try to make peace with the possibility we won't make it to the plant swap.

"I miss the things a man and a woman do together," Perry told the Regenderate list. "And I don't mean just sex." He didn't elaborate. But I think I'm starting to understand.

I open the bottle, take a swig, and wait.

ELEVEN | MAY
LOVE MY TRANSNESS

"She's beautiful!"

A jingle from my phone snaps me from my slow descent toward sleep. I roll in the direction of the nightstand and see the text from Paige in my notifications. It's late, and I should ignore it. But you're still reclining in bed with your phone—arranging a Dungeons and Dragons game with Lyle and Theo—so I undock mine to see what's up.

Scrolling to the top of a group chat, I find a photo of an infant scowling in a pea-green onesie, propped up by Daddy's hand, her wisp of hair coerced into an oversize bow. "Ladies!" Claire announces. "May I present Luna Meredith Cooper." Eight pounds, six ounces.

"She's a doll," confirms Claire's friend Nora. More endorsements follow. So precious. Such tiny hands.

She's cute, I guess, if you're into squishy purple faces and fat arms. Unfortunately, I'm missing the feminine instinct to gush over a baby. But I'm happy for Claire—she's been pregnant forever—and I'll offer the requisite murmurs of approval. Tomorrow, when I've had some sleep.

Responses come rapidly, now, blowing up my phone. "What's happening?" you ask, looking over my shoulder.

"Claire's had a girl. Her name is Luna." That's the name of Nina and Lia's yellow lab, I realize, as I lower the volume on my phone.

"I didn't get the text," you say, checking your messages. You toss your phone in my direction, as if suggesting I confirm.

"Here you go." I hand over my phone, though I'm surprised you care.

"Ladies?" You click into the details and read the recipient list aloud—"Nora, Melanie, Darcy, Paige"—your voice rising in pitch a little with each name. "Claire did not include me!"

"You don't care about babies any more than I do."

"That's not the point. Claire doesn't think of me as a woman!"

So that's what's on your mind. I should have known it wasn't a sudden interest in the little bundle of joy.

There's nothing I can say here.

There's nothing I can say, because I'm sure *you're right*. I'm sure Claire doesn't think of you as a woman.

She *wants* to think of you as a woman. If you complain, she'll *try harder* to think of you as a woman. But when Claire shared the new arrival with the women in her life, you didn't come to mind. You've never given birth, taken a pregnancy test, or vented about the needs of a toddler over a bottle of rosé on a moms' night out. Nora, on the other hand, is due in the fall. Melanie has a boy and is trying for her second. Indeed, your rift with Melanie began with your disinterest in children.

You probably don't know Claire is dehydrated and iron deficient. Her feet are swollen. Her vagina's so bruised it hurts to take a bath. She's nursing a dozen times a day—lucky if she can squeeze in a nap. She can be forgiven, perhaps, for losing sight of your needs in this moment of her own.

But it's not just Claire. None of your friends think of you as a woman—not in the way you want them to. Your womanhood, so far, is language, not substance. It comes with no physical manifestation, no set of shared experiences. For twenty years they've known you as James. You still look like James. Thinking of you as a woman is an act of will, not an act of observation.

"Maybe the recipients are random," I offer, taking my phone from you and placing it back in its dock.

"The recipients are women." You put away your own phone, fluff your pillows, and turn, lying with your back to me.

"You should let Claire know how you feel." I say, placing a hand on your arm.

"I shouldn't have to tell her."

When it seems you're asleep, and I'm fading, too, I roll to my more comfortable side. But you start to sob. You wonder aloud how I can abandon you, like this, in your time of need. I roll back toward you, willing myself awake, though I'm running on empty. I stroke your shoulder until the phantom sounds of sleep ring in my ears like trumpets, and my hand grows heavy and falls.

The western hognose snake is eating itself. For a moment, I can't look away. Caged at some pet store, it's immersed in its water dish, its head upside-down, its eyes empty. Its gaping mouth, packed with the fat flesh of its tail, forms a grimacing smile. It tackles its task with purpose— with haste, even, as if hungry. A ribbon of blood drains from the corner of its mouth. It's a real-life ouroboros. Leave it to religion to frame self-harm as self-renewal.

Snakes do this sometimes, says my company's data entry temp, pausing the video. Especially when captive or overheated or under stress.

I was unaware and wish I had remained so.

I usually ignore our new hire's latest Internet find, but the clamor of the crowd gathered at his desk made it hard to focus. So I slid my chair over to take a look. Now, I slide it back. I don't want to know how the video ends. If I leave the office soon, I'll beat rush hour traffic.

I check my email one last time. We need to execute a server configuration change outside business hours, so my boss is asking me to work on Saturday. I'm exhausted, but I'm new, so it's important to look like a team player. I have to say yes.

I check the ticket queue. I check the due dates on my training. I gather my bags and remind myself my commute gets more miserable with each passing moment. Then I sit in a stupor, staring at the to-do list on my whiteboard.

It's as if I'm looking for work.

When I examine my motivations, I realize something that surprises me. *I don't want to go home.*

My new job is tough. As a consultant, I must get up to speed quickly and prove myself an ever-ready machine of productivity. The learning curve is difficult, mistakes are costly, and I get no sick days, no vacation and no benefits.

But my home life is worse.

The house is a mess. I'm behind on the bills. I'm busting my ass to plan our impending move: finding a mortgage lender, making appointments to see homes, packing up the basement.

My relationship with you was once an oasis in times of stress, but that's become more fraught than all the rest. Since you came out, we haven't had a single pleasant evening. Coming to terms with your identity was supposed to bring you peace; instead, you're a bottomless pit of need. You're obsessed with your appearance. You're fragile and quick to fight. You cry yourself to sleep. I can't remember when I last *relaxed.*

It's settled—I need self-care. I'll take a yoga class or get a massage. I feel guilty when I do such things without you, but I'll indulge myself, just this once.

I can't afford to take you, anyway. Your contract with the school has ended and your cash flow has run dry. My job pays well—a staggering amount compared with my previous one—but we're barely staying afloat. Marketplace health insurance costs a fortune. I'm funding repairs so we can sell the house. And I completely underestimated the day-to-day expenses of a middle-class lifestyle for two. The price of my tea latte doubles when I cover your cappuccino. When I want a pedicure, you want one too. What should have been an affordable brunch with Sheila nearly broke me when you tagged along; after three hours of conversation we'd consumed far more mimosas than the one I'd budgeted.

I need to make our evenings bearable, starting with tonight. If I do nothing else, I'll make tonight go well.

My route home is littered with construction. While waiting interminably for a flagman to wave me through, I plan our evening. I'll bring home comfort food. Crunchy fried chicken, mashed potatoes with gravy, mac and cheese and biscuits with jam. When I'm finally rolling, a vehicle pulls into my lane so abruptly we nearly collide. I honk reflexively. A detour leads me down unfamiliar roads where signs connecting to my route are few and far between.

After dinner, we'll watch a movie. I'll treat you as gingerly as possible and stay attuned to your moods. Lost in these thoughts, I miss my turn.

Scavenging my phone from the passenger's side floor, I launch my GPS. The battery's low and I fumble to find the charger. I pull into an empty lot to turn around, noticing too late the sign posted there: "Not a Turnaround." Interesting, isn't it, that labeling something doesn't make it so. I fiddle with the radio as I correct course, but I can't find a station. If only I could find the time to load a USB key with some songs.

Finally, I'm merging onto the highway. Without the distraction of music, my thoughts turn to the snake. Why didn't it stop? Didn't it feel the pain? Its fangs curve backward—perhaps, embedded like fishhooks, they left the snake nowhere to go but forward.

I wish I could unsee the video, like other things I've seen in the darker corners of the web: photos of crime scenes, body modifications gone too far. A defense of anorexia. The ravings of a cuckold aroused by his wife's romp with an HIV-positive lover. And "rosebud" porn. Not just women whose asses are sore from rough anal scenes, as I once believed—as if that weren't bad enough. But women who've acquired rectal prolapse, a disability causing incontinence and requiring surgery—to provide some sadist with his five-minute thrill. Much of the Internet threatens our humanity.

My eyes drift to the gas gauge; I'm running on fumes. It's another expense that's gone up since I started working in Indianapolis. I coast onto the exit just in time, eyeing a billboard for a jewelry store. It reminds me—some couples renew their vows when a partner comes out as transgender. I want to suggest it, and I want to present you with an engagement ring when I do. Women get rings, and if you're going to be a woman, you should have one. I'd love to have it for our anniversary this month, but there's no way I'll scare up the money in time. We haven't even saved for a vacation.

"Let's have a nice, relaxing evening," I say, arriving with armfuls of food. Stashing the plastic forks in the junk drawer, I set the table with real plates and glass goblets. I decant the food into serving bowls and pour a carafe of water. I light a candle.

You sit down listlessly, pulling the cloth napkin onto your lap. You fish out a drumstick. Poking at the potatoes with your fork, you seem unaware that this is good, that things can be good, that I'm trying.

But I have this covered.

"How was your day?" I ask, splitting a hot biscuit for you.

"Nothing I wear looks right."

"You look great right now," I say. "But we'll go shopping this weekend if you want."

"It won't help," you say. "I don't feel pretty."

"I don't feel pretty, either. I'm middle-aged and so are you. We're not always going to feel pretty."

You draw up your eyebrows, lower your chin, and raise your eyes to meet mine.

"It's going to be OK," I add. "I'll get you the hot sauce."

I want to make you feel better, I think while browsing the door of the fridge, but I don't know how. I've used up all the words I can muster on this topic. I've told you you're lovely just the way you are, that no one is judging you, that fashion is a pain and no woman gets it perfect. I can't say it any more creatively. I can't say it any more often.

"Do I look like a fool?" you ask when I return.

"Of course not."

But these endless evaluations of your appearance—they have not improved your mood or your confidence. Your self-esteem is a leaky bucket that no torrent of encouragement can fill.

"You're just saying that."

I take a deep breath. I don't want to do this tonight. I don't want to do this *at all*. But I need to have a good night, at least tonight. Just *one good night*.

"I don't think the women at the plant swap liked my dress," you say. "It isn't *fair*."

There's that strange appeal to fairness again.

"Let's have fun tonight," I say. "Let's pop popcorn and watch Netflix."

You wrinkle your nose. You sniff. You look like you might cry. Only that's not exactly right—you look like you're *trying* to cry. Your lips curl, your eyes, lowered, scan the landscape, searching for that sadness you once professed to like. You're poised with electrodes raised, ready to awaken it like Frankenstein's monster, eager to jolt new life into dead miseries.

My temples bubble like lava. My face feels warm. I make a conscious decision to breathe; I remind myself to watch my tongue. Maybe you're not courting drama. Maybe you genuinely need me right now. But there is no more of me left to give. The best I can do, at the moment, is walk away.

I move to the back door and peer out the glass, across the back acre, into the setting sun. People our age are not pretty. Pretty is for the young. Pretty is for those who've yet to mature into the grace of adulthood, who haven't learned you can't always get what you want.

I've long outgrown the days of lamenting my insufficient beauty. I'm forty-six with rosacea-stained skin, a weak chin, and a waistline that perennially tries to expand. I've got more important concerns, now: telling the truth. Cultivating courage. Building a satisfying life. If I worried about being pretty, I'd find no time to be human.

Besides, it's enough to possess the kind of beauty that's projected onto you by that one special person who sees you through the filter of love. For whom your personality animates your aging body with a glow that passes for attractiveness long after tight skin and lustrous hair have left their post. It's been enough for me. I don't need to be beautiful to everyone. I just want to be beautiful to you—as you are to me.

But maybe I can no longer count on that, either. You've become more interested in your own body than in mine.

I turn around, return to the scene. You've left the dining room table. Fair enough. We'll move on to the next phase of our evening.

"Choose a movie," I say, sitting next to you on the couch and handing you the remote. "Anything you want."

"It's not *fair*," you say.

I open my mouth to respond—with what, I'm not sure—and then it descends. It comes fast in a whirling fog, that fate that can't be fought. You become possessed, a mouthpiece for its agenda. Your head spins and from your lips issues the vomitous stream of negation that now haunts our every evening: how ugly you are, how dire life is, how futile the pursuit of happiness. What's wrong with your clothes, with your face, with your feet. With the size of your hands. With the sound of your voice.

I scramble to bring you back. I deploy compliments, affirmations, promises, *lies*. You reject each in turn. My reserves are exhausted. You need something I don't have.

You unravel. You sob. And I can't.

I just can't.

"I'm going for a walk," I say, slipping on a pair of sneakers and grabbing my house key.

I cross the road lined with grazing cows, where swallows dance and dive in my path. I pass the painted horses behind the split-log fence. I walk briskly. I jog. I lose steam and walk again. In time, twilight darkens the pockmarked asphalt, turns it leaden and wet. Flowering dogwoods fade to the color of wine. I walk past silos and dilapidated barns, fence rows, a trailer park. I may never return. I may walk off the edge of the Earth.

I don't want to think about your gender. I don't want to think about your appearance. I don't want to think about your clothes.

Frankly, clothes aren't that interesting to me. I don't care what you wear. I don't care if it's flattering or unflattering, if it went over well or if it didn't. I don't even care this much about what *I* wear.

I don't want to spend another night consoling you.

I want you to buck up. I want you to be *an adult*. There's life to live—I want you to walk away from your mirror and *live it*.

We can't stop the march of time. We shouldn't try. Remember the gold-veined bowls we saw at the museum last year? Kintsugi—the Japanese art of repairing broken pottery. Instead of trying to hide cracks and flaws, it makes them conspicuous—a part of the design. And it's not just an art, it's a philosophy. We can't eliminate our scars and imperfections, and we shouldn't want to—they make us unique. We are made *more* beautiful, not less, when we incorporate them into our sense of self.

I have the same preferences I've always had. The people I find beautiful have calloused hands and smile lines and frizzy hair pulled back from a sweaty brow. They are people who get dirty with the business of life. Their beauty comes from within, from vigor and honest living. That was you, when we met. Now you hate the parts of you that are real. You don't want to be the kintsugi, growing stronger and more vibrant with age. You want to be your grandmother's china, too good for use, endlessly gathering dust in the curio. How can I support you, while appreciating what I appreciate?

I hold the same values I've always held. They're the ones you once shared. The night we took possession of our house, you spoke of growing old gracefully. Now, you care about how you look. You care about image. You care what other people think. How can I support you, while valuing what I value?

I walk until familiar houses turn into unfamiliar ones. I take the back roads, pass the school. If I get too far away from home, I won't have the energy to get back, and there are no Ubers in these backwoods. But I don't want to stop walking.

I can't face spending the evening with you.

I pick up my pace. I walk until it's too dark to see the road, until my knees buckle. Eventually, reluctantly, I turn around and walk home.

But I do not outwalk my rage.

"I got a new shade of polish," you say, meeting me at the door with fluttering pink nails. They match the shirtdress I got you for Christmas, you demonstrate, fanning them across your chest. I stumble over ripped-up tile and stacked planks of laminate to drop an armload of bags onto the kitchen counter. I ordered the new flooring last week, as our broken kitchen tiles will not impress potential home buyers. Apparently the installers started today.

"That's great," I say. The server configuration change took longer than expected, then I stopped by the hardware store, so my Saturday is shot. I had no choice—Sam is ready to take photos of our house. Tall and imposing with short-cropped hair, Sam's not your average Realtor. She's a contractor who got a real estate license to help her flip houses. But I work with her wife, and when they learned I was house hunting, she offered to help.

Our wood cabinetry from the seventies needs a coat of paint, so I picked up sandpaper and a gallon of primer. And these matte black pulls and hinges will spell the difference between "dated" and "farmhouse chic." Since school's out, I hoped you'd do the shopping, but you haven't found the time.

I need to take care of some business, I tell you, and I don't want to do it amid this clutter. I'll be outside enjoying the last sliver of daylight. You glance down at your dress, your smile fading.

I settle onto the porch where a slant of evening sun stretches across the lawn, lighting up the budding daisies. Opening my laptop, I start an email to the loan officer I contacted today. I've been looking at houses this week, and there's one I want to show you. So I've started the pre-approval process. After a moment you appear in the doorway, now in a t-shirt and an old pair of knee-length shorts.

"Did you do the price tags today?" I ask, as you pull up the chair next to me. We've decided to have a yard sale over Memorial Day, to bring in some cash and offset our moving expenses. Our furniture is worn, anyway, and may not fit the new space.

"I'm sorry, I didn't."

"Did you see the job opportunity I sent you?"

"I saw it," you say. "I'm not sure about it."

I was sure you'd love it; it's an easy web design position that's right up your alley. Since it's on the north side of Indianapolis, we even could carpool.

"What's wrong with it?"

"I can't be sure they'll accept the real me," you say.

"You're afraid to interview as a woman?"

You shrug. "I mean I won't interview as a man."

I didn't think so—but now I'm confused. I assume living as a woman will not entail abandoning the world of work. But it seems you're afraid to interview "en femme" and unwilling not to.

"You won't know if it's an issue," I say, "until you try."

"It wouldn't have been an issue at Cuppajoe Media."

I can't imagine why you're bringing up that job—you received the rejection letter last fall. It occurs to me you've made no effort to look for work since.

"We can't live on one income in the city. Plus you've taken on a debt with the laser salon."

You stare into the distance.

The loan officer needs a ton of paperwork from me, so I get back to it. I've been chasing this stuff for days—contacting former employers, stopping by the bank, scanning documents at FedEx—and I'm still not done. I start setting up my cloud storage account so I can transfer my pay stubs and statements to the loan officer.

"Why can't you love my transness?" you ask, after a moment.

"What?"

I drag my attention from my work and try to refocus. I didn't quite hear—or perhaps understand—the question.

"Why can't you love my transness?"

I smile. Don't you know *this is the love that's meant to be?* I save my work and close my laptop.

"There isn't some part of you that I don't love."

You're unsatisfied with this response, though I'm not sure why. "Trans bodies are beautiful," you say, quoting a meme that Krystal shared recently on Facebook.

I agree that your body is beautiful. But it's a male body, not a trans body—you haven't modified it. And it is *you* who finds it less than

158

beautiful. You seem to hate it now, with its unwanted angles, its flatness, the redundant flesh between your legs. Does loving your transness mean agreeing that your body is wrong or inadequate? It isn't, and I won't.

"I love your body very much," I say. "I also love your mind. I love all of you, whatever your gender expression." And it's true. I love the way you rock a floral scarf or bake a homemade pie. And I love the way you take an ax to a limb that's fallen in a storm.

You exhale, your shoulders dropping. I have made a mistake.

I'm at a loss. What will make you feel supported? Am I to be blamed for loving all of you, including the parts you don't love? Or is there something *more* to you that I can love? Where is this transness, if it isn't in your body and it isn't in your mind?

"Tell me what it looks like to love your transness," I say. "What am I failing to do?"

"I mean..." You trail off, the words eluding you.

I don't want this to go unaddressed. I am willing to learn. Yet I fear neither of us can locate your "transness" to give it the love it needs. I fear it's not in your mind or in your body, but is the very schism that pits your mind against your body. Does loving your transness mean hating the parts you hate, the parts you deem masculine? Does loving your transness mean, in practice, *withdrawing* some of my love?

If so, I cannot help you. My love for you is not some favor I bestow, to be doled out or dialed back at will. It's a *reality* I occupy. I can't change it, even if that's what you need.

"You told me you wouldn't have chosen this," you say.

"That's because you're *unhappy.*"

But this unhappiness—its source *does* seem to be your transness. Before, you enjoyed plant swaps and aced job interviews. You were fine with your reflection in the mirror. You were comfortable in your skin.

"If there is someone here who does not love some part of you," I add, "I'd argue it's *you.*"

"I like being trans," you say.

Do you, though? Your nightly tears speak louder than your words.

"Let me ask you this," I say. "Do you want me to stand beside you as you look in the mirror, and go, ah yes, I do see some hair you should remove? Some flaws you should hide? Is that what it looks like to love your transness?"

"When you say it that way, I see your difficulty," you say.

But I am no closer to understanding what you need.

TWELVE | JUNE
TRANSITION IS FUN

"Jamie and her wife are here to see you," the receptionist says into the telephone, taking in your floor-length skirt and cuff bracelet. She searches your face for approval as she pronounces the word "her." Aloft Counseling prides itself on its gender-affirming stance.

Dr. Doris appears in the doorway and ushers us down a short hall. She's wearing a shapeless earth-toned pants suit, a sizable tunic-length cardigan and comfortable shoes. A mop of chin-length orange hair has been teased and sprayed until it sticks out too far on the sides, in an intentionally messy hairdo she probably hopes looks eccentric. But she reminds me of a grade school teacher.

She motions for us to sit and closes the door. "Why don't you tell me why you're here?" She asks in a slow, luxuriating tone that suggests she's entertained by the sound of her own voice. She looks toward you, opening a leather portfolio and retrieving a pen.

"I don't really know," you say, your eyes wide. "I guess Shannon kind of wanted to do this."

That's not exactly right.

"You're not doing well," I told you recently. "You need therapy." To my surprise, you agreed. You were willing to start couples counseling, too, and to discuss our flagging sex life. You even volunteered to find the therapist—a trans-friendly one in Indianapolis, so we can keep seeing her after we move.

So I'm a little annoyed by this sudden bout of amnesia.

Dr. Doris turns and looks in my general direction with unfocused eyes and an open-mouth smile that hides her teeth. I feel bad for thinking it, but she looks like she's not all there.

"Why don't you tell me," she says, choosing vocal intonations that please her, "what's going on." The two of you stare at me, your mutual feint of innocence suggesting I've gathered us here for no good reason.

"Well," I say, perhaps defensively. "Since coming out as transgender, Jamie has spiraled into an all-consuming depression." I bring Dr. Doris up to speed on your nightly meltdowns. Then I tell her that counseling was a mutual decision, and I resent you suggesting otherwise.

"Why don't you say that to him?" Dr. Doris suggests.

"Her," you say. When someone fails to use a person's preferred pronouns, you told me recently, it's called "misgendering."

Dr. Doris apologizes.

I voice my concerns to you, as asked, though you know what they are. When I'm finished, I expect you, or perhaps Dr. Doris, to respond. Instead, the two of you bore holes into me with your eyes. You both seem satisfied you've done what's expected. The ball, somehow, is still in my court.

"I'm worried about our sex life," I add, to break the silence. We celebrated fifteen years together last month, so I was hoping for an intimate conclusion to the evening. It didn't happen.

"I'm worried about it too," you say.

But it's your actions that have put it in peril, so it's your actions that must rescue it. You feign ignorance when I say so, though we've had this discussion many times.

"What am I supposed to do?" you ask.

"Make up for it. I don't know how—that's your problem. Get creative. Do the things I like and do them more often. I think it's only fair."

"I feel like a perv pursuing you when you're not all that into it."

That's admirable, I guess. Still, it's the only way things are going to change. Right now, you care more about looking sexy than you care about having sex.

Before I can respond, Dr. Doris closes her notebook and pats it. She says she'll help us overcome our difficulties. She says if you transition, she'll help you through that as well.

"That's the *fun* part, for me," she adds, with what my country-boy uncle would have called a shit-eating grin. "Helping you transition!"

I meet Dr. Doris's eyes. Her appetite for "fun" feels less than appropriate under the circumstances. When I fail to return her smile, her glee quickly fades.

"*If* you transition, I mean."

She rifles through some papers, noting we've signed up for individual sessions as well as couples therapy. "That's interesting," she says, looking pointedly at me. "Most couples want separate therapists."

"Why?" I ask.

"To avoid a conflict of interest."

I assumed we were both clients in our own right. Why mention this "conflict of interest" only to me? Does she plan to take sides? Is transitioning you simply more "fun" than counseling me?

"What can I help you with?" Dr. Doris asks, when she and I are alone together.

"Jamie plans to remove... her beard."

Her beard. Using feminine pronouns, in moments like these, feels silly—if not dishonest. But I need to get used to it.

"Her hairless face interferes with my attraction to her. Kind of *a lot.*"

Dr. Doris asks me to continue.

"Sex is important to me. If our sex life is compromised, our relationship is compromised. I need to tell Jamie, plainly: 'If you do this, I will lose my attraction to you.' But when I've tried, she's brushed me off. And it's hard to hurt her feelings."

"Why don't you say it *this* way," Dr. Doris suggests. She shifts in her chair and places her hand in the air, palm down. "'I'm afraid my attraction to you will *go down.*'" She draws out the words "*go down*" and slowly lowers her hand by a few inches. Then she grins, optimistically, as if she's happened upon an important revelation.

I wonder if I have failed to explain myself adequately.

I need to tell you something that's hard for you to hear. I'm not sure what adopting this odd phrasing is meant to accomplish. If anything, I think it will allow you to remain oblivious. Is she suggesting I *further* obscure my concerns?

"Just say your attraction will *go down,*" Dr. Doris repeats, seemingly pleased with herself.

"Are you going to want hormones?" I ask, as we climb into your truck. I know you and Dr. Doris will discuss it, and I want to be prepared. I boot up the GPS as you pull out of the parking lot. We have an appointment to see a house before we head home.

"I don't know what my transition is going to look like," you say. It's the same statement you issued the last time I asked.

"Hormones cause erectile dysfunction," I say. That's a hot topic among the women on Regenerate, most of whom are no longer having sex. "What's it going to take for you to know?"

You don't know that, either.

164

The house turns out to be adorable—with hardwood floors, a bay window, and a fireplace flanked with modern built-ins. There's a living room for entertaining and a den for cozying up to the fire. "I want to make an offer," I whisper, pulling you aside. You're as charmed as I am—there's even a room for your music studio. After a quick huddle we reconvene with Sam.

It's a wise decision, she says. It's priced right and someone will surely snatch it up. We'll need earnest money, she reminds us, as she dials the seller's agent. And a down payment.

I hadn't thought of this. We haven't sold our old place, so we'll have to scrape for the money. I have a little in savings, but you have nothing. Since school ended, the last of your cash has quickly dissipated—consumed by payments to your loan, clothing and other things. I retrieve a pen from my tote and do some quick calculations on the back of the listing page. If I allot the cash in my account and half my next two paychecks, and we forgo groceries and sell the lawn tractor, we can make it happen.

When I look up, you're shifting your weight back and forth from one foot to the other. "How are we going to pay off my laser contract?" you ask, without raising your eyes.

I lay down the pen. I swallow, the dry lump in my throat a slowly mounting anger.

We? I didn't sign your laser contract. I didn't even want *you* to sign it. "Surely you don't expect *me* to pay it."

"I can't help it!" You tell me I've drained your funds, calling upon you for this or that expense, even though you told me you were running low.

I don't recall this.

But if it's true—why is it *my* job to cover our expenses? Why must I foot the bill for everything while you throw money at beauty treatments you can't afford?

What was your plan when you signed the contract?

I guess I thought you'd get a job at some point. But I don't say this. I don't say it because I can't say it politely. Not right now.

When Sam's off the phone, I tell her we'll have the money. I don't know how, or if, we're going to pay off your laser contract. But I am buying this house.

An old queen in a sequined gown sashays past, stopping to give us the royal wave. A chunker wearing little but a rainbow-colored tutu rides piggyback on a hairy "bear" in a spiked dog collar. Someone channeling Jimi Hendrix swaggers by in a ruffled blazer and carefully groomed mustache, chest bared and "Kiss me, I'm trans" scrawled in lipstick across sculpted abs. And this isn't even the parade—Twyla didn't want to get up that early.

We make our way up the gravel road, past the ticket booth and toward the purple balloon arch. Raven and I bound ahead, unencumbered in our shorts and walking shoes. You and Twyla, both in heels, trail behind. You're decked out in a lace cocktail dress. Twyla's wearing an anime girl's smock, thigh-highs, and a pair of fuzzy cat ears. An outsize Deee-Lite impersonator in harlequin-checked pants and platform shoes steps into our path. Close behind, a lanky youth with waist-length hair walks like nobility, dragging a vampire bride's lace train through the dust, prominent nose and Adam's apple leading the way.

A new energy dominates Pride this year. It's theatrical. It's exhibitionist. It's sexual, but in a commodified way. It's Debord's "accumulation of spectacles."

It's a conversation between one male gaze and another.

Or is it? Some of these individuals no doubt identify as women. But until they announce their pronouns, the lines between gay men, drag queens and trans women are blurred. Judith Butler sees *all* as performers, each creating a reality as valid as the next. But in this the queer kids depart from the founder of their movement. Your online activist friends draw sharp distinctions between increasingly fragmented identities, approving of some more than others. Gay is not as "inclusive" as queer, and that's a problem. Drag trivializes the struggle of trans women.

We weave through the vendor booths, which have also evolved. Corporate behemoths crowd out activists with petitions. A cosmetic surgery practice cozies up to an anti-circumcision booth. Insurance companies flank a shop selling fetish gear. A major pharmaceutical company represents. So does Fox News.

Raven stops at an apparel tent to examine a rainbow-colored wristband that matches her Atari t-shirt. Does she identify as queer, or as an ally? Did she visit Pride before her partner began dressing? Twyla joins her, straightening her cat ears as she fondles a t-shirt that reads "Be Authentically You."

It's my first Pride in ages. I dragged you to one early in our relationship, but you were uncomfortable the whole time, saying you felt like a tourist. I had the opposite problem. I felt at home among folks I recognized from my gay bar days. But next to you, I *looked* out of place. I felt a pang of sadness when a lesbian said to me, "we appreciate our straight allies!"

"You two look fabulous!" a woman in a figure-hugging dress shouts, approaching from the rear. A gaggle of her friends, running in spiked heels, soon follow. "Can we get a selfie with you?"

"Of course," Twyla says, pulling her pigtail forward before pulling you close. The ladies crowd around, and Twyla commands all to smile, to purse lips, to look surprised. When several photos are snapped the group thanks you and hurries away.

You and Twyla chitter inaudibly as we make our way to the courtyard where the bands are setting up. "I'm not attracted to trans women," I hear you mumble, when Twyla points out someone in the crowd. I glance back. You shrug. "It's just the truth."

I'm dumbstruck. I've shouldered so much guilt for struggling to stay attracted to you. I've tried to "find a way" as you've admonished me to do. And now you admit, without flinching, that you find the look you pursue unappealing? Count yourself lucky, Jamie—you'll never be asked, as I am, to squash down your preferences and give your body to a trans woman.

I watch the crowd gathering before the main stage as we spread our blanket on the grass. There are more allies than in past years. More teens whose lapel buttons announce proclivities only recently named: sapiosexual, demigender, pansexual, polygender. But it's not just that there's something new at the festival. There's something missing, too.

Where are the athletic women in racerback tanks? The couples wearing Birkenstocks with matching spiked haircuts? The baby dykes with their hair combed forward? Isabel and I met up with dozens of women when we came to Pride. I see only a few here from the old gang. They lie on blankets at the periphery, under the lot's few shade trees, where a Joplin-esque folksinger is slated to play. They have children and thirsty dogs in tow. They aren't making themselves part of the spectacle.

We unload the last boxes from the truck into the new house. Moving required two long trips to the Ohio place, left us scraped and sweaty, and consumed the whole day. I'm just glad we were able to close on the house so quickly.

We sit on the floor and down the last of a case of bottled water as our thoughts turn to dinner. The clock on the oven reads eleven p.m. Could that be right? I throw on a different T-shirt and roll on a bit of perfume. You find a clean blouse and swap your tennis shoes for a pair of loafers with a heel. Then you grab the purse you recently ditched your messenger bag for.

There are tons of restaurants near our new house. But we're too late for the pho place with the great reviews or the fusion stir-fry grill. Even the Mexican grocery with the taqueria inside has closed for the night. Nothing's open but a chain sports bar, and we're in no mood to go afield. Applebee's it is.

It's crowded inside. You release your hair from its ponytail and clutch your purse close we approach the host stand. "Hello ladies," the hostess says, without looking up. You smile broadly. She mumbles instructions to two trainees hovering near her, then addresses another party before asking us to follow.

As we slide into the wide booth, she drops two menus in front of us, making eye contact for the first time. "Sir, I'm so sorry," she says, when she gets a look at you.

Your smile fades. "It's OK."

"No, it's not," she insists. "It's been so busy and I was in my own little world."

"Seriously. It's fine." Your chin crumples as she picks up the extra rolls of silverware and walks away.

Before you can comment, a server arrives with a pitcher and two glasses. Water is fine, I answer, when he asks what else we'd like to drink.

"How about you, sir?"

You answer through clenched teeth.

"By the way." I'm trying to distract you, but there's something we really do need to discuss. "I closed my account at the Ohio bank today. Have you closed yours?"

You nod toward a table of men in football jerseys. "Those guys are looking at me funny."

"Those guys aren't important."

"Even my friends misgender me," you say, growing sullen.

Your friends don't use your pronouns, I remind you, because you haven't asked them to.

"I shouldn't have to tell them," you say.

"I'll use your pronouns at my birthday party next month," I promise. "I'll see to it that they do the same."

This appeases you for now. And I'm more than willing to do it. But to be honest, I'm not sure it will help. People will forget. And there will always be strangers, like our hostess and our server, who have neither the time nor the insight to give you what you need. I wish you could find your validation from within.

"Does this look gay?" you ask, turning to show me your butt in a pair of cutoff shorts.

I sit on the edge of the bed to sort out a flurry of thoughts. There is derision in your voice. Clearly, you hope not.

I look for words as you pull clothes out of boxes, hanging some in your closet, reevaluating others. I know you're ashamed of your bisexuality, but I didn't think you had a negative opinion of gay people. Now, you seem to want to distance yourself from them. Do you think *trans* is better than *gay*?

"Those guys at Applebee's didn't get me," you say, pulling off the shorts and tossing them to the floor. "They thought I was gay."

Well, *yeah*.

You shop in the women's department. It isn't a behavior that screams "straight" to the average dude swilling beer. They know only that you walk on the wild side—the difference between *trans* and *gay* is not on their radar. The idea that you might, via wardrobe tweaks, get them to unpack your gender—or that you should even try—suggests your view of reality is very different from mine.

"And those women at Pride—they thought I was in drag."

That may be. For allies, one reason for gender expression is as good as another. Even a barista in rainbow suspenders drew hearts on your coffee cup yesterday, winked, and surmised he'd see you at "the bar."

Are you wondering if you pass? Surely you're aware you don't. Then again, you seemed unclear that night at Moon Garden.

"I know I don't pass," you say, before I can ask. "But you know how there's a difference? Between the way a trans woman looks, versus a gay man or a drag queen?"

I'm afraid I don't. I guess there are iconic gay clothes, like assless chaps. Beyond that, I'm not sure. Do trans women wear hot pants instead of short-shorts? Botanicals before florals? If I'm not attuned to the rules, I'm not sure who is.

"How about this?" you ask, pulling on a pair of pleated shorts. Does *this* look gay?"

"I mean..."

I don't want to lie to you. And I don't want the fight that follows discussions of this sort. And I don't know how you could be *at all confused* about how others see you.

You await my answer, your face blank with a sort of panic.

"I don't think anyone's making that sort of assessment," I say at last.

"I'm not a gay man," you say, breathlessly. "I don't want to look like one."

"It doesn't matter. Remember the incident at the coat store? You said you didn't care." Now, as you sling tight-fitting tank tops onto a pile of boot-cut jeans, you clearly do.

You've stopped dressing for yourself; you now invite the public's response. That's a dialog, not a monologue. People have free will. They can misinterpret, or even reject, your message. I'm misunderstood, too, all the time. That's the human condition.

If you're going to keep courting controversy, you'll need to grow a thicker skin. Some will balk when you wear women's clothes; you can't mitigate that by wearing *different* women's clothes. This idea that some who shop across the aisle look different from others who do, because of how they feel inside—it's *magical thinking*.

"Forget about them," I suggest.

We can't manage others' opinions. Most of the time, they aren't thinking that hard about us anyway. Letting go requires grace.

THE SHAPE OF A WOMAN

You zig zag all over creation rolling a large, gluey ball, picking up everything in your path: benches, bowling pins, sisters, brothers, cattle. Your ball grows bigger as you take up lamp posts and trees, buildings and mountains. You are on a mission to make a star.

You sink into the beanbag chair across from your game console, which lies amid a jumble of cords after a hasty unpacking. The furniture is shoved into one corner, still unarranged, and we've yet to find the curtains and lamps; a streetlight casts a glare across your thirty-two-inch monitor.

Like many Japanese video games, "Katamari Damacy" is absurd. And yet—I've played it—it's strangely cathartic. There's nothing in this virtual world you can't conquer, nothing you can't assimilate. You're a rolling landfill, converting useful objects into trash, reducing everything to a featureless blob with no attribute except that of being owned. It's an exercise in untrammeled greed. Nothing is sacred. Nothing is thinging.

You're directed by a bearded, Old Testament God floating on a rainbow, a portrait of excess himself. His open robe bares sculpted pecs draped with gold chains. His oversize belt buckle frames an oversize package stuffed in white disco pants. Like many Gods, he's an asshole. He binge drinks and brags of being "naughty." He berates you—his son— as you do his bidding.

Your ball becomes uneven, wobbling from side to side as you tumble through football stadiums and towns, amassing without appreciating, much as you and I do in real life: we buy yoga mats, shrimp forks, too many varieties of lemonade. We're no strangers to the crisis of modernity.

"Bloodless," wrote one reviewer, weary of shoot-em-ups. Maybe; there's more murder in Grand Theft Auto, whose dust jacket lies empty nearby. Or maybe we're just inured to the familiar violence that makes us who we are.

Lounging against a pillow nearby, I load *Presumed Intimacy* onto my laptop from the library's e-book service. Americans' drive to acquire isn't simple greed, sociologist Chris Rojek argues. It comes from our conflation of acquisition with morality. For Americans, there's heroism in adventure and adventure in plunder. God helps those who help themselves. Prosperity theology. Cowboys and prospectors and manifest destiny.

Such is not lost on the game's designer. Here is the East's impression of so many morally bankrupt Western gods, collapsed into a cartoonish composite. Your pillage is justified by the Creator himself, even if it's wasteful and joyless.

But the book's focus is actually our pursuit of "attention capital," something Rojek says proceeds from the same impulse. We now require approval to feed our "inexhaustible appetite," and droves of online friends—procured without the work or sacrifice of real friendship—stand ready to deliver.

A notification slides onto my screen. "Ladies' Bibimbap Club," it reads, the subject of an email from a friend-of-a-friend I've recently reconnected with. A few weeks ago, a Korean café opened on the north side, and I joined her, along with some other women, for its grand opening. We loved the lunch specials, the camaraderie, and the opportunity to rant about the dysfunction in our lives, so we gathered there again the following week. "Let's make this a regular thing," she suggests to the group. I love the idea. But my enthusiasm is tempered by a sinking feeling.

Your name isn't on the recipient list. That makes sense; you didn't attend before and you don't work in the area. But after seeing your reaction to Claire's baby announcement—sent to a group that overlaps a bit with this one—I know a gathering of women that excludes you is going to be a problem.

I could try to get you invited, I guess—but that would be awkward. Maybe the organizer wants to limit it to the original group. Maybe it's for north side workers, or for women—in the old-school sense of the word. Maybe keeping it exclusive—or, as your online activist friends would have it, "exclusionary"—is wrong. Or maybe it's just a way to preserve a vibe. But it isn't really my call.

So I'm faced with a decision.

If I tell you I'm going, you'll be upset you weren't invited.

If I don't tell you, I risk the fallout of keeping a secret.

And if I don't go, I'll resent having to change my plans to spare your feelings. I've so enjoyed the respite from my workday. Why should I have to give that up?

It feels gross to sneak around for an innocent lunch gathering. And it's crazy that I can't discuss it with you. But I know I can't.

Maybe I'll talk to Eunice about it.

"She isn't like other therapists," Paige said, when she made the recommendation. "She calls you out on your bullshit. She tells the hard truth and she gives homework." I'd never seen a therapist like that. And I needed someone with no "conflict of interest" to declare.

Eunice turned out to be a tiny, energetic woman in expensive boots, with a gleam in her eye and a specialization in sex and relationships. "I support you," she said, when I told her I was planning to stick it out. She spoke with a disarming directness that made her instantly likable.

"But you're in for a world of hurt."

I was moved by the candor. I know this hurt all too well, of course. But I'd been led to believe it was my fault. Shouldn't I be happy for you? Shouldn't I try harder? That's the message I get from Dr. Doris, from you, from your friends.

I scroll to the final line of the lunch invitation: "Who's in?" Every answer feels wrong. So for now, I don't respond.

"How do I look?" you ask, waltzing through the den. You rotate on one heel to show me a tight, ruffly skirt paired with an Easter-egg pink blouse and an immense, butterfly-emblazoned necklace.

"You look great," I say, looking up from the box of books I'm unpacking.

Your shoulders drop. "Tell me the truth."

Apparently my face betrays insufficient enthusiasm. I'm not sure what to do about that; the outfit doesn't appeal to me.

"What do you *actually* think?"

I'm growing tired of mincing my words. And telling you what you want to hear isn't working, anyway. And I don't like the way lies feel in my mouth.

So I give honesty another shot.

"I wouldn't wear it," I say. "But who cares? Wear what you want."

You drop to the armchair amid the parts of an unassembled bookcase. I can tell you feel like a failure.

"Why wouldn't you wear it?"

I take a deep breath. I'm not sure why my clothing preferences need to inform yours.

"It's a bit precious. I'm not a fan of pink. That necklace is awfully large, and it's a bit brassy. Why are you dressed up, anyway?"

"So it's not to your taste," you say, exasperated. "But that's beside the point. Should *I* wear it?"

I'm confused. I don't know what it means to evaluate your outfit without invoking my taste. Are you asking if others will be impressed? In a world where people expect you to dress like a man? They probably won't.

Are you asking if it's flattering? It isn't, though it's no worse than your other choices. You choose outfits that compress and redistribute your body, now, instead of those that compliment it.

In truth, I don't like this look on anyone. Those ladies at work who squeeze their butts into pencil skirts and their feet into stripper shoes—they look helpless and inept to me, always managing creeping hems and falling straps, the very *opposite* of cool and collected. I associate that look with a need to get ahead in a world controlled by yuppie men. Certainly I've played their game, wearing its uniform as a scuba diver wears a wetsuit. But I wouldn't wear a wetsuit if I wasn't near the water.

I shrug. I accept your presentation—isn't that enough? Must I be called to the carpet for my innermost thoughts?

"Why can't I get this right?" you ask, moving toward the mirror in the foyer. You look at yourself from the side, from the back, desperate to understand where you've fallen short.

But you are not made of ruffles and pink; a rejection of them is not a rejection of you. And I have earned my opinion. I learned at a young age that dressing sexy was my job. That in pants, I was too shapeless; without makeup, too blotchy and plain. I stopped shelling pistachios to preserve my manicure. I stopped climbing trees to wear heels. I learned to express my opinion less and smile more. Then, a little too late in adolescence, I realized that shit was holding me back. I needed to navigate the world with my hands and feet unfettered. I needed to experience and to grow. I started unlearning my socialization. And I am still unlearning it.

So these fabrics and pigments don't hold the magic for me that they hold for you. They bore me, at best. At worst, they mean submission to the male gaze and life unlived. I don't owe a reverence for femininity to conservative geezers who wish I'd "put in a little effort." And I don't owe it to you.

But a more immediate problem plagues me.

You saw through my polite fib. But my honest opinion crushed you. I'm out of options. How can I respond when both truth and lie are wrong? What words can I choose that will save us from this death spiral?

As I watch you slump in the chair, your lower jaw shoved forward, I realize something important.

You don't want me to tell you what I really think.

But you don't want a lie, either.

You want a truth, but one that isn't mine.

You believe your clothing, shored up by self-identification, transforms you. You want me to *see* this transformation. And you want me to be *into* it. Neither the truth nor a well-meaning compliment will suffice. What you want is for my perception itself to change.

You want a different *me.*

The fact is, you are no shapeshifter. Your hips are still narrow, your shoulders still broad. Bits of sewn fabric cannot mold your form, as if it were clay, into a female one. And that's fine. There is nothing wrong with your body. You agreed, mere months ago.

I am who I am. I'm not interested in seeing your waist grow smaller or your hips expand. These are *your* wishes. I prefer the you of a few months ago, the easygoing one, the one who might have liked that necklace but would have paired it with straight-leg jeans and a five o'clock shadow.

My opinion, though you ask for it, isn't welcome. There is only one valid answer: your clothing is beautiful. Because your clothing is no longer a matter of taste or preference. Your clothing is a stand-in for you.

I survey the grounds of our old place, picking up sticks and arranging lawn chairs. The gardens have faded. Coneflowers droop, morning glory vines choke the basil, and tomatoes rot amid yellowed leaves. The Adirondack chairs your dad made lie busted and strewn across the lawn, thrown about by a recent storm.

We're throwing one last bash for Independence Day—and my birthday—at the Ohio house. It hasn't yet sold, and its expansive backyard is perfect for pyrotechnics. Every year we host an all-day affair here, treating your family, your friends, and their kids to Jake's famous paella and an epic fireworks display. Next year, Jake and Rosa have promised to host. Our new yard in Indy is too small.

Guests begin to arrive. Jake has barely stopped the car when Nina and Lia make a beeline for the toybox, dragging it outside. Melanie appears, and her son joins the girls, driving Matchbox cars up the length of the deck. You emerge from the house eager to show off embellished jeans and a girl-cut t-shirt. Your face is clean-shaven, but not for long. We've made a pact.

I'm still sad you're having laser surgery, but since you haven't yet made it to an appointment, I proposed a compromise. You'll grow out your beard for two weeks, and I'll say goodbye to it. I'll get to spend a little time with that face I love so much. And then you'll do what you have to do. I'm not happy with that part, but it's a battle I'll never win.

At first, you hated my suggestion. You got evasive; you scrambled for an excuse. But I begged. "It's temporary," I said. Eventually, you relented.

"It's fair," you wrote in your blog later. "It's the least I can do, when she's been so supportive."

Your friends and I assemble near the fire pit. Darcy's admiring the weather—"perfect for a summer party," she says—when we see you and your dad cross the lawn with purpose. He hands you a trash bag and scissors, then digs in his pocket, producing a lighter and a small candle.

"What is he doing?" Darcy asks, when she sees you stop and cut into the thin plastic.

Today's the day I promised to enforce your pronouns. No big deal—I'll say something. I open my mouth to respond, but Melanie chimes in.

"He's making something," she says.

"I think—" I say, but Lyle interrupts.

"He's probably modding some fireworks. Maybe I should get involved."

Theo cuts in—he wants to help—then Paige says something, too. I'm losing the room.

"I know what she's doing!" I blurt out, a bit louder than necessary. "She's making a Chinese lantern."

Darcy shifts in her chair. Lyle looks thoughtful. Theo and Paige take in the implications. I have been heard.

"Cool," Melanie says at last. "I hope she can make that work."

When the boys get up to assist with your project, and Paige wanders away to fetch a drink, Darcy turns to me.

"If you two split up," she says, "I'll still be your friend."

"Me too," Melanie says. "You didn't sign up for this."

I'm touched. It's the first time anyone's acknowledged the challenges I'm facing.

As the crowd thickens I walk around and snap some photos. This is the last time we'll enjoy this stunning country view. The last time friends will gather at our picnic tables, plates piled high. The last time Nina and Lia will turn cartwheels across the lawn.

Jake steals up behind me to see my photos of the girls. "Any chance you can babysit on Thursday? Rosa's working and I have to cater a party."

Of course, I tell him. I'm always happy to watch the girls.

I'm snapping a fluffy cloud beyond the fence row when you grab Darcy and pull her into my camera's field. "Take a picture of us," you say. She's wearing a dress adorned with T-Rexes, her hair died a fresh shade of blue, and the two of you make a cute, counterculture pair. When I've taken several shots, you grab my phone and scroll through them, choosing your favorite. You ask me to email it to you.

"Let's get an ice cream," I say. We've hardly explored the neighborhood and a gentle breeze has rendered the evening perfect for a walk.

You lift a finger. Hunched over your laptop, you type with a familiar intensity: someone on the Internet has made you angry. It's a thing that happens more and more these days.

"Being transgender is not a sexual thing," you say, without looking up. You're "educating" someone who thinks otherwise.

"But your identity *is* related to your sexuality," I say. You've talked about it. You've blogged about it. Perhaps you believe a little white lie is justified in the service of your PSA.

"It's not like that," you mumble.

"What about the tranny porn?"

You look up, your face a wounded animal's. "I was trying to find people like myself represented in the media," you say, softly.

"Oh come on. To jack off to." Post-agriculturalists have nothing on you with their Great Forgetting.

The flesh around your nose turns warm and red.

"Don't be embarrassed," I say. "I'm not kink-shaming."

"But it isn't sexual," you insist.

"Jamie. It's *me*."

I get that you want to present a certain image to the public. I really do. But have you forgotten who you're talking to? Don't lose your ability to be honest with me. Don't lose your ability to be honest with *yourself*.

You shake your head in confusion—real or affected, I'm not sure. So I remind you, gently, of your interest in the strap-on. Your desire to be dominated. *Your request to be called a "tranny" in bed.*

You recoil. These things don't count, you tell me. You can't discuss it anymore. You don't feel "safe."

But I am your haven of safety. Who else knows these things about you? Who else would understand? It's the rest of the world you're lying for—your secret's safe with me.

Maybe you're unaware of what femininity really means to you. You still balk at "chick activities" like Wine and Pottery Night. You have no use for children and you're less into housework than ever. You're into wearing lace though. And lying on your back in bed. "Feminine," for you, means "sexy."

I kissed a woman for the first time in the early nineties. It happened behind a semi-truck in the parking lot of Sho-Bar, a drag-bar-turned-college-haunt in Evansville, Indiana. She was a straight girl with an unsown wild oat and she was dressed like one in capri pants, fuchsia flats and a cropped sweater. Her eyes were the same walnut brown as the spiral curls that fell to her waist. She was twenty-one. Her name was Karen.

The kiss took me by surprise. One moment she was telling me about her job at the bank, and the next, she was pushing me into the truck, planting her lips onto mine. No warning. No segue. She attacked me like an animal, moving from my lips to my neck and back again, running her fingers through my hair, chewing my ear. She whispered of suppressed desires and time lost as she unsnapped my bra way too soon. I was flattered but overwhelmed. I hadn't prepared for this. I wasn't ready.

For a minute, I mean. I'd long daydreamed of this moment so I wasn't about to squander it. I praised my good luck and hauled myself on board, returning her kiss, moving my curious hands to her waist. I'd expected a woman to feel soft and small, and she did. I'd expected to enjoy the silkiness of her hair and her breasts pressed into mine. But I hadn't expected to be intrigued by the curve of her lower back.

Under the fabric of her short blouse, my fingers slipped into the crease dividing the musculature there, the unexpectedly deep groove running vertically from her neck to her bottom. Her torso felt nothing like a man's; it wasn't simply a smaller one, but one ordered by foreign rules, by the trigonometry that governs the proportions of a woman. I imagined da Vinci's anatomy diagrams, all circles and angles and lines, as I followed the dimples where her back met her bottom, traced the steady widening of her hips.

I'd have other, more titillating encounters. Like my tryst with Gayla, the dancing freak with the shock of pink hair and the conical bra. Or with Lynne, the Lady Diana look-a-like with the endless stamina in bed. But I'd remember the shape of Karen's back more vividly, and more fondly, than many of these.

"It's lucky you're attracted to women," Raven wrote in a recent email, "since your husband is becoming your wife." It's the conventional wisdom. And it seemed true enough at the time. You've said it yourself, to me, and to your transgender support group, and on your blog: how lucky you are to have me. A wife who is supportive. Adventurous. A wife who encourages you to be yourself. A wife who's *queer.*

But here in our bed tonight, as you pull me toward you, you need for me to *not* know the touch of a woman.

I come to you with my eyes open, still inflamed for you despite our passage through fifteen years, ready to appreciate every inch of your body. But that makes you uncomfortable now.

You want me to see you only in candlelight and to squint. To focus on your eyeliner and to overlook your receding hairline. To pull your long hair in front of your chest and avert my eyes from its flatness. You want me to *map woman onto you.* To not just say but *to believe,* as though I'm not familiar with that crevice in a woman's back.

I try to concentrate, but forbidden thoughts surface: that a woman is a thing, and not an absence of a thing. That a woman is a woman in every cell of her body, too complex to fashion wholly from something else. More than hair removal, carmine, white lily, lace. That you are already perfect and need not hide from me. I suppress these thoughts, redouble my efforts. But the illusion is tenuous, too easily broken. After so many years, my body knows your body, whatever our brains and mouths may say.

You move, or face the light, or speak, and I *see* you.

So I do the unthinkable: I go ahead and love the you I'm not supposed to love, the one I've always loved. I love the stubble you want to remove, the freckles you cover with foundation. I love the jawline you stroke disapprovingly when you look in the mirror, the strong arms that can lift me onto the pillow.

I search out that sensuality that's actually *yours*, the one you work so hard to neutralize. I bury my nose in your hair and seek your smell, the one you scrub away and replace with Angel Dream. I close my eyes and let my hands find the truth you try to conceal.

But you forbid this kind of love, so I hide what I'm doing.

It wasn't so long ago that this bed saw laughter, play, unbridled passion, *lust*. But these have been displaced by your one and only preoccupation. Now there is work to do; there are roles to play.

It's hard to get off these days. I'm alone in it, floating disconnected, no longer allowed to drink you in, to just *feel*. Instead I flatter you, perform for you, censor myself, *lie*. I wrangle my pleasure from you on my own, use your body to masturbate to a memory of you.

We've made do, in our way. I've learned you can't be here for me anymore, that it's my job to work around that. But what happens when I can no longer be here for you?

I haven't adjusted to being your actress. I still long to be your lover.

FOURTEEN | AUGUST
ME TOO

Lesbians. Drag queens. Feminists. You're *furious* with them.

Light from the floor lamp strains to reach the armchair, where you slump over your laptop, typing. One side of your face is cloaked in darkness. Light and shadow form sharp angles on the other, carving out cheekbone and jaw. Your fingers skate over the keyboard, expertly, as when you write code on a deadline. You spend a lot of time on the Internet these days, spoiling for a fight. But it isn't right-wingers or religious zealots who stoke your anger. It's liberals and activists. They aren't using the right terminology for trans people. Or they aren't including trans people. Or they aren't dating trans people. You're mad at Ru Paul and Boy George, and you reserve your strongest hatred for women over seventy.

I don't understand.

You call yourself part of the **LGBTQ** movement, now. These are its founders. They opened the first gay bookstores and nightclubs. They remember Stonewall. They've been writing letters and passing legislation since before you were born.

These are your allies.

I sit by the window, watching the slow fade of dusk. I recall Wisteria performing in a floor-length beadwork gown. Older ladies in boots and bolo ties. Jaqquee and Pandora, whose attic bedroom received me after many a late night, wigs and jewelry on pegs adorning its velvet damask walls. Girls dancing in their bras. I remember leather vests, glittered lashes, Madonna's *Erotica* on repeat. You've hardly set foot in a gay bar. Now you're ready to lead the queer movement, correcting its ranks from within.

It's not a good look.

I get it. I, too, have been sucked into virtual sparring matches. In the thrall of liquid crystal, we sit up all night, confident in our flawless reasoning, determined to get the last word. We persist through stiffness and eyestrain, losing perspective as we lose melatonin. Even now, I clutch my phone, poised to respond to vibration or beep. But it isn't good. We need to learn to sit with ourselves. We need to unplug.

I think you're especially vulnerable. You hate to lose a debate, and online, the debate never ends. There's always one more comment, and each comment demands a response, and each response is an escalation. It's like scratching an itchy scab.

But you aren't just reacting. You're on the offensive, searching for posts to disagree with, firing off hasty and poorly thought-out rebuttals. You emerge at intervals to solicit my approval. I can't always give it to you. You aren't always charitable.

The last thing we need is this endless ruminating. I miss the days when you showed me a book you were reading or a song you were writing. I miss the days when we snapped green beans on the porch. Concerns about your gender consume our days and keep us up at night. I've no energy left for the gender troubles of strangers.

You feel it, too. "This thing is an insatiable beast," you write in your blog. "I feel like I'm dying." The more you write, the more "this thing" looks like an unhealthy obsession. You *are* dying, in a way. You all but forbid talk of who you once were. You refer to "James" as your "deadname." You implored me not to share a recipe from our old homesteading blog with a coworker; he might discover I once called you "my old man"—and you once liked it.

I always thought good mental health meant *integrating* the parts of the self—the past and present, the noble and the embarrassing, the body and the mind—not fracturing them further. *Healing* from the regrettable, not disavowing it.

My phone jingles—it's a text from Nora. She wants our address so she can invite us *both* to her baby shower. She wants you to feel like "one of the girls." She'll understand if you decline. The discussion will be lame. Infant formulas. Postpartum pain. Childrearing trends.

She's saved me from navigating a minefield.

It's true that you don't care about these topics. But you'll still want to go. Maybe Paige told your friends about your need to feel included. I confided in her about your reaction to Claire's baby announcement.

"Jamie."

You raise a finger and continue to type.

Failing to wrest your attention from the virtual world, I join you there. I find you on Facebook, where the #metoo movement has gotten underway. Women share personal experiences of sexual assault, using the hashtag to expose its ubiquity. I've started drafting a post, myself, but it's taking a while to complete.

You've joined in. "I was almost molested once," you write. I know the incident you speak of. A Boy Scout chaperone invited you into his tent during a camping excursion. You declined, and thankfully, nothing came of it. But your next line is as troubling as it is confusing.

"It happened because I was seen as a girl."

Do you believe this, Jamie? That nearly forty years ago, at a boys-only event, a man saw in you a gender identity you've only recently adopted? The one that so confounded the men at Applebee's and the women at Pride? And how would this matter? Do you believe that *girls* are for molesting? #Metoo is an injustice to fight—not a club to join.

Browsing your timeline, I see what I've started to suspect. You're developing a love affair with *oppression*.

"I have the right to exist," you write in one post, echoing something Krystal said recently. But I don't understand who has brought your existence under threat.

"A stranger took my photo while Shannon and I were grocery shopping," you write in another. But I was not aware of this.

"My genitals are no one's business." But as far as I know, no one has asked about your genitals. Then, in a discussion of the democratic primaries, it is *you* who says "I don't vote with my vagina." If you don't want speculation on your genitals, why go out of your way to mention—let alone *misrepresent*—them?

Then, a little further down in your feed, you move beyond the implied and the exaggerated to introduce the bald-faced lie.

"I was harassed by security at the Miami airport," you write.

You were treated well by the TSA that day. So well, in fact, that it put a bounce in your step. You tag some trans friends, perhaps in a show of solidarity. But I can't get behind dishonesty as a means to that end. Those officers did what they thought would make you comfortable. What *did*, in fact, make you comfortable.

It's evil to recast that as harassment.

They'll never read what you wrote—maybe you're counting on that. But this is bad karma. Why invent trouble in a world that doles out more than enough of its own? I can skip participating in this discussion, and I will, but what if this comes up in my presence? I'm not comfortable pretending you were treated badly when I know you were treated well.

I'm not comfortable contradicting you in public, either, though. Being your partner means standing by you, to some extent, even if I challenge you privately.

I need to mention this to you—staying quiet feels like acquiescence. I suspect you'll brush it off as a little white lie. But it's a little white lie on a growing heap of little white lies. You say transition brings you closer to your "true, authentic self." Then why does it seem to require so much dishonesty?

Even I've become entangled. You want me to compliment your clothing when I don't like it. You want me to pretend you aren't aroused by tranny porn. You want me to deny that you look male, or, God forbid, gay.

You want me to *pretend you have a vagina*. To thrust at your crotch, with my hands and my pelvis, as if it were there and it were real. You want me to pretend that *I* have a *penis*—when I don't even have dysphoria. You want me to act out the story you've written, never breaking character, carefully shielding you from a reality you've come to reject. Even disclosing a lunch invitation has become a problem.

I want to be *my* true, authentic self, too.

And yet I know if I confront you, I'll invite another fight into our already turbulent lives. A fight that will ruin our night. A fight we'll be lucky to recover from.

I've never had to choose between honesty and compassion. There's always been a way to present the truth diplomatically. But this is something new. This way of life you've come to need—it leaves no room for honesty.

You were once a disciplined debater. You had no patience for the kind of person you've become. I can't count the number of times you argued some poor sap into submission over his "unsupportable dogma." The dude at the Irish pub who invoked Pascal's wager—the argument that it's safer to believe in God than to risk punishment—still won't speak to you or Lyle.

"Your God practices extortion," Lyle chided him, placing a hand on the bar only inches from the man.

"Your God rewards dishonesty," you chimed in, crowding him from the other side—Lyle's bravado rubbed off on you when the two of you were drinking. "He demands a *profession* of belief," you added, "but that's not the same as real belief." If the man couldn't defend his views, the two of you later gloated, he didn't deserve your mercy.

Now, *you're* the one who cries foul when interrogated. You're the one who ignores unpleasant facts. Maybe you believe your lie about the TSA; your relationship with reality seems a little shaky. Remember what Nietzsche said: a strong mind endures the truth.

Sometimes I want to grab you and shake you and force you to confront the many truths you now refuse to face.

You *do* look like a man, Jamie. Why wouldn't you? You *haven't transitioned.* You *do* look gay, to some people. *So what?* Your motivations, though complex, *do* include sexual ones. You can't force others to perceive you as a woman. You can't force others to *believe.*

I want to drag you back to Earth, for your own good, and for mine.

I don't, of course. I can't keep hurting you.

And yet, there is no respect in hiding reality from you as if you are some fragile child. You are an adult. You are capable. You deserve my honesty and my full participation in this relationship.

Wincing from your discomfort feels like giving up on you.

Thrash swaggered over, fist-bumped you and plopped down next to us in the semicircle booth. It was years ago, when Hellbilly Happy Hour was a regular thing. You often played the Melody Inn with a cowpunk band Fuzzy had slapped together. On this night, though, we were spectators. A one-man cello act was opening for the Drunken Deacons.

Thrash was dressed as usual in worn cowboy boots, jeans, and his signature leather jacket, a true work of artistry. Large sections were covered with studs and spikes. Amulets and chains dangled from the shoulders. An anarchy symbol covered one arm, an upside-down cross the other. And Thrash's mohawk was the tallest in the joint, fanning from the nape of his neck to his forehead in twelve-inch spikes that stood straight as arrows. From my closer-than-usual vantage I examined its translucent, gluey surface.

You made a show of welcoming Thrash though you'd always scoffed at him behind his back. You remembered him as Jeff, a man who wore khakis to a monthly folk jam session you hosted at a local coffee house. He took on his punk persona overnight, you said. Popping into a Nashville boutique, he traded half his savings for the jacket. Then he flipped through the catalog at the tattoo parlor next door and spent the other half on the skulls and roses that cover his arms. He christened himself Thrash and slipped into the local punk scene, swiftly and undetected, as if he'd always been there.

"He's kind of a dork," you complained. "Punk has a DIY aesthetic. You *make* your clothes. You don't go broke buying them." Thrash wasn't even a musician, you said—a prerequisite for the kind of cred he seemed to be lapping up. Why should you respect him for acquiring and putting on a costume?

You lambasted inauthenticity in those days. You hated the Tori Amos album I blasted while cleaning house. You said she put on an "affected lilt." Such is not good artistry, you charged. Tori wasn't original. She wasn't interesting.

Your fave Bob Dylan faked his accent, I reminded you. Joni Mitchell called him a "plagiarist," and Heathcote Williams said he stole his personality from a Welsh poet. You knew this, but you held Bob to a different standard. His was an act you admired: a hobo, a busker, a rambler.

Your friend Meat Loaf, so appointed because of his resemblance to the musician, dropped by the Mel that night. He dragged a chair toward the table, unable to squeeze his several hundred pounds into the booth. A bald spot had spread prematurely across the top half of his head, as if worn bare by a ball cap. The dome was surrounded by a fringe of unkempt hair that reached the middle of his back, partly covering the dates of a Mighty Mighty Bosstones tour.

More friends appeared. Men in Western shirts embroidered with birds. Women in halters printed with cherries. Everyone in horn-rimmed glasses. Fuzzy in a purple suit; Claire spilling over a plus-sized burlesque dress.

"Nice butterfly," I said to Claire, eyeing her new fascinator.

"It might be a moth," you said with a wink.

Those were good times. But Fuzzy's band, like so many, was short-lived. And no one goes to the Mel anymore.

"Maybe I was too hard on Thrash," you said, some years later. "Is there really any difference between a fake punk rocker and a real one? At the end of the day, maybe people are what they say they are."

I was reading sociologist Erving Goffman, who would have agreed. He thought of social life as a theater where people perform the selves they want others to see.

"Sincerity is when the performer is taken in by his own act," I agreed, paraphrasing the author. But I wasn't so sure. Certainly, people can create themselves. But they can hide themselves behind their creations, too. "Persona," after all, is the Latin word for *mask*.

You emerge from your latest online feud and flop down on the loveseat next to me. A story is being passed around. You're outraged but unable to conceal a faint smile.

A person who looked male, by all accounts, entered the women's dressing room of a recreational park. Inside, some high-school girls were getting dressed for basketball practice. The individual stripped naked—revealing a fully intact male body—and took a leisurely stroll around the facility, striking up conversations with the girls. Mortified, they dressed hastily and bolted. Later they told their coach and parents.

As it turns out, the person was transgender.

"Was this in the news?" I ask.

You're not sure. You pull out your phone and open the Facebook playlist group, where it's being discussed. But there's no link. Someone heard it from someone else.

"Anyway," you say, tossing your phone onto the loveseat. "Those girls should not have reported the incident!" Your tone is at once proud and condescending. "They need to *educate* themselves about gender identity."

"Oh come on," I say. "As far as they knew, that was a random dude."

"That was a *woman*," you say. "Those girls need to learn that there are different kinds of women!"

"It isn't that simple."

The dark underworld of my childhood, so recently frothed to the surface by my half-written #metoo post, floods my memory.

I am nine years old, sitting on the shag carpet. My brother is beating on his bongos while his friend Vick flips through a Mad magazine. Vick is a stocky boy of eighteen with a crew cut, bad skin and squinty eyes. A cone of incense chokes the air with the powdery scent of sandalwood. I cough. But I love my brother's room, with its beaded curtain and bubbling lava lamp. My brother wishes I'd leave, though. I'm cramping his style again.

"Vick is my boyfriend," I sometimes announce to my family. They chuckle at my youthful fantasy. But my relationship with Vick is not my idea.

It's Vick's idea.

When my brother leaves the room, Vick grabs my tiny hand, interlacing his fingers with mine. "Don't tell anyone," he says. I understand that it's our secret.

My family treats me like I'm underfoot, but Vick makes me feel like an adult. My brother comes back and Vick releases my hand, his advances confined to these brief touches.

I'd stumble across the sex offender list in the newspaper twenty years later, and learn that his sisters weren't so lucky.

I'm eleven. I sit against the lockers with Trish and Tiffany and two other girls with posh names and Jordache jeans. As a bony kid with glasses, I'm honored to be tolerated by them. A boy in our class strolls slowly in front of us, sizing us up. He speaks authoritatively to the friends who flank his left and right.

"This one has nice firm titties," he announces, gesturing to Trish. His comrades giggle. We girls giggle, too.

"This one also has nice firm titties" he says, with a languid wave toward Tiffany. We show our approval with more tittering.

"This one ain't got no titties," he says when he gets to me. His friends laugh.

I laugh too.

I understand this game. There are fuckable girls and unfuckable girls. I'm an unfuckable girl. My role is to be the ugly tagalong, never threatening the popularity of Trish and company. In truth, I'm an early bloomer, with breasts larger than Trish's and Tiffany's. But I wear a baggy t-shirt my mom wants me to "grow into." The boys aren't interested in my shapeless attire or its contents. But it doesn't matter. There's no way to win this game, with or without a better rack than the average fifth grader. Which is worse? To have boys ogle you each morning before class? Or to have them ridicule your shortcomings? It isn't clear. So I chuckle along with the others, as though it's clear that I have no tits, that I am a sexless and useless being.

I'm twelve. Me and my new locker partner, Renee, have just gotten new bikes. We're testing our geographical boundaries for the first time, making a circuit of the gas station, the graveyard and the arcade. We buy Dr. Pepper and Hubba Bubba at the grocery store. We hike the woods behind the cemetery. We play Ms. Pac-Man, run out of quarters, and walk outside to lean against a graffiti-covered wall, smiling and waving at the boys who pass.

Deedle and Damon descend like raptors. They're three grades above us but their swagger suggests they're even older. "Hello ladies," Deedle says, crushing a cigarette under his heel. The two begin horsing around in front of us, shoving each other, cursing, showing off.

Deedle puts his arm on the wall next to Renee. "What are you doing tonight?" he asks.

She says she's shopping for school clothes with her mom.

"That's too bad," Deedle says. He puts his face close to hers, cocks his head and looks straight into her eyes. "I was hoping to eat your pussy."

We're paralyzed by the audacity. We say nothing for a moment, then force a laugh. When they disperse we walk to Renee's house in silence and stay in for the day. We never speak of it.

I'm fifteen. I'm swimming in a cloudy city lake with friends. Someone, swimming unseen under the water, grabs a handful of my crotch and squeezes hard. Mortified, I hurry to the shore. But eventually I rejoin my friends in the lake.

The perpetrator gropes me a second time. I look around, eagle-eyed, determined to catch him rising from the water. But he never emerges. My friends remain untouched; it's a targeted attack.

When I enter the water again, I'm armed with a plan. I stand with my legs apart, mortified to offer myself as bait. When I feel the offender's touch I dig my nails in, scratching deep groves into the length of his arm. Still, he gets away. I scour the shore for someone injured and bleeding. I never find him.

I'm sixteen. I'm in the family bathroom, peeing. I hear a scraping sound outside the window and I know it isn't normal. I jump up from the toilet and flip off the light just in time to watch a shadow scramble away.

My mom calls the police. My dad scours the area. He finds the culprit: a local man who lives with his mom. When the police arrive, my parents decline to press charges. I stand at the window of the squad car in shock, searching for my voice. Maybe my parents don't want to see him go to jail. Maybe they think that'll complicate relations with the neighbors.

I'll never know what they were thinking.

Girls live in a battle zone. They fend off a constant onslaught of lecherous behavior from predatory men. Their limited defense strategies include watching their back, saying no, walking away and telling an adult. In a world where one in three women is sexually assaulted, asking girls to suck it up when they feel threatened is not the answer.

"It isn't that simple," I repeat.

"Of course it is," you say, sweeping your head forward in a manner that evokes a goose protecting her brood.

But you have no idea.

"Look," I say. "We raise girls to be leery of men. And for good reason. We can't very well do that, then spring on them that some men don't count."

"Trans women aren't men!" you say.

I take a deep breath.

I understand that self-identification makes a person a woman. I understand that, in polite society, we've chosen to equate the words with reality.

What I *don't* understand is how words are supposed to stop men from victimizing women. Much stronger measures have failed. Maybe we can talk about that sometime.

For now, I concede your point.

"*This* trans woman was indistinguishable from a man. How can a girl tell the difference?"

You shrug.

"You are aware, aren't you, that men lie?"

"That's not the issue!" you say. "The issue is that trans women are treated as second-class citizens!"

That's not the issue?

Whether a garden-variety pervert watched some teenage girls undress—and got away with it? That's the issue for *me*. It's the issue for those girls, too. It's an issue they can't safely ignore.

But fair enough. There *are* two issues, I guess.

There's the issue that trans women can feel less than welcome in public facilities.

And there's the issue that men prey on women. *Every minute or two*, #metoo reminds us.

I shouldn't be surprised that the former feels closer to home to you. But you can't just dismiss the latter.

The adult in this situation can be expected to do a bit of adulting. The woman in the room, if there was one, should empathize with young women. I would never dispute a girl's need for privacy. It's inviolable. At best, this person failed to grasp what it's like to be female—and at worst, willfully ignored the girls' discomfort. It's fair to question the motives behind such behavior.

"Sometimes a person exposes their penis to a minor with ill intent," I say.

And then I feel sick. At the sheer obviousness of the statement. At the need, once again, to defend a girl's right to her boundaries.

"You can't assume this person was going to commit a rape," you say.

Rape, Jamie? It's hard to believe you aren't being disingenuous. Are you *minimizing* sexual assault that stops short of penetration? Or are you actually *unaware* of the faces of abuse?

"Voyeurism is a sexual violation," I say. "So is exhibitionism. They're meant to intimidate women. They are crimes."

Well, they used to be. They've just become difficult to prosecute.

You fold your arms and glare at me.

I don't get it. Your empathy is something I've always loved about you. What's happened to it? Maybe you really *don't* understand.

"Let's do a thought experiment," I say. "Think about your niece Nina."

"OK," you say, but you look away.

I take you back to the Fourth of July. She ran through the yard, swinging sparklers. She drove Matchbox cars over chalk roads. Turned cartwheels. Filled a jar with fireflies.

She is a child.

"Yes," you agree.

"But girls Nina's age have pubic hair. And developing breasts."

You purse your lips and look at the ceiling. "I don't need to think about that."

I remember what it was like to be her age, I tell you, defenseless as a child while carrying the burgeoning body of a woman. A body we quickly learn is too alluring for strangers to ignore. A body that invites commentary, that emboldens grown men to point and stare. It's awkward, if not frightening.

"When I babysat the girls last week," I say, "I took Nina to swim practice at the YMCA. I have a question for you. What if Twyla had entered the dressing room while she was changing? Would you be comfortable with that?"

You jump up and wave your arms wildly. "You're contributing to a harmful trope!" you say, your voice climbing an octave. "You're suggesting that trans people are sex offenders!"

"I'm not *suggesting* anything. I'm asking a question."

This isn't about tropes, Jamie. This is about *reality.* A reality you've had the luxury of overlooking. In the time you've spent analyzing tropes, I've snubbed wolf-whistling creeps and changed routes to avoid being followed. Tropes are the least of my worries and the least of Nina's. I want you to see beyond the esoteric realm of literary devices and into the real world girls inhabit.

"It's not an accusation," I say, when it seems you don't intend to answer. "It's a question. I'm listening and ready to learn."

198

"No you're not. You're calling me a pervert!"

But I'm not talking about you, Jamie. I'm talking about Twyla—a former bodybuilder with a criminal record. And I'm talking about Nina, a little girl we both love. I have to wonder if you're arguing in good faith. Will you sacrifice your niece to some bogus protection of your honor? Is your ego so fragile?

"Could you stop thinking about yourself for a minute?" I ask, my own voice now rising in pitch. I consider my tone and soften it. "I'm asking you to think about Nina."

"I will not hear this," you say. "I don't feel safe!"

And just like that, you're done. You dismiss another conversation, completely and unceremoniously. It's becoming a habit.

And I *do* want to know your answer.

If you don't want Twyla in the dressing room with Nina, you should say so. Be honest. Truth should not be subordinated to ideology.

If you *do* think it's OK, I'm disheartened. Twyla is sketchy, at best. Nina is a *child*. She's your own flesh and blood, and she needs the support of those who love her. If *we* don't back her up when she's feeling uncomfortable—*you and I*—who will?

I remember the man who watched me pee. He got away with it, because nobody wanted to call it out. Not even my *own family*. I couldn't imagine, at the time, how that was possible. I knew my mom and dad were fuckups. But I thought they'd protect me from a peeping tom if they did *nothing else* right.

They didn't.

I will not become one of the adults who forsakes Nina.

I will not become one of the adults who betrays those girls who want to dress for practice in peace.

In a world where sexual assault is endemic, I will not become one of the adults who finds a reason—*any* reason—to say to a female child yet again: I know you feel threatened. I know you have very real reasons to feel threatened. *But what about the adults?* What about *our* discomfort? What about the social costs of protecting you?

A month before her college graduation, Renee was killed by a drunk driver. Feigning mental and physical illness, the man responsible showed up for trial with a wheelchair and a slick lawyer, buying himself a short sentence.

That's how I begin the next segment of my #metoo post.

Renee was buried in the cemetery the two of us used to explore. When her grave still bulged with fresh dirt, the stone littered with teddy bears and tributes, I paid a visit. I serenaded her with a ditty we once found amusing. "Please don't take my sunshine away," I sang, reaching a lyric that no longer seemed lighthearted. I dropped to the grass and sobbed.

Old man Rodriguez staggered over the hill toward me. I knew him as the single dad of Tommy, a nice boy in town who avoided having friends over. Drunk, he waved a handful of bills in my direction. I could barely make out his slurred speech, but soon realized he was offering me ten dollars for sex.

The next year a friend I trusted offered to rub my aching back, and I fell asleep sprawled across his lap. I awoke to find him fingering me through the leg of my shorts. Appalled, I jumped up and read him the riot act. I had squirmed, he claimed, so he assumed I liked it.

As a young adult, I was on fire to make a name for myself professionally. I stayed with an aunt in St. Louis so I could take a job with a startup preparing for its grand opening. As the first employee, I worked alone with my new boss in a sparsely populated industrial park. I rebuffed his subtle advances, but one night he grabbed me and kissed me. Terrified, I fled—and moved back home.

I'd try my hand as an entrepreneur, then. I opened my consulting business out of a low-rent shared office space. A man twice my age pursued me relentlessly, suggesting that an "independent woman" like me might enjoy dating a married man. When I told him married men should date their wives, he pretended to be joking. Afterward, my faxes and photocopies disappeared and my clients were reported for loitering. My business couldn't recover so I permanently closed up shop.

Then there was the gentle-looking, brown-eyed guitar player I met outside a gay bar, who invited me to sit in his car and hear his demo tape. He shoved me hard onto the seat when I resisted his kiss, and put his fist through the dash when I called him out on it.

Then there was your friend from college, who pulled down my top at one of Theo's Halloween parties and grabbed a handful of my bare breast.

Darcy had a slumber party a few years later. All your female friends were there. When talk of our periods, relationships and breakups began to wane, someone brought up sexual assault. Every woman present had been a victim—many times. Except me. That's what I said, anyway.

I didn't think about the underwater swimmer or the friend with the roving fingers or the man at the Halloween party. I failed to count them *all*. Such incidents are all too commonplace, after all. As women, we're trained to wonder if we invited them.

That college friend of yours later filled a hard drive with images of men choking and raping young children, police reports say. Lyle stays in touch with him. Your other friends decline to take a stand. They've learned that sexual assault is part of the landscape.

You remain glued to the Internet all month.

I get that you feel different. I get that you need support. But looking for it online hasn't lifted you up. It has, instead, marred your perspective.

You are lucky, after all. You are white and able-bodied and no one has given you *any* grief. You blogged, only recently, that you've gotten "universal support" from your social circle. This is something you should celebrate.

Your friends have complied with your pronouns since the party. Your family has placed no limits on your dressing. You've collected hundreds of transgender friends on Facebook and Twitter. Your fan base has blown up. Online allies call you "brave" and "beautiful" daily.

You're a college graduate with marketable skills. You're currently drinking single-origin Sumatra as you hammer on the keyboard of an Ultrabook over lightning-fast Internet.

Many trans women face homelessness or racism or turn to sex work for survival. But these aren't things that you, yourself have faced. It would be admirable if your work aimed to lift them up. Instead, you try to join them in their shackles.

"I have something to ask you," I say, breaking your focus from something you've been typing for the last half hour.

You half-close your laptop and look up, blinking hard, as if to clear your head of what was there before.

We no longer speak frankly. Our sex life hasn't improved. You've stopped job hunting and keeping house. We have a huge amount of work to do, and your online activities distract from that work. They're making you angry. They're making *me* angry, too. I'll be honest—I can no longer stomach the suggestion that you're more vulnerable than a little girl half your size.

I'm doing my best to exercise patience as you work through this strange new world. But I need for you to meet me halfway. We need to address our own problems before we worry about Caitlyn Jenner's or a high school basketball team's. We don't need to cultivate our anger. We need to de-escalate it.

"It's about social media," I say. "Activism. Politics. They're taking a toll on our relationship." I want you to take a break, I tell you. I want you here, with me, focusing on *us*.

You flare your nostrils, chew your lip. You don't want to, you say.

But then you sigh, and you tell me it's fair. Nothing, you say, is more important to you than our relationship.

Relieved, and full of gratitude, I jump up to offer a hug.

"You never sent that picture of me and Darcy," you say, as I wrap my arms around you.

FIFTEEN | SEPTEMBER
ALL IN THE WRIST

It was a blistering afternoon at Delaney Park when we tipped the canoes. You and I got wet. Lyle, who was berating Red for his squeamishness about hooking a worm, got wet. Most importantly, Belinda got wet.

I believe Darcy and Melanie got wet, too. But all were mosquito-bitten, exhausted, and scorched from a full day of sun. We dragged our boats ashore, our collective thoughts turning to long-overdue nourishment and something cold to drink.

"Let's just get changed and go to the burger stand," someone said. We were resourceful campers, some former Scouts, who prided ourselves on our endurance—and we seldom did anything the easy way. We'd refined an elaborate dinner routine: building the perfect long-burning fire, chopping fresh vegetables and herbs, simmering stews "low and slow" in dutch ovens over carefully prepared coals. The idea of simply going to the burger stand was brilliant. We didn't have to cook, after what we'd been through. We could even get ice cream afterward!

The proposal was met with enthusiasm, and we hurried to our tents to change. But Belinda had a problem. It was her first outing with the group—Melanie and Darcy had gotten over their grudge—and she was the only woman present who wasn't an unrepentant tomboy. She'd gotten her only pair of jeans wet, and since she hadn't shaved her legs that morning, shorts were "not an option."

We didn't care if Belinda's legs were unshaven. We were camping, for God's sake! None of us looked our best. One day of hair growth, at any rate, would be imperceptible. With these and other arguments, we enjoined Belinda to get over herself and get dressed for dinner. Our efforts failed. Belinda's leg stubble would not be making an appearance at the burger stand.

We rifled through bags, offered pants for loan. One was too small, another too big, another not quite clean enough. Belinda and Lyle retreated to their tent to brainstorm. Muffled bickering ensued. The group grew hungry and annoyed as dinner was delayed.

I don't remember if Belinda found cover for the offending legs, or even whether we made it to the burger stand. I recall only our self-righteous recap later in the tent.

There was no excuse for Belinda's behavior. So hair grows on her legs—as it does on everyone else's. She was willing to inconvenience everyone to conceal that she's *human*? What a profound failure of perspective. Vanity had made her a shell of a woman.

She was only hurting herself, anyway. Her slavish dedication to image—an image no one even cared about—robbed her of the good things in life. A flame-broiled burger, the company of friends, bare legs drying against the sun-warmed pine of a picnic bench: it was the kind of day we lived for.

We'd never let anything so trivial stop us from living our lives. We'd forever stay curious and brave and open to adventure.

"What's up with our order?" I ask, dipping my steak knife into the softened butter and spreading a layer onto a slice of bread. It's taking a while for our dry-aged ribeyes to arrive.

You tilt your head at a steep angle, raise your eyebrows, and lift the corners of your mouth, forcing a soft laugh. I can't make sense of this response. It's as if you've decided to try out an expression you've seen somewhere, without practicing it in the mirror, so you don't know you're getting it wrong. I think you're trying to look coy, or perhaps flirty, but it's a poor execution.

And anyway, what's up with our order? I'm starving. This is an occasion to commiserate, not to preen.

Light from the chandelier picks up a silver thread in your dress, and your eyes move in the direction of the sparkle. You admire the fabric, then catch your reflection in the hammered tin panels lining the wall.

You seem distracted.

"I know," you say at last. You jut an upturned palm into the space between us, and for a moment it seems you might ask a question. Instead, you curl your fingers delicately, as if balancing a teacup, and gaze lovingly at the curve of your wrist. You seem pleased with yourself.

The server deposits more bread, apologizing profusely. "I'll see to it that you get your food as soon as possible," she promises. There's been some mix-up in the kitchen.

You move the upturned hand toward her in a show of impatience. It's unsettling—despite our grumbling, we've never been the sort to take out our frustrations on the wait staff. We try to stay humbled by the first-world privilege of accessing fine food and having it served to us.

She braces herself for a complaint. But you lower your chin and intensify your gaze, peering at her over the ungracious wrist. The tension in the air grows thick, your silence impressing upon her the gravity of her offense.

She can only apologize with more vigor.

"It's fine," I assure her. "We're fine."

"Did you have to give her attitude?" I ask, when she's fled the scene.

"What do you mean?" You tilt your head—this time in genuine confusion.

I motion toward your hand, still occupying a disproportionate share of the space between us. Then I realize with amusement where I've seen this gesture before.

It's a "valley girl" thing. In junior high I'd sometimes affect the same pose, jutting my lower jaw forward, rolling my eyes, and dismissing some "grody" idea in a voice journalists now call "vocal fry." I was from the Midwest, not the coast, and I'd never laid eyes on a surfboard. But it was stylish, at least among the early teen set in my small town, to emulate the California surfer girls we saw on MTV.

Now I understand. You weren't angry with the server, after all. Though she was in your line of sight, you weren't even looking at her. You were looking at your wrist. She and I were busy interpreting social cues; you were busy demonstrating your charm. The display of feminine grace was lost on us both.

"Oh, *that*," you say, observing your hand as though it belongs to someone else. You pull it limply toward your chest. "I didn't even know I was doing it."

I doubt that. It would seem, from where I'm sitting, that the placement of your wrist is your primary concern.

"The server thinks you got on her case."

You shake your head dismissively, as if that interpretation's wholly without merit. You regret giving her the wrong impression, you say. But there's a sort of smug amusement dancing in your eyes.

"This is just *how I am,*" you say, extending the hand. You hold that these new gestures are so innate you can't suppress them. Any misinterpretation is a failing on the part of the observer, perhaps due to latent bigotry.

In the midst of your monologue you catch a glimpse of your reflection in a pane of chrome surrounding the nearby bartop, where we've promised to meet your ex-wife, Melanie, for an after-dinner drink. You crane your neck for a better view, touching your hair, and lose yourself in thought again.

"They've almost perfected the uterus transplant," you say to Melanie, when we've settled in at the bar. You try out the flirty expression on her, curling your lips and twisting a lock of hair with the newly softened wrist.

"I saw something about that," Melanie says. Her brow wrinkles, almost imperceptibly, as she takes a sip of her malbec.

"That means women like me could get pregnant," you say. "I'd *love* to carry a baby."

Melanie raises an eyebrow, but behind her eyes I see profound sadness. Have you forgotten the two of you divorced because she wanted children and you didn't?

Rows of candy bars in shiny foils call to me as I unload my reusable shopping bag onto the conveyor belt, starting with a package of ladies' cotton briefs rolled tightly in a grip-seal bag. I worked late again, and I'm hungry. But I don't want to regain the weight I've lost so I resist.

You haven't washed a load of clothes since we moved. You haven't even unpacked—boxes line the garage and we're living with a subset of our belongings. I barely manage to find and uncrumple both halves of an outfit for work each morning. I don't have time to do laundry, and besides, it's *your* official job. So I've taken to small rebellions. Last week I washed only my clothes, passing over anything that was yours. The sinful little indulgence required a hefty suppression of female guilt. This week, I'm buying more underwear. I'm holding my ground on this one little thing.

I empty the bag and dispatch the plastic divider. Six cans of tuna, a squeeze bottle of mayo, a box of crackers, a honeydew. And a can opener I can leave at work. I can't find time to make lunch, so I'll assemble it at my desk. And I certainly can't afford to eat out. We still own the old homestead, so I'm covering two house payments and two sets of utilities on top of a Marketplace health insurance policy that costs more than our mortgage. Plus I've started giving you a bit of money. It was Paige's suggestion. You helped me when I was in school, she reminded me. It's a reciprocal thing that married people do.

It's dark when I get home. I drop my purchases on the kitchen counter, along with today's mail, and fill Carrot's bowl. "Carrot Top," I call, as you wander into the kitchen behind her. "My Little Caribou!"

As I browse the fridge you leaf through the mail, tossing aside bills and a letter from your bank. A hand-addressed envelope catches your eye.

"Jamie," I say, scarfing down a piece of salami. "Will you do me a tiny favor in the morning?" I've just about given up on asking for your help. But I could sure use it right now.

"Sure."

"If you do nothing else," I ask, "will you do this one thing?"

"Of course," you say, furrowing your brow, as though perturbed I'd doubt you.

"Cut up this honeydew and put it in a container for me?" The melon should last the week, keeping me out of the vending machines when that afternoon snack urge strikes. It'll save me money and calories.

"Of course," you say, cradling the envelope. Then you rip it open.

"Nora's having a baby shower!" you announce.

"Ah, yes. She mentioned it."

"Is this one of those co-ed showers?" you ask, tempering your enthusiasm. "People are doing that now."

"I don't think so. I think it's only for women."

You beam with pride, then look worried. "I don't know if I have a dress for this," you say, dropping the card and making a beeline for your closet.

"What a hateful bigot," someone posts on the *Achewood* forum, sharing a link to an opinion piece. "She's making the world hostile to people like us."

I lay my phone on the counter—I'll read the article later—and open the refrigerator. It's Saturday night, and it's getting late, and I'm getting hungry. But you're not here. I'm not sure where you've gone; you don't always tell me now.

Finding little of interest, I peel the plastic wrapper from a stick of string cheese and lean against the cabinet, regarding the state of the kitchen. The honeydew sags into the countertop, a smudge of syrup spreading where its flesh meets the granite. When you didn't cut it up for me on Tuesday I asked, again, if you'd cut it up on Wednesday. But Wednesday turned into Thursday. And the week turned into the weekend. And the melon did not move.

The pile of mail hasn't budged, either. I move aside coffee mugs and crumb-covered plates to make space for sorting. I stack the bills and toss the junk mail. Then I open the letter from your bank and pull out the single sheet of paper inside.

It's an overdraft notice. You never closed your account in Ohio. And it isn't the first one—there are fees upon unpaid fees, stretching back for months. The amount you owe, now, is shocking. I unfold the letter and leave it where you'll see it. It isn't my responsibility—it's yours.

My responsibility, right now, is to find dinner. The Mexican grocery with the taqueria is walking distance; it's become my go-to when I don't feel like cooking. I call in my order then pull up the *Achewood* post to kill a minute or two.

Who is this vile person, I wonder, and what has she done?

I open the article: "A Rape Survivor Speaks Out About Transgender Bathrooms." Hardly a formidable opponent, I think. But the news outlet seems conservative and I see the word "God" early on, so I brace myself for some Westboro Baptist-style rhetoric.

Instead, I see the story of a woman struggling with memories of childhood sexual abuse. In its aftermath, she's slept with the light on. Showered in her underwear. Lined the crack under the bathroom door with a towel so no one could peek under. She still battles with trauma, still knows its "horrific language of shame and rage and grief." So far, she has my sympathy. She was so young—and there's no wrong way to process that kind of ordeal. But I guess the article's about to go south.

To my surprise, she expresses "a deep sense of empathy" for transgender people. She's instead worried about *ordinary men*—who could leverage lenient bathroom policies to prey upon women and children at their most vulnerable. Abusers will seize any opportunity they can, she writes, and when gender is a matter of self-identification, there's "zero screening" to prevent it.

Indeed, your online friends oppose screening of any kind. No one should have to prove their gender, they say, *ever*—whether with a birth certificate, a medical intervention or a "panty check." They call such measures "gatekeeping" and say they're an obstacle to transgender care.

Reactions from the *Achewood* crowd pile up. If bathroom inclusivity results in violence against women, one writes, that's an acceptable trade-off. Another offers to personally do the author such violence. "Bigots deserve to die," writes a third. Not content to simply critique her position, they seem to relish ripping her to shreds. They're a mob with torches, but to be fair, they're young. Their prefrontal cortexes aren't finished growing. Their sense of empathy is not fully formed.

I pull the front door closed in time to see you pulling into the driveway. "I forgot something," you say, as you jump out of your truck, releasing the stench of stale smoke into the yard—though last I checked, you're not a smoker. In your passenger seat is a pale kid with a large forehead and sunken eyes, around nineteen years old. He slumps forward in a posture of low self-esteem, his long black hair unbrushed, and he's breathing through his mouth. Though he's dressed unremarkably in a punk t-shirt, he reminds me of the goth kids of the eighties or the Marilyn Manson fans of the nineties. As styles change, this look remains perennial for a sullen sort of youth. You aren't teaching anymore and we're a long way from your old school district. Who is this teenage boy and why are you hanging out with him?

"This is Allie," you say. The kid waves, regarding me with glazed eyes. "Her mom is away so I'm giving her a ride to the meeting."

And so I learn I'm mistaken about Allie. Allie is a woman.

And I remember now: You've found a transgender support group in town. I return the wave, and skipping the small talk, lay a course for Mi Familia. Maybe I'm wrong, but I don't expect to have much in common with Allie.

"You're going to have to learn to be kinky."

I ponder the presumptuous opening of Viv's email—its breathtaking ignorance of my history—as I walk into my new hair salon.

Cameron greets me with a hug. I haven't seen him since the meeting in Dayton, but I stumbled across his profile on the staff page of a nearby salon and reached out. He's moved to Indianapolis to care for his sick mother. He needs clients. I need a hairdresser.

You're out for the evening, at an art exhibit of Twyla's. It's the latest in a string of events standing between me and that two weeks of beard growth. Before that, we walked around Gen Con with Paige, and I guess that wasn't a good time either. "I'll do it afterward," you say each time you postpone. "I'll keep my promise."

Cameron drapes me with a chair cloth as I fill him in on my needs—
a professional look requiring minimal fuss. "This would be fabulous,"
he says, opening an album to a photo of a simple cut with highlights. I
know he's right.

It's time for you and me to address our sex problem. So yesterday, I
asked my support list for help. Viv, who says she and her partner keep
the passion alive, promised to get in touch. I can't resist pulling out my
phone and returning to the email when Cameron steps away for
sectioning clips.

I'm desperate. I can't figure out how to engage you sexually when
you hate your sex organs and have lost interest in mine. When you
require role-playing to stay aroused but can't maintain your suspension
of disbelief. When you need clothing to feel whole but must remove it
to do the deed.

"Cherry *does* have erectile dysfunction," Viv admits. "And her penis
has shrunk from hormone use. But we work around it."

Work around it. Her words evoke a phrase I saw in some
postmodernist's ramblings: "post-genital sexuality." I'm not impressed
with its connotations. I don't want to "work around" my lover's body. I
want to *enjoy* it.

Cherry needs Viagra and a cock ring to stay in the game, my mentor
goes on to say, though it seems that barely helps. Viv must ride on top to
maintain penetration, a position that doesn't really work for her. So
when she's ready, she rolls off Cherry—who does not offer to help—and
uses a vibrator on herself. Still, Viv writes, she feels lucky to have her
"play toy" at all: she's completely straight and Cherry wants bottom
surgery.

It's a reminder that we need to talk about hormones—a topic you
keep evading. Even you know it's time. "Shannon wants to know what
my transition will look like," you recently blogged. "And I owe her an
answer."

I'm glad you're ready to talk. Dysphoria alone has made you a wilting daisy; hormones would surely drive the last nail in that coffin. Would you compromise a vibrant sex life, fifteen years in the making? It's hard to imagine the person I fell in love with doing that. You—who have always devoured me ferociously. You, who denounced "impossible beauty standards" and Belinda's vanity. If it turns out you value feminizing your appearance more than you value our intimacy, I'll be honest: that's a self-indulgence I can't wrap my mind around.

What really saved her marriage, Viv writes, is kink. BDSM. Swinging. Sex parties.

"I need to learn this town," Cameron says, returning to part my hair. He wants someone to visit a new poké place with. He thinks we should hang out.

I agree. We should!

Humming quietly to himself, he paints and wraps sections of my hair as I return to Viv's email.

The fact is, Cherry isn't interested in sex anymore—and must be dominated to achieve arousal. So Viv's bought handcuffs, a leather paddle, and a blindfold. She doesn't love playing dominatrix, but she finds it has its advantages. To get what she wants, she simply issues commands to Cherry: to give oral, to take off the distracting clothes, or, when impotence prevails, to strap on an actual dildo. Viv works her ass off to stimulate Cherry's reluctant body, and barely wrangles her own orgasm out of the deal. She's a "domme" in name only; she isn't the one getting her way. She calls it a good sex life. It isn't the sex life I want.

Maybe I'm old-school, but I expect my partner to *care* about my needs. Maybe even to be *driven mad* by them. I want to be wanted, and I don't think that's too much to ask. For me, sex is a place of bliss, it's communication, it's communion. For Viv, it's services rendered—in piecemeal and without a smile. I want sex to arise naturally because we both yearn for it. I don't want it to mean winning a negotiation, drafting a game plan, and gearing up as if for battle.

Viv's advice isn't practical for us, anyway. When we met, I'd had my fill of polyamory, and you were even less amenable to playing around. I'm all for kink as an *enhancement* to making love, not as a replacement for it. We need to get our intimacy back before we turn to whips and chains.

I think about the women of Regenderate as Cameron secures the last foil. I've watched them go down this road countless times—and it seldom ends well. First, someone announces that her partner wants to be tied up and dominated. Why so many trans women need this treatment to get off is anyone's guess. She starts scratching that often insatiable itch, giving more and getting less in return. Then her partner wants to open the marriage—often to pursue men. She gives in to this, too. Her heart isn't in it, but she looks on the bright side—maybe she can get her satisfaction on the side. Soon after, the relationship implodes.

I once called you the most sexually well-adjusted person I knew. You loved sex, yet you remained free of the hangups about it that plague so many. Your reluctance about porn, though it sometimes spoiled my fun, was part of that healthy sexuality. You didn't expect me to have a Brazilian wax or a rail-thin body. You thought porn looked fake, the actors unhappy. You wanted authenticity. You valued consent. It was an expression of your compassion.

But if you were sexually healthy then, you've sure made up for lost time. And your hangups aren't the kind most people have—the kind that lead to interesting, if controversial, sex. You have the kind that *kill* sex. Making love to transgender Jamie turns out to be like making dinner for an anorexic.

Laden with rules and anxiety. Never embarked upon with full enthusiasm. Enacted with an almost ritual sacrifice of joy.

And what's the point of sex without joy?

Raven is struggling, too. "Edgar is transitioning," she wrote in her last email, using her spouse's given name with me for the first time. "I've never felt so straight in all my life." She dislikes her partner's shaved chest. She's afraid transition will drain her financially. "My best days," she wrote, "are when we don't talk about it." Her worst are plagued by panic attacks.

It's another change, I think, as Cameron carefully releases each foil. Another change, among many, in the small transgender world we've come to know.

Rhiannon, who once claimed to be "gender euphoric" and happy either way, now says she's a woman and has known since she was four. "Sometimes you have to cut toxic people out of your life," she blogs, explaining she's recently divorced. I remember Alex from the restaurant—with her ardent defense of Rhiannon's right to "do what she wants"—and wonder what happened.

Your friend they call Meat Loaf now identifies as a woman—and chairs that transgender support group you found. She hasn't given up her wrinkled band t-shirts, covered her bald spot, or made any other changes to her appearance, citing perpetual "bad timing." Even the support group has trouble with her pronouns, to say nothing of her appointment to the post. "We should be represented by someone who knows the struggle," one complained.

Some of the *Achewood* folks have switched identities more than once, selecting from newly minted genders as if they're varieties of lemonade.

Then there's Krystal—or should I say "Kris." Not a year after completing every gender confirmation surgery on the books—including genital surgery—Kris has stopped taking hormones and resumed living as a man. He claims he no longer has gender dysphoria.

Even Margot, the author from Regenderate who says she's "hard-wired" for monogamy, has agreed to open her marriage. She isn't ready to discuss it and she's put her new book on hold. It's hard to shake the feeling she's made the decision under duress. As a famously trans-affirming author, can she even complain?

Cameron hasn't changed, though. He smiles as he lowers my head into the shampoo bowl, the pink tint on his lips a perfect match for the ruffled cuffs of his blouse.

"I saw your blog post," I say, trying to straighten the sheet without stripping the bed. "Can we talk about hormones?"

"I know." You turn over your pillow, hiding a mascara stain shaped like a smashed spider. "But I haven't decided anything."

"We can't keep sidestepping the topic." I flip off the lamp and we lie in silence, bathed in the pallor of a neighbor's dusk-to-dawn light.

"Fine," you say, after a moment. "I don't want to take them off the table."

That means you're interested.

"What's stopping you?" I pull the quilt toward me, noticing its weft is growing brittle.

"I look pretty good right now. But I don't want to turn into an old man."

Not so long ago, back at the farmhouse, you *longed* to become an old man. You dreamed of growing out your beard and playing Santa at the mall.

Now, I can't get two weeks with that beard.

Now, it seems hormones are in our future. And though you say you don't want surgery, I must prepare for that possibility, too. It seems you will pursue the body you want, whatever the price.

And when you achieve that body—that altered, flaccid body that approaches *your* ideal but neither arouses my interest nor responds to my touch—what's left for *me*? I don't want to have to browbeat you into sex, like Viv does with Cherry. I don't know what's going to happen, but I won't subordinate my needs to yours.

"Can we talk about the beard promise, then?"

You sigh. "Ren Faire is coming up."

I get it. I do. It's a chance to dress up. But I want you to *make this happen.*

"When is a good time?" I ask. "You choose."

"It's complicated," you say.

But it isn't complicated. It's a matter of picking a date and keeping it. You've scheduled a laser appointment, I remind you. Soon there'll be no hair to grow out.

"It won't take effect right away," you say.

"It isn't going to happen, is it?"

"I can't help it!" You launch into an embarrassment of excuses. But to me, they boil down to one. You won't make it a priority.

"You know what." I roll away from you and the ceaseless security light, toward the nightstand, where my phone flickers in its dock, waking with a soft glow. "If you can't do this for me, just fucking forget it."

But I don't want you to fucking forget it. I want you to keep your promise. I want you to suffer through two measly weeks, just for me. I'll get two weeks of what I want. You'll get a *lifetime* of what you want.

I undock my phone, prop myself up, and swipe to unlock it. I'm not even sure I'm bluffing. I think I'm just coming to terms with the fact that I can't actually count on you. I want my needs to matter to you. I want you to at least pretend, right now, that they matter. I want you to at least continue to feed me the bullshit line that you're trying.

That's the best I can get these days.

Instead, you roll toward me and say: "OK."

You muse on the color of the bedroom wall, new since Labor Day, when I hired your sister Jill to paint throughout the house. Cheer creeps into your voice as you appreciate its hue in the dim light, happy to forget we ever made that pesky little agreement. Savoring your ill-gotten reprieve, you excuse yourself, again, from the tedium of compromise.

My browser opens to the last page I visited—the *Achewood* post. Comments have grown ruder and more hyperbolic. The author of the article is responsible for trans people's deaths, the group says. The author's a privileged cunt. The author can die in a fire.

At the end of the thread is a comment from you. You think she's a bigot, too. You think men are going to creep on women with or without laws to discourage it. You think she needs to "sit down and shut up" and listen to trans people.

It's shaping up to be a night of broken promises.

The seduction of online brawls, it seems, is stronger than your ability to keep your word. But now it's stronger than your empathy, and that's even more disheartening. A *rape victim*, Jamie? That's where you're directing your anger, now? She is no threat to you. Her vulnerability is palpable; she may as well be curled in the fetal position before us. And maybe the last thing you feel like doing is offering a hand. But can you do me a favor—do all women a favor—and refrain from *kicking* her?

The person with a soul walks away from her story feeling heartbreak, not anger.

I ask you about your comment.

"We don't need that kind of rhetoric making trans women look bad," you say.

"What rhetoric?"

"The rhetoric that we are perverts."

I hand you my phone. "Can you show me what you mean?"

"I don't remember." You push the phone away.

"She explicitly said otherwise."

You shake your head, then pummel me with a monologue about transgender bathroom access that sounds well-rehearsed.

But this isn't about politics, for me. It's about *empathy*.

It's something everyone deserves, not least a sexual assault victim seeking a compromise that keeps all parties safe. Without empathy, we can't build a world that's safe and accommodating to *anyone*.

But I want to understand where you're coming from. I really do. So I ask you, again, to show me what you found problematic.

You exhale sharply.

"Fine," you say. "I didn't read the article."

My heart falls.

I'm disappointed that you've broken your promise. I'm more disappointed that you've chosen a rape victim as the target of your wrath. But to convince yourself of her guilt without reading what she has to say? That's most disappointing of all. Where's the integrity in this?

You get inordinately angry about what you read online. Now, it seems, you get angry about what you *don't* read, too. Why? Do you enjoy turmoil?

I don't. I want my life back.

I want to have real conversations again. And maybe we can't have them about transgender politics. Maybe we need to start someplace else. I ask if you agree. I ask, again, if you can shelve social media and activism in the interest of working on our relationship.

You sniff. You didn't think the webcomic group counted, you tell me. And anyway, you're not sure you want to. And anyway, you don't think it's reasonable for me to ask.

You've just been informed of a volunteer position with an LGBTQ organization. You'd be working with Caleb from your support group. I struggle to decipher the glimmer in your eye when you pronounce Caleb's name.

"Our marriage is in crisis," I say. You can live without this position. There will be others.

You roll away from me. "I'll think about it," you say, with a flip of your wrist.

SIXTEEN | OCTOBER
GROWING COLD

A chill pervades the gray October air and seeps into my bones. I pile on sweaters and sip mugs of tea but I can't keep warm. My skin feels paper-thin. I ache like I've been trampled by horses. I want nothing more than to immerse myself in a bath infused with my favorite sesame scented oil.

Instead I lean over the sink, recoiling from an electrostatic shock as my fingers make contact with cold stainless steel. I shake it off and turn both handles full steam, splash my face and rub it dry with a clean-enough looking towel. The bathtub's full of crumbled drywall after Jill sanded and painted the room. At the family discount, I can't complain. But for weeks we've been using the cramped shower stall in the second bathroom.

I haven't cleaned the tub because I can't slow down. My employment contract ends soon, and since you've been unemployed since spring, we can't afford a lapse in my income. Plus, we've gotten an offer on our old house. So job interviews and real estate matters have consumed my every waking moment.

You haven't cleaned the tub because you've been crying.

Crying's replaced all your former pursuits. Your crying jags are punctuated by breaks, but not by activities. You can no longer be seen opening a piece of mail or rinsing out a coffee mug. Your sorrow's become an indulgence from which you'll brook no distraction. You enjoy enumerating its causes; most involve your appearance. You don't look right in a particular dress. Your neck is too wide. Someone shared an unflattering photo of you.

You appear in the doorway and mumble good morning. I stop rifling through a drawer to respond. I know you've wanted to talk and I know I haven't been fully present. The young couple who's made the offer is expecting their first child and they barely qualify for financing. But I want the deal to go through so I can wash my hands of that second set of bills. That means answering questions, responding to inspection complaints and assembling counteroffers. I've spent a lot of time preparing for my job interviews, too.

And we were up past midnight again. You were ruminating on your gender. I was consoling you. It's Friday, so rest is in sight, though we have plans this evening.

"Tonight is Joel and Maria's anniversary party," I remind you.

Joel often played the folk jam session you used to host—his feel-good Americana complements your rustic blues. His wife shares my love for Mary Oliver and the Indigo Girls. The four of us have gathered at farm-to-table restaurants after shows, discussing Camus or the latest Flaming Lips album over vegan tacos. When you first stumbled across a photo of Joel in gold brocade in front of a mural of Coptic art, we were astonished to learn he's a priest. But the pair isn't dogmatic. Their values align with ours: gratitude, simple living, a passion for social change. They're good people who feed my soul, and I'm looking forward to seeing them tonight.

I glance at the time; I need to get going. If only I could soak in a hot bath tonight. I won't have time to clean the tub between work and the party, but you will. You'll be home all day with nothing to do.

I close the drawer and turn toward you, looking into your eyes. "I know you're depressed. But could you do me a favor today?"

"Of course."

"Will you clean the bathtub?"

"I'm sorry. I've been meaning to."

I feel bad, but I'm unconvinced you'll follow through. I search for words to relay how fervently I desire a bath.

"Can you make it a priority?"

"Of course." You lean against the sink, face me, and return my gaze. You seem utterly sincere. I realize I've been clenching and I choose to breathe. I thank you and allow myself to look forward to the bath.

"Where in the world is my hairbrush?" I mumble to myself, trying another drawer.

"I borrowed it. It's in the shower."

"Again?"

Last time I found it smelling like gym shoes, a fine black mildew covering its foam base. I threw it away and bought another for each of us. What have you done with yours? I don't have time to wonder; I drag an old comb through my hair and get myself out the door.

When I've slogged through a workday I'm sure will never end, I stumble home, pass you drowsing on the loveseat, drop my bags and make a beeline for the bathroom.

The tub is still full of drywall.

I catch myself grinding my teeth as I head for the shower. Irritability bubbles up, manifesting as a scalded, hollowed-out sensation at the top of my skull. I crank up the hot water and focus on the warmth, trying to mask the burning in my fevered head. I *will* get centered. I *will* have a good time. I succeed, somewhat, in cooling my ire. But a hopelessness floods in to take its place. And the hopelessness is worse.

I emerge to find you laying outfits on the bed, enthused about dressing for the party. When you've settled on an ensemble, you model it for me, asking which purse and heels I prefer.

Abe and Chana's home floods the street with a warm, yellow light that breaks amid a scrabble of power lines. Inside, it's abuzz. Flushed guests cradle wineglasses of pungent reds, huddle near a candlelit table arranged with smoked salmon, caviar, crème fraîche, plump dates wrapped in hickory-smoked bacon and blackberry-chèvre tarts. White lights lie strung across a blown-glass pendant. Our coats are whisked away by a stranger.

We don't know anyone except the guests of honor, who are nowhere in sight. Not even our hosts, who now materialize, plying us with hugs and introductions and a whirlwind tour of their historic home. We're deposited near a selection of open wine bottles on a midcentury-modern console, where we make fast friends. With antique collectors, bookworms, gourmet food aficionados. With Maria's sisters. With Joel's classmates from seminary.

Then, members of their parish and singers in its choir. Sponsors and witnesses from their bridal party. Friends of the pair, from childhood, high school and beyond, all belonging to a few interwoven congregations. Everyone present, we come to realize, is Christian Orthodox.

Everyone.

Are we the only libertines Joel and Maria know? Will there be no music scene buddy, no neighbor, no friend from a gardening club?

It turns out not to matter. No one flinches at your barrette or your jacquard skirt. I shouldn't be surprised Joel and Maria's friends are as cool as they are.

"What part of the city do you live in?" a woman named Leslie asks. She's new in town and looking for a place to rent.

I describe our neighborhood on the north side. It's diverse, I say, and close to shops. And friendly to joggers and dog walkers.

"We love it there," you chime in.

Leslie tilts her head and studies your face, then mine. "You two live together?"

Later Abe regales me with a story of how he and Chana met while serving as counselors at church camp. "Are you married?" he asks.

"For eight years," I say, moving toward you and placing a hand on your waist. "Together for fifteen."

Abe apologizes.

It isn't his fault—we don't fit the mold. The men here are dressed like men, if with a touch of class. A chartreuse scarf. The soft leather of a Wolverine boot. They smell of cypress and tonka, colognes picked out by wives who, thirty years ago, were their high-school sweethearts. You're not even wearing your wedding ring—it hasn't fit since you lost weight.

It's a repeat performance of Nora's shower. Her mom eyed you skeptically, sure you'd wandered into the wrong church basement. Then a friend of hers settled in next to you and held forth on her brother's husband's catering business. When Nora praised the fare served at our wedding, the woman apologized and offered me her chair.

We don't look like members of Joel and Maria's tribe.

We don't look like married people.

We're invisible to bar patrons and gay baristas. Why should we be recognized here? The pink smudge of an eraser mark lies where our relationship was once written. I just haven't gotten used to life as a ghost.

To be taken for carpooling buddies, again and again, after the epic we've lived—an epic as grand as Joel's and Maria's, or Abe and Chana's—proves the final blow to my flagging morale. Defending our marriage becomes a burden I can no longer carry.

The crowd swells. Maria appears. Joel pops a bottle of champagne and fills one flute after another. Chana whisks away serving trays as guests swarm to a living room lined with pillows and comfortable chairs. You take a seat on the sectional and I squish myself into the corner next to you, where I can recline. I take off my cardigan. The room is warm.

Once, in a Japanese restaurant, the server walked backward from our table, her hand concealing a giggle. "You two are in love," she charged, wagging her finger. "Everyone can tell."

Once, we clobbered the other couples playing a "Newlywed Game" knockoff at a Valentine's Day party, because we knew each other so well.

Once, your youngest sister said we were her proof true love exists.

"To my wife," Joel says now, raising his glass to the sound of cheers. "My love," he projects over the clamor. "My best friend."

Someone is sharing a memory. A wake, held in the living room of a home, where Joel spoke and Maria held space for the bereaved. Others follow. A late night of studying. The challenge of the ascetical fast. A prolonged labor and uncertain birth. Each thread pulled spins into another. And now the explication of romantic love: the double dates, the awkward proposal, the wedding cake that came a day late.

I want the crowd to know that we, too, appreciate the joys and sorrows of navigating the world with one person for a very long time. We've been at it for a decade and a half—we're no amateurs. But I can't find the words. My attempts to rescue our marriage flounder, here as at home. The public failure mirrors the private unraveling.

I find no words, even, for celebrating Joel and Maria. We haven't shared the right sort of history with them. That time the four of us ordered more tapas than we could eat—it just isn't that compelling now. My silence feels conspicuous, though it needn't. No one looks our way when a story ends and it's time for another to begin. If we share in this tradition, no one can tell.

And it's possible, I realize, we no longer share in it. It's possible the path we embark upon, now, has nothing to do with the one that came before. These misconceptions I fight—maybe they aren't misconceptions at all.

Some of the men retrieve guitars from a corner. Your face brightens when Joel hands you a spare Fender. You pluck, checking the tuning, as conversation gives way to a jam session. You slide easily into the familiar role of entertainer.

Joel cuts the noodling short with an assertive riff. It's a rushed-tempo version of a song I've heard before but can't place. "Wake Up," someone announces, as you find the chords. Joel hums the first refrain. Others join, growing louder, growing boisterous. Then voices rise, shoring each other up, giving shape to lyrics.

"Something! Filled up! My heart! With nothing!"

I want to join in, but I don't know the words.

The singing turns to shouting. In the care of Joel, "Wake Up" begins to sound like the human spirit prevailing over all evil.

I sink into the sectional. I'm the only person who isn't playing or singing. I clap once or twice, but my heart isn't in it, and the show of participation feels like work. I'm an outsider, ill-equipped to access, or even fake, the spirit of the room. I'm not a musician. I'm not a childhood friend. I'm not a kindred spirit of the church.

To this crowd, I'm not even a spouse—the minimal requirement for a sense of belonging. Cracks form like spiderwebs in my happy facade and my faith in our marriage begins to wane. With effort, I fight back tears. This is not the time or place. But when is the time, where is the place? I've been holding it together for you for so long.

"Someone told me not to cry,"

the crowd sings, laying bare the absurdity of my plight. And I'm Sisyphus buckling behind the weight of the boulder I keep pushing up the hill, knowing it will roll back down.

Feigning allergies, I retreat to the bathroom. The levee is breached, and for five full minutes I release raw emotion over Chana's reclaimed art-glass basin. Then I pull myself together and return to the scene with wet eyes and a blotched face. For once, you notice. You offer to take me home. I'm in no condition to decline.

Pushing aside dresses and belts, I retreat into the mass of unwashed blankets on our bed. You ask what's wrong. But I have no new answers for that question.

I shiver against the cool sheets as you deliver your lecture. My sadness is offensive to you. My sadness means I don't accept you. Why should this be hard? Aren't I happy for you? You change into your kimono, tighten the sash. You want to stay together. But you're not sure I do.

I'm not trying hard enough.

You climb into bed. What about *your* problems? What about *your* feelings? You shouldn't have to address my sadness. I should be addressing yours.

Your injured self-esteem, now the star of every show, takes center stage. *Aren't you good enough? Are you even pretty?* Midnight comes and goes before you're finished with me.

Maybe I can't expect happiness. Maybe I can't even expect rest. But warmth is attainable. I crawl out of bed, fetch the dustpan and the cleaning supplies, and get on my knees in front of the bathtub to scrub.

Grease runs from the foil packet, flaring amid the coals as I rotate my dinner with a sharpened stick. Sun glances off the single tent between me and a weather-stained Winnebago. A biting cold seems slick with steam and light.

I've got no vacation days left but I can commute from River Bend. I've hung five career blouses from the handrail in my car. I'll wear the same black pants and loafers every day. I'll twist my hair and hide it in the folds of an oversize scrunchie, as women do on "bad hair days."

I had to cut some corners. I had to get away.

Every evening starts the same. I give myself a pep talk as I cross the office parking lot. Crushing down the impulse to drive in any direction but home, I start my car. I dig deep into my dwindling reserves of patience and optimism. I greet you at the door. I try to sense your needs. I try to yield to them.

Then the thing happens. You notice a patch of hair on your body. You read an upsetting news story or tweet.

And you spiral.

I try to salvage the evening. Because I care. But also, if I'm honest, because I need a break. I need to have that evening where we savor a simple meal, linger over conversation, climb into bed before the clock gives way to single digits. If I don't get a full night's sleep I'm going to wrap my car around a telephone pole some foggy morning.

My efforts fail. You start sobbing. Sometimes you start yelling. You land on your body—what you think is wrong with it, what a freak you are. Then you speak of mistreatment, sometimes real, more often imagined.

Then we're fighting. Sometimes you start it. You blame me for not finding you attractive. You blame me for doubting your womanhood. You're angry because I humor you, but you're also angry because I make you confront the truth.

Sometimes *I* start it. I beg *not tonight, not again.* I tell you being pretty doesn't matter, for fuck's sake. I lose my shit. I remind you that you haven't worked or washed a dish in months, and that I'm tired, and overworked, and I want you to step the fuck up. I *beg* for a decent night's sleep.

Then you cry softly on the bed. If I'm unsympathetic, that's another fight. You need me to reassure you. But it's two a.m. and I have to get up in four hours, so I roll over and switch off the light and disappoint you yet again.

Now I unroll the foil packet, emptying charred meat and fork-tender potatoes onto enamelware. After an ill-advised bite that burns my tongue, I leave my dinner to cool and pull my tote across the dust, away from ash and spark. Pushing aside the spiral-bound notebook knocking around inside—I have a letter to write, but that can wait—I retrieve *The*

Dialectic of Enlightenment by Max Horkheimer and Theodor Adorno. Raven mentioned it in a recent email.

What ails the world? According to its authors, man's need for "blind domination." Over nature. Over others. And over himself. Modern man doesn't *accept*. He wages war against anything and everything that thwarts his desires.

When there's food in my belly and a critique of modernity in my head, I walk away from the fire and Horkheimer and a woodpecker that clacks overhead, coaxing nutrition from a moldering oak. Re-wrapping my scarf, I follow the gravel road until fading autumn leaves hang in damp shreds and a gang of barefoot boys splash in the cold sludge of a puddle.

"Some people abuse their partners with tools other than violence," a woman named Harper posted on Facebook yesterday. We were friends when she lived in town, but she's moved to Columbus and we've fallen out of touch.

"They perform sad feels," she added. "And have breakdowns when things don't go their way."

It made me think.

I know your feelings are real. But your feelings, alone, control our dialog. They're setting the agenda for our evenings. They're plotting the course for our *lives*.

And maybe motivation is a fuzzy thing.

Maybe an abuser isn't always a shadowy figure in a trench coat, twirling his mustache, devising punishments. Maybe, sometimes, he's someone who wants, who grabs, who chooses not to think about repercussions, who waits until it's too late.

But it doesn't matter. Injury is injury, intended or not, and I've had enough for now.

Ahead, where the park grows thick with RVs and little yards are cordoned off with tarps and garden gnomes, my eyes drift upward. In the towering branches of a northern white cedar, a million glowing fireflies have come to rest.

But that can't be, of course—it's too late in the season.

"Magical, isn't it?" asks a man with thinning mutton chops, parked in a folding chair below. His wife, wrangling a profusion of pale hair into a bun, shows me the LED projector from which it emanates. Who knew a device from the drugstore could evoke bioluminescence, foxfire, a curtain of fallen stars?

They offer me a chair. I learn that after fifty years together, they're fulfilling a shared dream—to visit every state in the country. Together they've seen the mountains and the desert and the giant redwoods. I'm impressed by their spirit; they're curious and brave and open to adventure. You and I have discussed retiring on the open road. It seems unlikely now.

With reluctance I leave the warm cocoon of their camp, pulling my cap over my tingling ears and looping around the park toward my temporary home. And then, flanked by spent milkweed and huddled geese, I reach the White River.

And I see the dragon.

Its gaping mouth is the truncated fork of an upended tree. Muscular vines form legs that lift its body from the muck below. Its torso surges upward, twists, reaches for the firmament. From knotholes in scarred bark angry nostrils protrude, exhaling a crimson flare that streaks the sky and sets the horizon on fire. Once a downed tree, it has risen again. Once vanquished, it triumphs.

When the chill of late fall has chased me into my tent, I retrieve my notebook and pen. "I want you to write a goodbye letter to James," Eunice suggested at our last visit. "Not to *Jamie*. But to your *husband*. Because that person doesn't exist anymore."

I think that's a shame. James was worth knowing. Worth loving. What makes a perfectly good person vanish into thin air?

Dear James,

I write,

My first taste of real sadness was when we broke up for those four days early on. I was in love with you, though I didn't know it yet.

The years we've spent together have been my happiest. I never thought I'd find someone so compatible with me, let alone so compassionate and kind. It was easy to love you because your goodness runs deep.

For so long I've lived inside a bubble of contentment I was sure nothing could rupture. I felt secure. I felt sure you'd always be there for me. But now you're gone, and it isn't fair. I've held up my end of the deal. I was once your primary concern. Now there's something you value more.

They tell me there is nothing I can say or do to bring you back. I have to say goodbye to you as if you had died in some stupid war.

This letter is probably supposed to help me forgive you, but I don't know if I can. I can't even get to the part where I say goodbye. You are an asshole for leaving.

And I would do anything to get you back.

When I catch my breath I flip the page.

The letter was Eunice's idea. The lists are mine. Three of them, to help me strategize. First, a list of the things I love about you. It'll help me remember what to see in you when I see only turmoil.

Second, the problems we must overcome. I want to tackle them methodically.

And finally, the potential outcomes of this journey. It'll help me understand what my possibilities are, what I need for them to be.

When I finally turn off the lantern, I dream I'm standing before a portal to the past. It's open—I can put my hand in it, touch what's inside. Present-day you is here, next to me, looking into the portal too.

The you from the past appears inside. That you is dressed in flannel, wearing a beard, moving about like a ragdoll. Vibrant and happy, he doubles over in uninhibited laughter. Then he comes near the portal. He's so close I could touch him.

I'm overwhelmed. Wistful. I want nothing more.

But you're standing beside me—the you of now—watching. And you don't want me to touch that person. You want me to reserve my love for your transness, now, and nothing more. You stare at me, compel me to resist. Your lip trembles. And hurting your feelings is the last thing I want to do.

But I love that person in the portal, and I can't change that. It's a *reality* I occupy. And why must I suppress love? I look at the you of now and the pity I feel hurts my soul. But I have longings, too.

I reach into the portal and touch James.

In the morning I rekindle the fire and warm a kettle for tea and instant grits. It's cold as hell. I flip open my notebook and review what I wrote last night, starting with the list of things I love about you.

"You're a good conversationalist." But we haven't talked about anything but your gender for months.

"You love the outdoors." But you don't want to camp or backpack anymore. How would you keep up your makeup? Unisex clothes, like boots and cargo pants, trigger your dysphoria.

"You're great in bed." But those days are gone. The last time we had sex, like the time before, was made possible by a couple of stiff drinks and my willingness to forfeit my own pleasure.

"You're good at your work." But you haven't worked for much of the year. And you don't believe you can find work. And you no longer seem interested in work.

How does a person change so quickly, so completely? The authors of *Dialectic* know. You've declared war upon yourself. I shouldn't be surprised—I've seen your self-hatred scrawled across poster board.

A war upon your strong face—which you're trying to soften with makeup and laser surgery.

235

A war upon your body—the one you once hauled over harsh terrain, shirtless and sweating, determined to outlast your hiking buddies. The one you squeeze into spandex, trying to mold it into the soft, slight frame of a young girl.

A war upon your raspy voice—the one you once belted out blues songs with. The one you now replace with a whispering lilt.

"Jamie will outgrow this unhealthy phase," your youngest sister insists. But what does it look like to be transgender and healthy? How do you care for yourself while detesting the substance you're made of?

You say you reject your *gender*. But that isn't right. Your gender is whatever you make it. It is your *sex* you reject.

It is your sex you recognize when you like your dress but not the way it fits. It is your sex you try to hide when you tuck your penis or tighten your corset. It is your sex you hope to alter with hormones.

But your sex is your flesh. You are no poltergeist enmeshed in skin and bone and brain. You *are* skin and bone and brain. A war upon your flesh is a war upon yourself.

War protests have fallen out of fashion. Hating your body was once a tragedy; now it's "transness." Self-love isn't part of the mission. That folksinger who sang of dirt and whiskey? A casualty. That geek who lost himself in computer code? Acceptable loss. I mustn't grieve the fallen, I'm told. The right thing to do is join the war. To prove how progressive I am. To prove my love.

I flip to the next list: the possible outcomes of this journey. We break up. We stay together. You fulfill your wishes and I give up on mine. We open our marriage, like so many women on Regenderate—or we lose our intimacy and live as roommates. There's only one path that doesn't fill me with dread. It's the path in which you compromise. It's the path you haven't been willing to take.

As I dress for work in the camp shower house, I ponder the list of problems we must overcome: our marital bed death. Our diverging

236

interests. Your depression. Your financial dependence on me. Your unwillingness to put aside distractions and focus on these problems.

It's a big list. It's a hard list. It's a list that chronicles a steady decline in our quality of life.

I haven't been able to save a dime for your engagement ring, I think, as I start my car. It's possible, I realize for the first time, that we won't make it long enough to renew our vows.

When I boot up my phone and launch my GPS, I'm flooded with notifications. You've been texting me since I left, asking when we can talk again.

"I need to be a participant in my own life," I say. Still nursing a tea from this morning, I take a seat on the loveseat, cradling the ceramic mug in my hands.

Though I left my retreat early—it was just too cold—it helped me hone my thoughts. If we're to make it, we need to have a frank conversation. You haven't been open to that, but I've thought carefully about what I want to say. Surely you can understand that this is my life, too. My life needs to work for *me*. I slosh around the last sip in the cup, glancing in the direction of the fireplace. Though it's chilly, we've never made a fire in our new house. It hasn't even crossed our minds.

You circle the room and stop in front of me, blocking my view of the unsoiled hearth. "What do you mean?" you ask, your lips curling into a scowl.

I know you know what I mean.

"We only have the kind of sex *you* want to have. We only talk about what *you* want to talk about. You even dictate what I can say to *other* people. Our life has become 'The Jamie Show' and I'm expected to sit back and applaud."

"That's not true!"

I expected you to defend your tyranny, but I didn't expect you to *deny* it. You've been unwilling to budge on *anything*. Can you really not see that?

"What am I missing?" I ask, with all the restraint I can muster. "Can you name a compromise you've made for me?"

"What sort of compromise am I supposed to make?" You shake your head, your eyes narrowing.

"I've given you what you want in bed," I say. "I've asked for a little extra attention to *my* needs in return. You couldn't give me that."

"We talked about that."

"I asked for two weeks with your beard. You couldn't give me that, either."

You search for words, but fail to find them.

"I asked you to take a break from social media. You said you would. But you didn't."

"I compromised with you about hormones," you say.

What? Was I *present* for this?

"You said you wouldn't take them off the table," I remind you.

"But I seriously considered it."

"So you *almost* compromised," I say, "but didn't."

"It was hard to even consider it!" you say, with rising indignation. You take a seat on the loveseat and turn your body away from me. "You don't know how hard this is!"

"I don't doubt it. But this needs to work for me, too. My life doesn't even *belong to me* anymore."

"What do you want from me?" You get up and cross the room again.

"What can you offer me?" I ask, reining in a sarcasm I know will be unhelpful.

How about inclusion in your plans? A peaceful evening? A glance of appreciation?

"Do you know how long it's been since you looked at me?" I ask. "Really *looked* at me, because you're *interested* in me? Not because you want to borrow what I'm wearing?"

You lower your eyes.

"You've stopped demonstrating your love for me. People can't even tell we're married. They think you're gay and I'm some fag hag friend."

"You're calling me a fag?" Your tone suggests I've threatened your dignity. But you smirk as if gratified to catch me in a misstep.

"Please," I say, refusing the bait. "I'm gayer than you are."

"You need to be tolerant. I'm going through a thing!"

"Oh yeah?" I say, my patience wearing thin. "Well I'm going through the *same god damn thing*. Except it's more fun for you than it is for me. And people check on you daily, but no one asks how I'm doing."

"I'm also working forty-plus hours," I add, walking toward you. "I'm paying our bills. Two mortgages. Two sets of utilities. Marketplace health insurance. I'm buying groceries. Selling our house. Keeping this place in order. You couldn't even *cut up a honeydew* for me. Don't tell me about going through shit." I look into your eyes, directly but calmly, pressing for your response.

Tears well in your eyes, but your face betrays anger. You walk away briskly as I gulp down my final swallow of tea.

"Anyway," you shout from across the room. "What does this have to do with you!"

A red heat floods my cheeks. The sheer depth of your willful disregard sinks in.

Until now, I assumed you'd lost sight of my needs in the urgency of your own. Maybe you even *resented* them. But it's worse. You actually seem *confused* by my agency. I'm a human being, Jamie. I'm real. Had you forgotten? I wondered if you saw me as an equal in marriage. Now I wonder if you're able to recognize a fellow *soul*.

You've been self-centered for a while, but this is incredible. This seems *pathological.* I assumed you'd need a reminder that I deserve to have a life. I didn't think you'd need *convincing.*

I can't even process this. What's happened to your compassion? Has my support been a waste of time? Have the last *fifteen years* been a waste of time? A slow rage begins to boil and my hand presses against the mug I'm holding. In an instant I imagine flinging it. Against the wall. Through the bay window. Smashing it into pieces. Shattering the goddamn house, taking a baseball bat to the drywall. Razing it to the sinking foundation upon which I've built my one wild and precious life.

Instead, I tighten my grip, cramped white knuckles pressed to porcelain. Because Shannon doesn't throw things. She has too much foresight. She sees herself sweeping up the shards, paying a repairman, apologizing. Instead, she screams. She screams in an otherworldly wail I hear from above her, safe on a distant astral plane.

"Are you *fucking kidding* me?"

She screams without my consent, unwilling to be steered. She marches into the kitchen in a fit of fury, stands above the sink, and hurls that mug, impotently, across the sixteen inches in front of her, into the stainless-steel basin, where it rocks and stops, dislodging a small chip at the rim.

"Are you seriously fucking kidding me?" I repeat, now inhabiting my body. I pivot away from the sink to face you and step into the doorway, where you huddle after following me into the kitchen. I look you squarely in the eyes, dare you to answer.

You draw your wrists limply toward your chest, hunching forward, feigning terror. A subdued smile betrays that you relish my loss of control.

"You're scaring me," you snivel, raising the back of your hand to your face, as if to shield it from a physical blow. *As if I might hit you.* I've never even been in a high school scuffle and you know it. You back away from me on tiptoe, making a show of your weakness.

"Are you seriously fucking kidding me?" I repeat, into the impenetrable fog that surrounds you. You've excused yourself from every important conversation this year. I won't excuse you from this one.

You bolt for the bathroom and I follow. You try to shut the door. I slam it back open, knocking it from your hands. *"What does my fucking life have to do with me?"*

Several hours after "taking a drive" you enter the bedroom, banging a drawer loudly enough to wake me as you change.

"I don't feel safe with you," you say, climbing into bed next to me.

"Bullshit."

"Trans women face high rates of violence," you say.

I tell you no one has threatened you, here or anywhere else, and I'm not in the mood. You tell me you're sad. I tell you I'm sad too. And everyone considers your sadness an important civil rights issue, but no one gives a shit about mine.

You start to cry. Because every night must end with your crying. Instead of consoling you, I allow myself the indulgence of letting it go. I invite sleep to take me before I can feel guilty.

But now you're saying more things: a blur of things I lose track of. Complaints and admonitions. How hard life is for you. How much I've fallen short. Then you tell me, again, that I'm not trying hard enough.

And now, against my better judgment, I'm saying things too. Inadvisable things.

You jump out of bed, wave your arms wildly. "Maybe I should leave for a while." You cast about the room for your duffel bag and ceremoniously throw a couple things inside.

"Maybe you should."

The thought brings me tremendous relief. Since my aborted camping trip, I've craved time alone.

You gasp, drop your bag, stall for time.

"I'll leave in the morning," you say at last, climbing back into bed.

Most Halloweens, we watch scary movies together. You choose the same ones every year: *The Fly, Alien, Invasion of the Body Snatchers.* You're fascinated—and horrified—by the idea of an outside force controlling someone's body for its own ends. It resonates, you say, in a way you can't explain.

This Halloween, I'm home alone. You took a few days to make good on your bluff; you dawdled around the house, pretending not to find things.

I've enjoyed the downtime. This morning I lingered over a cup of Earl Grey, reclining in a blush-colored ray of sun. I went to the winter farmer's market and bought late-harvest corn and a pumpkin for fisherman's stew. I filled a basket by the door with candy bars and dusted off a wreath I made years ago, its blood-purple roses cradling a skeleton crow. Since you left, I've slept well and woken rested.

You haven't fared as well.

"I don't think I can do this," you texted on Thursday. "Can we talk?"

I asked you to give me some time.

"Can we meet for lunch?" you texted on Friday. I declined. "Will you give me a date?" I said I'd let you know.

When I met with Eunice, she wondered if I miss you. "I haven't had time to," I told her.

It's a slow night for trick-or-treaters, so I call Cameron to shoot the breeze. "Let's go to the haunted houses," he says. "I'll pick you up."

We're leaving Nightmare on Edgewood when my phone jingles. "I miss you," you text. I lower my volume. We've got a corn maze to navigate, and I'm not ready to talk. As Cameron pulls into Haunted Acres, I watch your texts pile up. "What's going on?" you ask. "Will you please respond?"

"I'm tied up," I type. "Talk later." I'm sick of trying to solve the puzzle of our future. Perhaps in a few days I'll have fresh ideas and renewed faith. But I am not there now.

"Get some sleep," Cameron says, when he drops me home at midnight. "You need it."

I'm dreaming of soaring across the night sky on a stick when I'm jolted awake by a startling noise. Adrenaline rushes through me like dread. Is someone in the house? I sit up in bed, considering my next move. Then I see a figure in the doorway, backlit by the night light in the hall.

"Shannon?" you call, plaintively. "Will you talk to me?"

Spent and drowning in the deluge of your needs, I scream.

"Leave me alone!" I beg you. "Please just leave me alone!"

You sob in horror, apologize, and flee.

"I was out of line," you text later. But only a day passes before you're asking, again, when we can meet.

Your brother has invited everyone to a family-style Italian restaurant for Nina's birthday tomorrow. It's a neutral setting. Beaten down, I relent.

We can talk afterward, I say.

SEVENTEEN | NOVEMBER
THE DEATH DRIVE

"I never wanted to be a woman," you practically spit. "I fought it kicking and screaming!" You lower your head into your hands, lean forward until your forehead touches the dash.

I engage the key and turn on the defrosters as our breath fogs the windows. I'd hoped we'd chat here for a moment, then part ways for the evening. Rosa and the girls file out of the restaurant clutching to-go bags. Jeremy floats around the parking lot, practicing tai chi. Jessica walks our way. This is no place for this conversation. I give the group a wave—we'll see them at Thanksgiving—then pull out of the parking lot and circle the mall.

"When I admitted I was a woman that day in Dr. Doris's office," you say, "I was *horrified*. I curled into the fetal position and sobbed over the *awful truth of it*."

I thought I understood, to a degree, what's going on with you.

But now I don't understand at all.

What is transition for, if it does not bring you closer to what you want and need and love? This thing you once described as "fun"—the thing you're tearing our home apart for—is it now some curse?

And you *"admitted"* you're a woman? *Admitted?* Why *admit* something that brings you pain, when its truth lies *solely in your confession of it?*

Your activist friends say you're a caterpillar transforming into a butterfly. Tonight, you seem like a moth drawn to a flame.

Who's navigating your life? Are you not at the helm?

It was good to break bread with your family. It was good to see *you,* actually. For a moment I forgot about all this. As I passed the baked ziti your way, our eyes met in simple acknowledgment. I felt a glimmer of optimism, more hope than anything. I was reassured by your family's warmth: your dad's firm hug, Rosa fussing with Mylar balloons, Lia resting her head on my shoulder. Then the singing: happy birthday to Nina, sitting on her hands at the head of the table, eager to tear into the double chocolate cake. I let my guard down. I stuffed my face. It was like old times.

I *missed* you. The *old* you. The one who laughed loudly and loved passionately and sometimes grabbed my hand or stroked my hair. I remembered chopping vegetables for dinner with you, playing the alphabet game on a long drive, sleeping face-to-face with our legs intertwined. Those days seem so long ago.

Now you tell me, between sobs, that you never wanted to be woman. That you uncovered this truth in therapy, though you wanted no part of it. "I feared for my future," you say, wiping your eyes with the back of your hand.

Womanhood isn't something that arises from the body, you've told me. Womanhood is a matter of self-identification. But tonight, it seems, neither is right. Tonight, "woman" is something set in stone by powers bigger than us both. A fate you can't escape.

Yellow bars of light break up the shadows as I wind behind the theater, here and there illuminating your scowl. I survey the facts on the ground. The ever more *inscrutable* facts.

You don't *look* like a woman.

You don't *behave* like a woman—whatever that means. You aren't, after all, the natural homemaker. You don't like children. You aren't demure or deferential—you've bulldozed everything in your path.

Transition doesn't help your love life. You say I float your boat; you say I'm your one and only. But I'm not into shaved legs or a practiced falsetto. I was won over by *you*, not this alter ego. You pursue womanhood not for sex, but *in spite* of it. You do it not for love, but *at our love's peril.*

You weren't bullied as a child. No one's ever called you gay or questioned your manhood. So this isn't some path of least resistance. There's lots of resistance: the funny looks. The confusing interactions. The misgendering.

Nobody's asking you to be a woman.

And now, the mystery deepens. Even *you* do not want you to be a woman. Who is it up to, then? If it's so awful, why not disavow it? Is identity so immutable? Don't people like you live as men, and more often than not? You did, until very recently. Surely the option remains open.

I follow the road to the industrial park, where beige garage doors conceal unknown wares. You lean your head against the window. Your brow ridge flickers with the reflections of pylon signage, a procession of 3D blocks and trend lines in blues and greens. You seem enfevered, like the pet store snake—staying your course, even as you suffer. Is your gender an expression of your true self, or a set of fangs now so embedded you can't back out?

What happened that day in your therapist's office? Did Dr. Doris pressure you to confess? To what end? You were given no brain scan, no MRI, no chromosome test—those are at odds with affirmative care.

247

Where, then, was the evidence for this womanhood? Was it your sensitivity, your love of poetry, your interest in lace? What sorcery confirmed your diagnosis?

"When can I come home?" you ask.

"How about Sunday?" I offer. But not because I feel ready.

"That's perfect," you say, relief settling in your eyes.

Then the worried look returns.

"I should tell you—I don't want to live."

This is bad news.

It's also familiar news.

When I was a sophomore I broke up with a man I'd dated for a week and never kissed. In response, he swallowed a bottle of pain killers. My mom found him unconscious in our garage. Instead of calling an ambulance, she asked me to check on him. To make sure he'd revive. To comfort him. This was my fault, I was to understand.

He survived. He stalked me for years, following me home from school, knocking on my bedroom window. My fear of someday finding his death on my hands left me ill-equipped to fight. To be raised female is to know you hold a lethal power over men. To be held responsible for their pain and the relief of it. To shoulder their crimes—you inspired them, after all.

A few years later I broke up with another man. He left a blood-smeared letter at my door, professing his love and his intent to die. The familiar guilt resurfaced. Then *he* stalked me. Anyone showing an interest in me was invited to a fist fight.

There were others. And it wasn't just manipulation. It was real. I'm sure it's real for you, too. There's an outcome I failed to consider while camping. Another dreadful outcome for an already bleak list.

You lower your head; you start to sob. This is different, of course. You are no mere teenage fling. You're the person I vowed to spend my life with. But I am as helpless to save you as I was to save the others.

And if this relationship is failing me—something I haven't decided, yet—then I can't let this news affect my plans. It took time and therapy, but I know, now, that I'm not responsible for the actions of others. I don't have to go down with you in your sinking ship. The thought feels empty and awful anyway.

"Dr. Doris asked me if I have a plan. I do."

Psychologists say if you have a "plan" for suicide, you're more likely to follow through. I don't ask you about your plan. I don't want to encourage that line of thought.

I vow to stay strong, but that won't save me. If you do this, I will feel guilt and I will grieve. I'm a casualty of your decisions, now. Because I am here and because I have loved you.

I arrive home in silence, dropping SQL Server manuals on the table. The database administrator resigned today. I'd be the best person to absorb her duties, my manager decided. Perhaps he's right. But it's outside my comfort zone and will take serious study.

"Hi," I say, looking your way as I head to the fridge. You're so often in a volatile mood, my optimism is well tempered.

You smile faintly. You, too, seem beaten down.

I bring my sparkling water to the den and sit across from you. "How was your day?" I ask, taking in your pink batwing blouse.

"It was OK," you say, glancing absent-mindedly toward the window. You've nothing terrible to report. Have you managed a day without plummeting? Will your despair manifest as a slow boil tonight, instead of an eruption?

"Do you want to order pizza and watch *Project Runway?*" you ask.

I do. I very much do. A casual dinner in front of the tube shimmers before me like an oasis in the desert. I pick up the phone and order your favorite: pepperoni and jalapenos. I'm not a fan of the combo, but topping choices are the least of my concerns. Getting through an evening with you would be amazing.

We throw together a salad and open a pinot noir. The warm smell of bread suffuses the foyer as the driver transfers our dinner. Perhaps this is how a good day can arrive in our lives: in the resigned exhaustion that can tolerate no more bad ones.

Sinking my teeth into a fire-grilled slice feels like a real indulgence. We put our feet up. We debate about the finalists. Mondo's work is more striking, you argue. But I think Gretchen's shows sophistication. We grow animated comparing his geometric prints to her flowing chiffons. For a moment we're beside ourselves. We actually laugh. A tight coil of stress in my chest unfurls. This dwelling together—this communion—if we could only go back to it. I think we could make it.

I pour myself another glass on the heels of the first. You lean against me. I miss sex. The tension and the release. The satiation and the exhaustion. I miss the intimacy, just you and me, touching, expressing our desire. I miss the spontaneity, back before it all became so fraught.

I close my eyes, sink into the cushions. I explore your skin with my fingertips, willfully ignore its prickliness. You cuddle up closer and caress my hand. I pour the last splash of wine and belt it back. When you can't get me there, alcohol can. And right now, while I'm frustrated, while I want so desperately to savor this moment, to savor this relationship—to *save* it—that's good enough. When you click off the TV and lead me to the bedroom, I'm where I need to be.

You do nothing creative; you just use your body as it's intended. But that's good enough. I only need for you to last long enough, and you do. When the tremors subside, I bury my head in your chest. I want nothing more than sleep and I hope you feel as satisfied as I do. But I glance up and find trouble brewing behind your eyes.

"Are you ever going to have sex with me again when you're not drunk?"

It's the fucking audacity.

We both know why this is happening. I can no longer see you, the you that gets me going, in this persona you've created. I need a little help, now. I've asked for it. You've failed to give it. Call it what you want, Jamie, but you've lost interest in pleasing me.

And now the way I cope offends you? What choice do I have? To live out my days without sex? To lie down for you when I'm not in the mood?

"Possibly not," I say, shoving down the nastier responses that come to mind.

It's truer than I know.

I sat in the cafeteria, staring at my tray. I was bleeding on the seat. The knowledge was a shadow in my periphery I hoped would go away if I didn't look right at it. There was nothing I could I do. I was going to have to get up and walk away, in front of hundreds of people, leaving blood on the seat.

I didn't look back. When I got to the restroom, I found two smears of soppy blood on my butt cheeks, each the size of my hand. I don't remember how I got out of there. I had no jacket to tie around my waist; it was summer.

I tried not to think about the other students who had been sitting next to me. What they thought when they saw the pool of blood, what they said. Whether they laughed nervously or were grossed out. I don't know whether they looked at me funny for the remaining two weeks of art camp. I don't know who they were, or what they looked like, because I blocked it out.

At fifteen, I was too old to be starting my period for the first time. And I was deeply homesick. The campus was far from home and I'd never been away from my family for more than a day.

The incident wasn't the last. I dripped on the floor while coeds played cards on my roommate's bed. I bled through in painting class. I doubled up on tampons and pads, per the pamphlet from fifth grade. But before the end of every hour I bled through the products, my underwear and my pants. It was a proper hemorrhage, I'd learn, one requiring medical intervention. At the time, I only knew letting other people see your menstrual blood was *not* OK. I had failed fundamentally as a human. At my age. In front of everyone.

Back home, my mom took me to the gynecologist. Gripped by anxiety, I allowed her in the exam room. The doctor emerged from between my legs with both hands drenched in blood, like a scene from a slasher flick. My mom, usually a master of stoicism, could not hide her shock.

The bloodletting continued another twenty-nine days. I got more exams, each as messy and traumatic as the last. No boy had so much as pawed me at a drive-in theater, and now men were spreading my legs and inspecting me every few days. I was stripped of dignity and completely demoralized.

Tests followed. Hypermenorrhea. Low hemoglobin. Blood transfusion imminent. "Any chance you're pregnant?" I was asked for the first of a dozen times. "I'm a virgin," I answered. The nurse looked at me askance, sent my mom out of the room, and asked again.

I was scheduled for surgery. My cervix would be dilated and my uterine lining scraped "with a spoon-shaped curette." A nurse met me outside the hospital with a wheelchair. Adults filled out paperwork while I stared at my intractable body. I could bleed to death, one mumbled. Death would bring relief, I thought, for the first time in my life.

The staff placed me in a pediatric ward, per their policy for patients under sixteen. I shared common spaces with kids—lobbies, playrooms, a sun deck—as I waited for my procedure. A young boy divulged his leukemia diagnosis while his mom spoke hopefully of new treatments. I was too mortified to confess my own condition, and after all they'd shared with me, my silence seemed an affront. But I could hardly speak freely. The boy wouldn't understand and the mother wouldn't approve. It happened again with another kid and another mom. The children around me walked close to the specter of death, but only my period was shrouded in taboo.

At my mom's insistence, the staff moved me to a gynecology ward, where I shared a room with three other women. As they spoke of their sex lives, their pregnancies and their miscarriages, I exhaled. I found camaraderie, at last, for a condition that no longer felt so freakish. One of my roommates shared that she'd gotten a heavy period on a plane, having to climb over her seat mate repeatedly to visit the lavatory. When he assumed she'd gotten "stomach issues" from Caribbean fare, she let the misconception stand. It was easier to admit to diseased bowels than to a functioning uterus. So I was starting to learn. It's easier to admit to *anything else* in mixed company. Lost gym gear, headache, *cancer.*

On my doctor's advice, I've taken hormonal birth control ever since. Thirty-something years. I punch a little pink pill from its blister pack, convinced it's causing the migraines that plague me every month at this time. If I stay on the pill I'm at risk for stroke. If I stop taking it I could bleed to death.

"You don't think of me as a woman, do you?" You're sitting on the edge of the loveseat in the den, as if about to rise. Earlier I referred to you as "he" while talking to my mom on the phone. You heard.

You're dressed to the nines in high-heel boots and a slinky wrap dress. You've put on a full face of makeup and have fixed and sprayed your hair. I'm not sure why; I wasn't aware you had plans tonight. You come toward me now, taking on the s-shaped posture of a tall person who struggles to walk in heels.

No good can come of this discussion. But I will not be allowed to opt out of it. I own up to the mistake.

"I'm sorry. I have respected your pronouns since we talked about it this spring and I will continue to do so."

"But you don't think of me as a woman."

You're right. But I can't help what I think. And I don't think rewiring my brain is a reasonable goal for you. I think respecting each other, in all our difference, should be our goal. I don't say this; honesty too often rankles you now. But I'm not giving up on honesty. If I can't speak with you frankly, but compassionately, then we no longer have a relationship to save. I don't want to grow used to the way lies feel in my mouth.

Still, I can't help but employ every technique at my disposal to protect your feelings. Avoiding unproductive discussions. Stretching the truth to its breaking point. Meeting your questions with questions.

"What *is* a woman, anyway?"

"*I* am a woman." You motion toward your body with both hands. "*This* is what a woman looks like."

"But what makes that true? I'm genuinely curious, I promise."

You're thinking.

"Is it your clothing?" I ask, when it seems no answer is forthcoming.

"Of course not! I'm still a woman no matter what I'm wearing. Clothing is just an expression of my womanhood."

"OK," I say. "And you've said you don't believe women have different brains..."

"It's not about sexed brains!"

"If it's not in your body, and it's not in your brain, where is it?"

Instead of answering, you say: "Trans women are a subset of women."

But a subset has *all* the traits of its parent set. What traits describe females, plus you? At best, people like you and people like me belong to a superset—"women-in-effect," or something. But set theory is probably the wrong framework for this discussion.

Still.

"What do you have in common with Sam?" I ask. Our Realtor works as a contractor and wears men's clothing. I can't think of any trait the two of you share.

You start to pace.

"I have a female *gender identity*," you say, after a moment. "Same as you."

"Wait—no. I don't have a gender identity."

"Sure you do." You seem offended, as though I deny it to prove some sort of point.

But I'm sure I don't.

"You dress like a woman!" you say, waving your arm widely.

"I buy what's on the rack. My clothes aren't some extension of my psyche."

"Then you don't identify with *femininity*," you say. "But you feel like a woman, inside."

I know you want that to be true. But I don't know this feeling.

In fact, I'm alienated by what's supposed to interest women. The "biological clock" that hastens their plans to have children. The desire for jewelry. The talk of putting husbands "in the doghouse." And I'm taken aback when I realize I'm being *treated* like a woman. Like when I returned to college, sure I wanted that computer science degree, and the guidance counselor smiled condescendingly and warned me there was math involved. Or when the window installers wouldn't talk to me because they thought "the man of the house" should make the decisions. It's *other people* who notice I'm a woman, not me.

You scoff when I tell you this. "You don't have an internal sense, in your brain, that you're a woman?"

"I don't." I see a female body when I look down, but there's nothing more to it for me.

"What if someone thought you were a man? Wouldn't that bother you?"

"No. I imagine men are less often second-guessed by guidance counselors and contractors."

You eye me skeptically.

"I know I'm a woman," you say, with an air of finality. "It's an *article of faith.*"

That's quite the invocation, coming from you—the atheist, the strict materialist, the debate-team whiz. Once, a friend visiting Melanie defended her "faith" in your presence. You interrogated her until she left in tears.

"Anyone who identifies as a woman is a woman," you remind me.

But aren't you, indeed, some substance or other, with or without your saying so?

"It's a question of semantics," I say. "If you're a woman, it's by definition." Even *your* definition keeps evolving.

"It's *not* semantics," you say. "It's in my brain's mapping of my body. When I look in the mirror, I expect to see a woman."

"But a woman is not someone with an anomalous brain mapping." I say. "Except by an expansion of the definition."

I know this doesn't sit well with you. And I don't want to ruin your night. But I don't want to humor you, either. There is no respect in that.

"I will not hear this," you say, peering at me through narrowed eyes. You walk toward the foyer and fiddle with the coats and scarves hanging there. "I will not tolerate this cruelty! I will not let you insult me!"

"Jamie. Come on. 'Man' and 'woman' are descriptors, not insults."

I can't question your womanhood, you tell me. It's something I'm simply not allowed to do. It's a "denial of your humanity." Your eyes glaze over as you speak, as if you're parroting words you've heard elsewhere. What I've said, you tell me, is a kind of *blasphemy.*

This would go more smoothly if I lied to you. But lies are for bosses and guests who stay too late. I don't lie to the people I love.

"Look," I say. "I'm not going to contradict you in public. I'm going to refer to you as a woman. I'm going to use your pronouns."

I take a deep breath.

"But I'm not going to tell you, here in our home, in private, that I see you as a woman. Isn't it enough that I accept you and respect your wishes?"

You rifle through the coat rack with purpose, breathing through clenched teeth.

"Why is it important to call yourself a woman, anyway?"

"Jamie will not kill herself for you!" you hiss.

The confusion on my face must be palpable; you step away from the coats to explain. "James, the man, was suicidal. Jamie, the woman, wants to live."

But is that true?

For a decade and a half, James seemed happy. Down in the dumps once in a while, like all of us, but largely content. James was a musician and backpacker and gardener. James never cried himself to sleep. Only Jamie seems to be in crisis. Jamie's the one who brought up suicide. And as recently as last week, she had a *plan*.

"I have known I'm trans my whole life," you add.

I wonder if you recall saying and writing otherwise earlier this year. Explicitly. Enthusiastically. Under no apparent duress. Am I to understand that that was fake, and this is real? Am I to understand that the you of the past fifteen years was unhappy, but pretended not to be? And that the you of now is happy, though she wants to die? Am I to understand that making the you of then into the you of now was a good thing? Even though *you*, yourself, "never wanted to be a woman?"

I watch as you remove a coat from the rack, tears filling your eyes. And I see something in you I've been trying not to see.

I see that you're *courting* tragedy. That you're *interested* in it. I see— though I don't understand—that happiness is not everyone's goal. I see it isn't yours.

I've been believing, naively, in Freud's "pleasure principle"—the idea that everyone acts in ways that create pleasure. Such ensures survival. It drives people to pursue life-affirming activities like creating art and making love.

But even Freud saw the limits of that. People sometimes behave destructively, his critics charged, and he couldn't disagree. So he devised the "death drive." It pulls people *away* from joy and vitality. It "denatures" them.

Denature. I remember when I first saw that word as a kid, on a plastic bottle at the pharmacy. *To strip away its nature,* I thought, knowing neither what the product lost nor what remained. It was such a sad word. What are you without your nature? How powerless that must make you. How impotent.

The death drive explains compulsion, and addiction, and masochism, Freud said. I can see, in retrospect, that you've been in its grip for months.

You fancy yourself an ouroboros: god of your own world, epicene, self-made. But you are more like the captive snake, succumbing to the heat and the pressure of the cage you've wandered into. Gender norms. Social media. The fetishization of choice. The crisis of modernity.

Your pursuit of womanhood turns you inward, away from women. Your introspection becomes self-absorption. You are killing James, from excising his flesh to snuffing out his appetites: for adventure, for sex, for living. And now, you're apparently unable to go anywhere but forward, even though it hurts.

You say it's self-renewal. It looks like self-harm.

I'm starting to question my role in this. Have I propped up a charade that's brought you to this death wish? You have the right to self-destruct, but I don't want to be an enabler. My love for you is stronger than my need for your approval. My love for you is stronger than my need for your love.

"I love you," I say.

"Maybe I shouldn't have burned it all down," you respond, slipping into your coat.

I open my mouth, but words won't come. Because I don't know where to begin. What the fuck have you burned down? And no, it probably isn't prudent to burn things down. And why is whatever you've done so irreversible?

"I will not quit activism," you say, placing a hand on the doorknob. "I will be taking that job."

I follow you, try to touch you.

"I am literally a woman" you say, mechanically. "And *not* someone who identifies as one." A cold blast of air fills the foyer as you slip through the door.

MUST HAVE BEEN LOVE

You're crying again.

You're afraid I'm going to leave you. You know I'm sexually frustrated. You know I want answers about your transition plans, and you know you haven't given them to me. You're afraid I'm no longer in love with you.

Something about this list sounds familiar.

A little *too* familiar.

It's the same set of worries I brought up yesterday on a message board for women's issues. I don't know how you would have found my post.

But I've had partners who snoop. I know what that feels like. I know what it *smells* like. And I'm sure it's no coincidence the worries you bring up today are the ones I voiced yesterday.

You end up admitting it before I can call you on it.

"I noticed you typing intently yesterday. I walked behind your chair and looked over your shoulder. I took note of the website and your screen name. I found and read your post."

I have every right to feel angry.

But somehow, I don't.

Not because what you did was OK. It was an asshole move. It was a complete and utter invasion of my privacy.

Not because I don't care how you feel. I *still* don't want to hurt you.

And not because I've given up on you. I *still* want to make this work.

I don't know why I'm not angry, at first. Then it comes to me.

I'm *relieved.*

I'm relieved that my true feelings, the ones I suppress at every turn to protect you, have found their way, through no fault of my own, from my head to yours. I'm relieved that I no longer need to walk on eggshells because all the eggshells are broken. I'm relieved to be standing here, bathed in the brilliant light of honesty with you, unable to hide. To be, for the first time in over a year, *living authentically.*

I can't tiptoe around the truth. I can't pretend I didn't write what I wrote. We'll just have to *face* it.

I feel resigned but hopeful, like it's one of those projects at work that's important but in danger of getting canceled. I'll give it my best effort without investing my full hope.

You want to know if I meant this and if I meant that. You want to know what this means for our future. You want to know if I still love you. You bring up each point in turn and I try to respond with what I think will make it better.

But it turns out making it better isn't what you want to do. What you want, more than anything, is to *feel* better. You want to talk around and around each point until it doesn't hurt anymore.

I've always thought of the truth as a bright light that, once revealed, no one could ignore. I've been afraid to bring you from your seclusion into its fullness. As though, in your fragile state, the exposure would blind you. But my fear was misplaced. You conceal a secret weapon I hadn't counted on.

All you had to do was close your eyes.

"I don't know what you want from me," I hear you say into your phone, as I toss my shopping bags into the back and climb into the driver's side seat. "I have problems of my own. My marriage is on the rocks."

It's your brother. We're planning a small holiday gathering to show our new home to old friends, so we stopped by the mall for a cheese board and a festive table runner. When I sensed the gravity of Jake's call, I left the engine running and went inside alone to give the two of you some privacy.

"That's not *true*," you say now, moving the heating vents around. You are defensive, maybe even incredulous, as you confront some apparently unfair accusation. "I'm still the same person."

I leave the car in park and move my seat back, settling in with my phone. I don't want to be driving when this call ends—I suspect you'll need my support. You remain silent for a stretch of time as Jake apparently has a lot to say.

"Dad could just as easily call *me*," you say at last. "Why is it my job to call him?"

You turn to look at me as you lower the volume on your phone and stash it in your purse. There's fear in your eyes, as though you're under some sort of attack, and I can tell you need for me to validate your version of whatever just happened.

"Jake says he doesn't recognize me anymore. He says the whole family agrees with him."

Thank goodness someone else has said it.

"I haven't changed just because I've changed my clothes," you add, scrambling to fill the seconds of silence that elapse as I search for words. It's a phrase you've been repeating since you joined your support group.

"Jamie, will you stop with that line? This is not about your clothes. No one has given you any shit about your clothes."

"I am the same person!" you protest.

"You kind of aren't." You grow sullen as I list the activities you've lost interest in: camping, singing, gardening, web design. In fact, you're aware of this. "Sometimes I don't recognize myself," you blogged, not so long ago.

We had a better way of life, Jamie, before your Great Forgetting.

You pull out your phone and type rapidly with two thumbs as I drive us home.

It's evening when I stumble across what you've written: a lengthy Facebook post. You're not accepted for who you are, you lament. People "can't see past your clothes."

Activist friends come to your rescue. "You don't need them," one asserts. "They are not your real friends," warns a second. You are beautiful, assures a chorus of voices, and "valid"—and "sometimes you have to cut toxic people out of your life."

No doubt that's true. But your brother isn't one of those people. Nor is your dad, who'd go to the ends of the earth for you. Nor is anyone whose only crime is noticing that you've changed. You've known these online friends for less than six months, and some you've never met in person. It's irresponsible for them to coach you to abandon your oldest and closest relationships. But in the comments you promise to cut ties with anyone "problematic." The reduction in your friends list shows you kept your word.

"You are truly blessed with friends," I tell you, "if you can afford to drop so many of them with so little thought."

I have never had such fortune.

A couple days before Christmas I realize I don't have a single present for you.

I look in my wallet and allot the amount of cash I see to the task. Leaving you slumping over your laptop, I point my car toward the Victoria's Secret at Clay Terrace, a small shopping center north of town. I find the fragrance you want, add a handful of body sprays from the impulse bins near the register and get it all gift-wrapped. Within ten minutes I'm done and under budget. So I wander next door to a shop that sells hippie dresses with a Western flair. I sweep through the clearance area and leave with three prairie blouses and some jewelry.

It's unlike me. In years past I planned your gifts months in advance, picking up trinkets while running errands, scouring the Internet for hard-to-find items, hiding in my office to paint the pieces of a handmade board game. I labored under a feminine notion: that it was my job to make Christmas special. Now I toss my acquisitions into gift bags and deposit them under the tree, thinking about the men I know. They brag about the sort of shopping I'm feeling ashamed of. To them, gift-giving is a monetary responsibility. Shopping quickly isn't thoughtless—it's "efficient."

In a few days, none of this will matter. But no one wants a shitty Christmas. So I plan to wait until it's over to bring up divorce. I'll spend the holiday as I always do on odd-numbered years, hanging out with your family. I'll eat glazed ham and pumpkin pie. I'll collapse on a recliner in front of *Elf* with whoever's become too sleepy to eat. I'll crawl on the floor, building Tinkertoy empires with the girls. I might as well enjoy the last Christmas I'll spend with your family. After all, they are important to me. The loss of all I hold dear can wait until the twenty-sixth.

We wake up early as always for Usmas and start the hot chocolate. You hand me the small stash of gifts you've acquired on your limited funds: bracelets, an adult coloring book with pencils, a set of Guatemalan worry dolls meant to take on the concerns of their owner. You've done all your shopping for me at one store, but it's one of my favorite stores, and I don't blame you the way I blame myself. We're tired and we can't hide it, but you perk up when you see your new blouses and you choose one to wear for the day.

The day proceeds normally, if in a blur. We drive to your dad's house in silence. Once there, I steer clear of you, visiting with your sisters, finding a quiet corner to poke at my phone. A dark foreboding keeps me from fully appreciating my last hours with these people I love. You seem sad, too. In the evening I call my mom and wish her a merry Christmas. Then I log onto Regenderate, thank them for their help and tell them I no longer need their services.

As we climb into bed, I tell the worry dolls, telepathically, that I don't want a divorce. I tell them I can't continue on this path and I'm out of ideas. I put my faith in them. I invite them to reveal solutions. Maybe they belong to the realm of the sacred; maybe they can save us. As I place them under my pillow I look at you and see that you have seen.

The day after Christmas I tell you I can no longer live this way, as a mere spectator of my own life story.

You dispense with the conversation like you've been expecting it, more irritated than sad. You don't want a divorce, you say, but you won't try to make me stay. "I want Carrot," you add, though I could have guessed. It was you who rescued her when she was barely weaned, far from home in a meadow near your dad's.

I tell you I'm open to any and all compromises. You tell me you can never compromise.

As you pull your duffel bag from the closet, I ask you to consider what you're taking from me. I married you with the expectation that we were forever. That I was investing in a family that would always be there for me. You are lucky. You are one of five and you'll always be supported. My social network is frighteningly small, I remind you. My father has passed away, my brother is estranged and my mother lives far away. And now my favorite cousin has developed a rare heart condition.

"I need a better reason to stay," you say, coldly, "than that you will be lonely."

Fair enough. What about us? The life we've shared, the feelings you once had for me, the promises you've made. Why is it easy to leave that all behind?

"You said this would never come between us."

"I was wrong," you say, folding a wrap dress and tossing it into your bag.

Must have been love, I think, *but it's over now.*

"I know you'll go back to women," you say, your eyes growing damp. "And that will kill me."

But it's not my choice to move on, Jamie. It is you who has abandoned our marriage. I signed up to be your *partner*—not your bankroll, your therapist, your sex prop. And do you speak of "women," now, as though they are a group you don't belong to? Isn't that the crime you can't forgive me for?

You zip up your bag and text someone. It's not what I want you to do.

What I want you to do is to fall at my feet, and cry, and beg me to stay, and tell me you'll do anything, everything, *something* to save us, you'll think again, you'll get creative, you'll find a way. I want you to love me that much. Because this isn't right. There's no way this love, *the one that's meant to be,* comes to an end. There's no way this is anything but a mistake.

I want you to fight for me, to exhaust *all* your options.

I want you to *choose love.*

I was in it forever. It's who I am. And it's who you seemed to be, not so long ago, the night we played around on Pinterest, the night you told me nothing would ever come between us, "least of all this."

I gave you all of me. There wasn't some thing that could have pulled me away. Not some latent thing, some unspoken thing, some unpredictable thing. Not even this thing, this important thing.

And maybe you didn't know about the thing that would come up. I don't think you did. You say now that it was always there. But I watched you get it. Your own blog is a testament to the days, not so long ago, when you were blissfully free of its grip.

No, you didn't have it eighteen months ago. I remember.

On the first day of my life without you, my face floods with heat and my palms begin to sweat. I'm driving away from an early appointment with Eunice, who for a moment infected me with her optimism, helping me build a plan of action as only someone like Eunice can do.

I'd volunteer at the feral cat shelter. I'd call two friends a week and arrange lunch. I'd save for a vacation. For an hour, cocooned in her office, I was protected and safe. I didn't know what it was like out here.

Now, as I embark upon a ten-minute drive toward a shelter that isn't open until noon, I panic.

Going home is out of the question; there's no one there. When I get to the shelter I'll make myself useful. I'll have people to talk to. But two hours and fifty minutes stretch between me and the safety of that moment. An intolerable expanse of time.

I drive anyway. I drive headlong into a morning that seems to shimmer and fracture into pieces before my eyes. Behind me are fifteen crumbling years. In front of me is a dark unknown.

And who am I? I am no more real than the morning. Without continuity, the thread that makes me who I am frays and snaps. I am a disembodied collection of thoughts, spinning in a capsule, hurtling into outer space. I could be anyone. Or no one.

I poured too much of myself into you. I lost too much. Even my life before you feels suspicious. My relatives are old and I have no heirs. I counted on you to take my memories, to be their witness, to give them a home. You were family. You were an extension of me. My past seems like an illusion now, the mad fancy of someone who no longer exists.

The Death card rarely symbolizes an actual death, the tarot reader said. Instead, it represents the loss of something big. A home, a job, a marriage, a family. Not one of these things, it turns out. *All* of these things.

"One day at a time," goes an Alcoholics Anonymous slogan—I know that from my mother's recovery. But in front of me is one minute I can't handle, beyond that another. I cast about for hope, finding instead a perverse idea: maybe a runaway eighteen-wheeler will spare me the burden of living without you. But I'm driving thirty miles per hour on a city street.

Hands that apparently belong to me dampen the steering wheel and go numb. I watch myself pull the car over; I hear myself scream. But that was a half-baked plan. I'm driving again. I consider the role of low blood sugar on my current state, and throw my anchor toward Fresh Market.

I don't remember grabbing the orange juice or the string cheese. I don't remember navigating to the register. A man materializes in line behind me. He says he used to work with me. He asks me how I've been. It would seem that I am real, and recognizable, after all. I utter some words, suppressing the tears that gather in my eyes. I do not ask him to hold me, though there is no one to hold me, no one for a thousand miles.

I rush to my car and call you. You do not answer.

You could have kept loving me. I just know it.

I can't believe what life threw at you was more urgent than love.

I can't believe that love, as I know it—that respect and admiration for the good in another, that burning desire to dwell within it—should fail over ruminations on sex and gender and whether one's personality matches the contents of one's pants.

You could have worn a dress, painted your face, cried at a movie, baked a cake, bombed at baseball, and spread your legs for sex without failing to love me.

AND BEYOND

"How many men, women and transgender people have you had sex with in the past twelve months?"

Tamika's monotone suggests she asks this question all the time. Near a frosty window behind her desk, plastic wall pockets hold glossy brochures; a poster proclaims "HIV Testing Saves Lives." The young woman shuffles a stack of documents between well-manicured purple nails and lets it come to rest on the desk between us.

"One woman and one transgender person," I report. I feel conspicuous, suddenly, with my beveled fringe and the cable-knit cardigan I chose for work this morning. Surely a client who looks like me more often cites a husband whose dalliance in Vegas brought her here. But Tamika's dark eyes remain unfazed as she marks the paperwork. Was that sex unprotected?

"Yes."

I'd been chatting up a woman named Eli on a dating app. Her profile photos were less than flattering, but she was career-oriented and a good conversationalist, so with tempered expectations I accepted her offer for a drink. My stomach dropped when she walked into the bar with a motorcycle jacket layered over a white t-shirt, hair styled in a pompadour. She took a seat across from me, all cheekbones and a wide, jaded smile, and hit me with what could only be described as a leer. It was irresistible to feel wanted. *It had been so long.* I could hardly believe my luck when I found myself in her bed, uncovered her sculpted body and felt its weight against my skin. She was gifted in the ways of pleasing a woman and wasted no time proving it.

Afterward, she ghosted me. I couldn't even get her to return the earrings I'd left on her nightstand. Still, I wouldn't trade my night with Eli for anything. She made me feel alive.

"Fill out the demographic information," Tamika says, pushing a form toward me. "I'll call your name when your results are in." She hands over a selection of brochures curated just for me.

I take a seat in a waiting room among young gay men who are busy averting their eyes. A dark-skinned teen wearing pink denim and a fade stares at a daytime soap. A wisp of a boy in painted-on jeans crosses and uncrosses his legs. A chubby youth slumps behind a mane of tousled hair, gripping his clipboard as if nothing else matters.

Almost a third of trans women are HIV positive, I recently learned. I don't want to believe you're at risk, but you've hardly engendered my trust.

When I stopped by a coffee shop on my way to work last week, I caught a glimpse of that photo I took of you and Darcy—on the front page of a local newspaper. It accompanied a story about you, and how you don't "feel safe" as a trans woman in our town. The paper plans its articles months in advance, I know from a stint at freelancing. So around the time you promised to take a break from activism, you gave that interview. You pestered me for a photo *I* took—and gave the paper permission to publish it. And you passed off Darcy as the "supportive life partner" mentioned throughout the article. Soon after, *you* snooped on *me*—as though *I* were the one sneaking around.

You also entered my house while I was away. And somehow, sections of our chat history have gone missing from my phone.

Then there's the elephant in the room.

You've cheated before.

On Melanie, with *me*. And with Blaze, for that matter. And with others, I'm ashamed to realize; I've dismissed each story as youthful indiscretion. Why should I assume you've changed? You kept our affair from Melanie by being careful and lying well. You're still capable of being careful. You're still capable of lying well. "If you marry a man who cheats on his wife," Ann Landers once wrote, "you'll be married to a man who cheats on his wife." I open a brochure to the face of an HIV-positive woman, and with a warm flood of shame, grasp just how foolish I've been.

When I'm finished with the paperwork I pull out my phone and browse Facebook, where I see your latest post. You've returned to the Miami airport incident. "I was detained," you write this time. "Because of a genital anomaly."

You've already twisted the TSA experience into harassment. Now, you embellish it further. We were not delayed—the manual scan took only a second. The officers said nothing about an "anomaly," nor did they mention your genitals. You were makeup-free that day, and dressed in a way that my coworkers, who'd seen you earlier, found completely unremarkable. Yet you imply the guards were *confused* by your body. That despite screening thousands of people from all over the world, they lacked the experience—or even the *imagination*—to recognize gender-nonconformity.

But there's something else about your post that's odd. Something about your choice of words.

It's *familiar*.

I Google "genital anomaly." I find a story on Shadi Petosky, a television producer who's filed a complaint against the TSA. You've

273

repeated the story as your own, using much of the same verbiage. *Why?* To advance your political agenda? For sympathy? For *attention?*

Tamika calls my name.

"Your test was negative. While that may sound confusing," she says—even though it doesn't—"it's the result you want. No HIV antibodies were detected in your blood." Her eyes brighten as she slips into the role of sex educator. "Tell me—what can you do to lower your risk?"

How about commit to a long-term, monogamous relationship, I think. *How about limiting partners to one you trust?* Nothing else comes to mind, so I keep my mouth shut.

"Practice safer sex!"

"Right."

"This is a dental dam," she says, retrieving a square of latex from a drawer. I recall these from the nineties, touted in safer-sex ads and erotica aimed at queer women. But never in the wild. Never in the hands of a real lesbian. Dental dams floated in and out of clubs of their own volition, hitching rides with kinksters, passing between sex workers. They waited in baskets by doors in solidarity with the condoms that promised safety to a generation of shell-shocked gay men.

When I've been properly educated, I ease my driver's seat back, blast my defrosters, and wait for the windows to clear. I saw you shortly after my encounter with Eli. You seemed angry with me—possibly even *jealous.* I'd mentioned the rendezvous in an Internet discussion under an anonymous screen name. If you found that comment, you're investing a lot more time and effort than when you could walk behind my chair.

A few days before your birthday, you call. I know better than to pick up, but I want to see you. I want to hear about your day. I want my life back.

In lieu of that, I want to be friends.

Before things went south, I'd planned to take you and your family to Pizza King to celebrate. Your brothers call the local institution a childhood favorite, recalling fondly its chopped pepperoni and big screen cartoons. You want to keep our plans, you say—but just the two of us. You dread spending your birthday alone.

So do I. Maybe, I hint, you can return the favor in July.

The day arrives with subzero temperatures and a blistering wind that chaps my lips and stings my eyes. I bundle up in my warmest coat and convertible mittens with an extra-long scarf pulled across my face. The chill seeps through the gaps and dampens my sleeves when my fur-lined boots hit the street. Parking is scarce and I see you in the distance locking up your truck.

You teeter my way in a miniskirt and stilettos, teeth chattering. A woman we know from the Mel walks by. "Nice legs!" she says, with a thumbs-up. You grin and feign embarrassment, tugging at your jean jacket. As I open the door to the restaurant we're hit with a frigid burst of wind.

"It's fucking freezing," you say.

It is. And you've chosen attire no sane person would wear in conditions rife for frostbite. I say nothing, because nothing polite comes to me. I have only questions: what *is* this need that gnaws at you, anyway? This craving to be seen—is it so unrelenting, now demanding the literal sacrifice of your flesh?

When we've settled in and ordered, I realize how much I miss you. Tears gather in my eyes, but you scowl and look away. Unsure what to say, we sit in silence until the arrival of the pizza provides a welcome distraction.

You're staying with your dad, you tell me, dishing hot slices onto our plates. But you're about to move in with some friends. I've seen them on your timeline: underemployed twenty-somethings with Disney-princess names. You've applied for a lobbyist job that should cover rent. You learned about it from your friend Caleb—whom, you say, as you twirl up strings of melted cheese with your fork, was "assigned female at birth" but takes testosterone and lives as a man.

"Caleb is my boyfriend," you add with a giggle. "He just doesn't know it yet."

I am a fool, I know.

But I am still in love with you.

And I am not prepared for your casual willingness to move on, nor for your insensitivity about it. Not today, on your birthday, after *you* wanted to see *me*. We spent a third of our lives together. I have not, in the mere weeks since we signed the divorce papers, put those years behind me.

I am, in fact, crushed.

I choke down a mouthful and excuse myself. I mean to wipe my eyes and pull myself together. Instead, I close the bathroom door behind me, fall against it, and feel the muscles in my body weaken and give way until I'm crumpled on the floor. I'm racked by sobs, breathless and soggy. Time stands still, holding space for my grief.

"I'll get my stuff soon," you say, ignoring the length of my absence. I stare out the window, raking pizza around on my plate with a fork, watching snow flurries bang against the glass as the wind changes direction. When the check comes, I pick it up. Because you don't have any money. And it's your birthday.

It's early on Valentine's Day when you come to get your stuff. I awake from a stupor on the loveseat, my shirt yellowed with coarse smudges of vomit, to the sound of you flinging things into boxes. I can barely lift my pounding head, so helping you is not an option.

"Sheila left me," Brent told me last night. "To explore the BDSM scene." Naturally, he needed a drink. As we weighed the options, he confessed an "unholy urge"—to visit the strip bar a stone's throw from his house. Grateful for company, he funded lap dances for me and bottomless cups of watery beer for us both. When the last fatigued young woman had listlessly writhed before me, her holographic bikini top grazing my cheeks, we staggered to his house and crashed in separate rooms.

You take a break, pausing in the doorway. You'll send your forwarding address soon, you tell me. You're still trying to get that job. You're still trying to get that apartment. You can't take Carrot right now, either.

"I'll get her soon," you promise.

"You might as well take the sex toys," I say, as you come into focus. They're contaminated by your memory, if not your secretions. I hope you'll blow off my passive-aggressive suggestion. I hope the fate of that lot of silicone is the least of your worries. But you head for the bedroom, and I hear the little vintage suitcase scrape the shelf as you pull it down and pop it open, tossing dildos and the expensive leather harness into a bag.

"I intend to have a sex life," you say, when you pass back through and catch the sadness in my eyes.

"I will get over you," I choke out. "I will move on." I say it more to convince myself than to convince you. I don't see it on the horizon.

I watch through a sliver in the drapes as you wedge and stack boxes into your truck, muscles flexing when you pull a rope taut and tie it off with your favorite Boy Scout knot. I doze off as you drive away, and dream of you walking toward me cradling a newborn. She's your daughter, a product of the uterus transplant you wanted. She has your fair skin and she's dressed in a polka-dot jumper. "I can't keep her," you say, passing her to me. She's warm and heavy as I gather her into my arms.

Rousing in the late afternoon, I reach for my phone. You've posted a photo of your piled-high pickup on Facebook, complaining of your "shitty day." There's a text from you, too:

"I will forever love you. I'm glad you can move on, because I never

will. I will always be looking out the window of this train, waving to you on the platform, watching you recede into the distance. But no matter how far you recede, I will always have my eyes on you. I will always miss you."

It's a punch to the gut.

It also feels manipulative. I am the same person who has loved you and loves you still. It is you who has boarded the train.

"This is not your fault," you text me, days later. You want to work it out. I want to work it out, too. We go out for sushi and I pay the bill. We exchange long emails over what went wrong and whether it can be righted. I write you a love letter. I give you money. For months, it seems there's hope. Then, after another impasse, you text and say you're moving on. With this we settle into the sort of civil relationship one hopes for when all else is lost.

In the spring our divorce is assigned to a judge, and he needs to send you certified mail. "I'm between homes," you say, when I call to get your address. "My roommate threatened me with a sword." It's an absurd story, and one you want to expand upon—but I'm not surprised if living with insolvents half your age didn't work out. I'll use your dad's address, I say.

"You'll always be family," your dad assures me when I call. Jake is visiting, and he takes the phone. "Come to our Fourth of July party," he says. "Yes," Rosa chimes in. "Celebrate your birthday with us!" Their generosity renders my future a little more hopeful.

But in the summer you come at me like a wrecking ball.

"Your ex-husband is being a cunt." I'm at a craft brewery watching Joel play guitar when I see Cameron's text.

"It's on Facebook," confirms Leslie, a woman we connected with at the anniversary party. She's recently divorced and new in town, so we've become fast friends. She pulls up the diatribe you posted earlier today. Maria looks over my shoulder—she didn't know. She unfollowed you a while ago, she says, because you seemed "unstable." She didn't want to "poke the bear."

"It's time to tell the truth," you broadcast to our friends. "My ex abused me." It's important to speak out, you say, because trans women face "high rates of violence." You claim I spy on you and harass you, too.

I've watched, Jamie, as your lies grow copious and strange. I've seen you attack people, often unfairly. But until now, I've maintained my faith in your integrity. Behind each of your lies, I've assumed, is some reason I could understand. Maybe you're advancing your cause. Maybe you feel genuinely unsafe. Maybe you've just lost perspective. Your soul is surely intact.

But this is a new low.

We haven't interacted since the day I asked for your address. And *you're* the one who wanted to prolong that call. And before that, Valentine's Day. The day of your effusive text. I've even stopped reading your public Facebook posts; they prove how little you resemble the person I once knew.

You post photos of yourself with Allie, the teenager from your support group, your hair in pink braids and a cigarette dangling from your lips. You promise to flash your "new tits" to the next person who doubts you're a woman. They're plus-size, so you didn't grow them yourself—I guess you've changed your mind about prostheses and surgery. You post that you're "into straight men" but they're "too cowardly" to date you. If this is the life you wanted, what was in it for me?

In response to your accusation, one of your trans friends promises to hunt me down and "shut me up." Another says I "deserve to die." These are people we've socialized with. They want to hurt me, now. And they know where I live. And I live alone.

"I'll monitor the situation," Leslie promises, taking some screenshots.

I start to shake.

"Listen," Leslie says, wrapping an arm around my shoulder. "This wouldn't be the first time a woman faced the wrath of a vindictive ex." Hers publicly denounces her as a liar and a cheat—after *he* had the affair. Now he's out "unicorn poaching"—offering free rent to any woman who'll join him and his new girlfriend for threesomes.

I've been arrogant. I've been unfair to divorced women, like Leslie and my cousins. I thought I was so impervious to their fate. But they fell in love sincerely, as I did. They were confident in their selection, as I was. I thought I was different. They thought *they* were different.

And you—you think you're different, too. So what if you took your leave just as the years etched their lines around my eyes? So what if you took an interest in someone new? *You're* not like those antsy husbands who ditch middle-aged wives for new lovers and new lifestyles. You're not even a man, so you can't be a husband—and this can't be your midlife crisis. We all think we're above it, we're not a statistic, our reasons are different, our reasons are *special*.

What's inspired your rant? My lowest moment was hurling that cup and slamming that door. But you weren't scared, Jamie.

Then there was my struggle with your pronouns—your support group calls misgendering "violence." But my track record wasn't bad. I changed my language at your request. I just couldn't change my perceptions—and I think that's what you wanted. Remember your critique of Pascal's wager? It was spot on. You can extort a *profession* of belief, but not real belief. You must find grace with that.

You went through something, Jamie. But I went through something, too. What I went through, all those years, was a heterosexual relationship. Not a lesbian one. Indeed, I *gave up* women for you. I stopped going to the gay bars and Pride events I loved. I made space for your aftershave and jock itch powder. I married you, legally, at a time when I couldn't have married Isabel.

I carried the housework, as wives tend to do. I picked up your socks and your boxer shorts. I cleaned the toilet—something you confessed, eight years in, that you'd never done. Not even once.

I had sex with you. Sex in which you penetrated me, as men do to women. Sex that left semen in me and on me. I slept in the wet spot. I endured migraines and the birth control routine that caused them. When I missed a pill, I unrolled a condom onto your penis. When I missed a period, I took a pregnancy test. It was I who dealt with these women's issues, not you. Change your future, if you must, but you can't change my past.

You think you feel like a woman, whatever that means. But I don't feel like I married one. I respect your experience; you need to respect mine.

And now? I would never tell you, but you still don't read female to me. Of course you don't. Breasts and braids haven't fundamentally altered you. You look like the man I fell in love with—is that my fault? My brother's friends wore long hair, too, and bracelets and fringed vests. Fashion didn't morph them into women. It would have been shocking, at the time, to suggest that it could.

I was not so mean to you. As far as I can tell, I was your unicorn. I loved you before and after your revelation. I indulged your kinks and kept your secrets. But you wanted more. You wanted me to indulge your kinks while pretending they weren't kinks. You wanted me to keep your secrets even from myself.

You took my support for granted—that I've come to terms with. That you now recast it as abuse is truly craven.

"What Jamie did to you was evil," Jake says, when I appear at his door. I'd planned to make small talk, but he leans in for a hug, and his support comes as an unexpected and sweet relief. The floodgates open and I'm racked by gut-wrenching sobs, soaking his shoulder with my tears. I hold onto him like he's my best friend, like he's my mom, like he's my lover.

"I can't afford this blow to my social network," I tell him. We move to the dining room; he offers me a cup of tea. Rosa's working and the girls are playing in their room.

My friendships, which were always precarious, are crumbling in the aftermath of your tirade. Melanie's grown chilly. Darcy and Lyle and Theo have dropped me cold. Willow sent me a nasty text and Claire unfriended me. Paige supported me at first; you were drinking too much for her taste. Later, she flaked out too. My best friendships are new, and my family has shrunk even further—my favorite cousin, once a phone call away, has died in open heart surgery.

"I rely heavily on friends," I add.

Your friends, that is.

Because you knew them first. And when I tried to make other friends, like the couple at the hibachi, you undermined me. And I guess I was too trusting. I guess I thought Melanie and Darcy weren't blowing smoke up my ass when they said they'd stick around.

Now, I don't know who I'd call if I woke up in the hospital.

"You can call me," Jake says. "You'll always be family."

I want to believe him. But your family will never really be my family again, whatever their intentions.

"If friends dropped you that quickly," some people say, "they weren't really friends." But that isn't helpful. It means I can invest my heart, and years of my life, into friendships I never manage to make "real." The fact is, they *were* my friends. They were just *your* friends, too. Good liberals are *supposed* to "believe survivors." Lying about abuse is beyond the pale—surely you wouldn't. Surely I'm just the monster you say I am.

You've always been the popular one. Now you belong to the trendier minority. Your lie is compelling. Your pain is interesting. You've decided to bully me. You can.

I ask Jake to call you off. Not for the sake of justice. But for my *survival.*

You're too blessed to understand, Jamie, but I need a ride to the doctor sometimes. A cat sitter. Someone to decompress with after a rough day. I need the standard relationships that keep people functioning and safe and alive. Have you ever faced a nighttime intruder alone? Have you ever coughed up blood and realized there was no one you could call? *I* have.

But you know this.

I'm faced with an awful truth: *you're exploiting it.*

When we talked about divorce, I begged you not to leave me without support. That night, you said I looked lonely. You said it wistfully, as though savoring some poignant scene in the movie of your life. I always thought your interest in sadness was pitiable, if mysterious. Now I wonder if it's sadistic. Are you so broken that you need to ruin me to feel something?

To see you descend to this level of depravity, from the height of intimacy we once shared—it shakes my very faith in love.

Jake wants to help. But he says no one can get through to you. You broke your dad's heart by refusing to call. You had a falling out with Jeremy, who said "men cannot become women." You skip family gatherings now, and when you do come, you bring Caleb and a ceaseless transgender awareness campaign. Rosa stopped hosting when she caught you plying Nina and Lia with photos from one of your political rallies.

"By the way," Jake says, his shoulders dropping. "About your birthday." You've issued an ultimatum—if I'm coming, you're not. I'm disinvited, though he finds nicer words.

And so, as in the story you penned, Lilith is exiled. You thought you wanted a strong woman. You just wanted a strong woman in bed. You wanted a strong that was sexy, a strong that could be throttled with a safe word. I was a speaker of my truth. You wanted a propagandist of yours. I was a participant in our relationship. You wanted a spectator.

You were Adam. You wanted to be Eve. Now, you play God. You can't suffer me living on my own terms—you demand retribution. You drag me asunder to the scorched earth, wall me away from all that's good and sustaining. I should have known Paradise is not for women like me. Not for girls who come out as gay, spinsters who marry late, barren women. All I am, and will ever be, is the witch who does not belong in Eden.

In the autumn of Carrot's seventeenth year her breathing becomes labored and her pace begins to slow. You never took her, of course. She starts eating less and vomiting more. Poor little Carrot Cake. My Baby Carrotine.

"Bronchitis," a vet says, because her lungs look cloudy on an x-ray. But that doesn't explain the nausea. "Kidney disease," says a second. But that doesn't explain the wheezing. I bring her home and give her the antibiotics and the prescription diet.

It's good to have her with me. I spend too many nights holed up in a darkened room, giving into my sadness. I cry until my face hurts, until my eyes are bloodshot, until I can't get up. Then I get up, because Carrot needs me.

Living without you has imbued the objects around me with sadness. The ice cream maker you wanted. Your moth-ridden Yoda shirt. The photo of us at Myrtle Beach in a crab-adorned frame, now a plastic trinket hollowed of meaning. Cold hard objects of science. No longer things. No longer *thinging*. I get choked up over the inexplicable: a postcard of a cottage in falling snow, its windows brimming with yellow light. A stuffed bear in a duck costume propped at the register when I take Carrot in for another x-ray.

The vet holds up the film, tracing a tumor that crowds her tiny belly and the space once occupied by her left lung. I give her a last meal of salmon and bring her to bed with me, ensuring her final night at home feels safe and warm.

In her final two minutes on Earth, Carrot protests. I'm the one who holds her face in my hands as the vet injects the drug. I'm the one who watches her little legs buckle and sees her fall like a wounded deer. As you continue to air grievances about me on social media, I wrap up your business. Caretaking is women's work; so too are deathbed ministrations. If we are both women, why did they fall to me? But I'm grateful for the solemn privilege of attending Carrot's death. It leaves a hole in my heart, though, a heart that craves nothing more than to keep loving something or someone. My loss brings a revelation: I miss loving more than I miss being loved.

It's *giving* love that quiets the self-serving inner monologue. And I can love without waiting to be loved. I can love with my whole heart.

I start right away. I babysit the girls so Jake and Rosa can have a date night. I take Cameron out for his birthday. I host a monthly supper club for Leslie, Maria, and Chana. We gather in my kitchen for an intricate dance of julienning, sautéing, and plating that culminates in a splendid feast. We gather around that oversize kitchen table, laden with French or Moroccan or Cajun fare, and we talk. Really *talk*.

Some days I don't want to rebuild. I don't want to make new friends. I don't want to live in this cavernous house.

Some days, I don't want to live at all.

But I apply for grad school. I join some clubs. I fill my calendar with whatever presents itself. Like the dragon at River Bend, I lunge forward, vanquished but rising from the muck.

Some days I drink and dance and numb my pain with empty revelry. Beneath the surface of my life, a rip current surges. I skim across it in a flimsy vessel, a change of wind between my joyride and a capsize into the deep.

I am unmoored.

I lumber against a warm, battering wind, my hair whipping into my eyes. Two hundred feet below, the sway of a thousand sea urchins stains the ragged edge of the Atlantic ink black. Ahead, the sky dips into cerulean water, a seamless luminescence without edges. The ocean surrounds me in two-hundred-seventy degrees. I recede in its presence, growing small. I can see for miles. I can see the curvature of the Earth.

Bruce has been driving me and my cousin Eric around St. Croix all day. I stopped asking where we were going. It was nicer, I found, to just stare out the open window, letting the Caribbean flow through me. Weeds and cacti blurring past. Mangroves and baobabs. An egret standing on the back of a goat.

So when we scrambled up the high, narrow summit, I was unprepared for what lay ahead.

"Point Udall," Bruce says, as if the sight does not defy description. "The easternmost point of the United States."

My new job with a major software corporation would make anyone envious. Free gym membership. A jaw-dropping annual bonus. Six weeks of vacation.

Six weeks.

As I completed my onboarding paperwork, I was filled with dread. Whatever would I do with it? There would be no trips with in-laws. No romantic getaways. My new friends have their own families. I'm trying to stay busy, not sit with my troubled thoughts. Not wonder, anew, what I'm living for. So when Eric planned a visit to a friend, and suggested I tag along, I had no reason to decline.

I see further, now, than I saw then: nearly to the Mid-Atlantic Ridge, nearly to Africa, up to the celestial vault and beyond. This is my backyard, a short flight away. There is a world out here. A world I haven't begun to explore.

And now, I have *too much* vacation time. This is no liability. I've got to get a passport.

To be unmoored is to be *free*.

"You can't write about this," warns a man half my age, leafing through my workshop contribution with canary-yellow nails. It's a short piece I've written for my first grad school class, on my difficulty buying into your feminine illusion.

"It's the truth," I say, passing a copy to Rachel. At twenty-two, she's backpacked across half of Europe. She's become not just a friend—who drags my exhausted ass to dance clubs and open mics—but an inspiration. With her encouragement, I've booked my first international trip, to Amsterdam. I'm taking a one-way ticket, a backpack and a global train pass. I'll fly home from wherever I end up three weeks later.

"That doesn't matter," nail-polish-guy says.

"It does to me." I hand a copy to Liza, an urban homesteader my age. She's become a friend, too.

It's been a good season for making friends. I've met some neighbors: a biker who takes me for rides, a gardener who shares cuttings from her roses. I've reconnected with Harper and visited her feminist book club in Columbus. And I befriended some ladies at Imbolc, a pagan celebration of light and fertility.

"Have a new experience," my professor urged. "Then write about it." The local Wiccan circle seemed adequately novel. Only when I brought the communion of milk to my lips—representing the life-giving force of female divinity—did I realize with a start I was practicing witchcraft. Then I was struck by the inevitability.

I've met people through Liza, too. Her wife performs biweekly at a local piano bar, a gig that attracts a rotating group of the pair's friends. I've even met someone promising there. That was unexpected—after a couple of dead-end encounters arising from the dating app, I'd put romance on the back burner.

She strolled in on a slow night and took the seat across from me. "I'm Grace," she said, offering her hand. She had the body of a former athlete and the platinum hair of blonde graying gracefully. I was immediately drawn to her sharp wit and fearless laugh.

Grace. What a lovely name. It's one of my favorite words. Or at least one of my favorite concepts.

Soon after, she called me for a proper date. That was a classy move—I'd come to expect covert meetings in bars with women who swiped right and showed up late, sometimes with a friend and an exit strategy.

Over sole meunière and lavender-infused champagne, Grace and I shared our vision of the good life: a hike in a meadow in late summer, when green fades to amber. Eggs over arugula on a lazy Sunday. Simple pleasures, living in the moment, cultivating gratitude. We hit it off so well, we broke injera around an Ethiopian mesob days later. Then we spent an evening at my house, trading childhood stories and tending a long-burning fire.

My classmate isn't finished lecturing me. I'm duty-bound to *politeness*, he insists, not to honesty. Like a pastor steering a young heretic from the path to hell, he counsels me. What I've said, he warns, is a kind of blasphemy. "You can't say it."

For a moment, I'm lured. It's the authority in his voice. But then I remember who I am. *Heresy is in my blood.* I speak the Ineffable!

"Audre Lorde calls the 'erotic' an 'assertion of lifeforce,'" I tell the circle gathered in Harper's living room, pulling the text from my tote and flipping to the pages I've bookmarked. "And pornography a *denial* of eroticism."

Cameron and I almost didn't make it to book club—luckily, we'd gotten an early start. Forty miles from Harper's home, my failing car engine sent us drifting to the shoulder. I phoned her to cancel, and to my surprise, she located a mechanic, called a tow truck, and insisted on driving out to pick us up. She even arranged our bus ride home.

I found Lorde's view counterintuitive, I admit to the group. But then I realized her dichotomy—eroticism as creative and feminine, porn as destructive and masculine—fit neatly with those of Nietzsche, Freud, Jung, and Fromm. The Dionysian and the Apollonian. The pleasure principle and the death drive. Anima and animus. Biophilia and necrophilia. Even Paglia, who kind of defends porn, calls it a masculine "protest" against the feminine. As I speak, I meet the gaze of a young woman I haven't seen here before. With a mane of messy hair and low-rise jeans that show off slender hips, she's attractive enough to stir an uninvited flutter.

"Porn does not celebrate the female essence," I suggest, inviting the group to discuss. It replaces the sexually mature woman with the hairless, adolescent waif. It trades vitality for heroin chic in chains. The acts of porn do not lead to procreation; they establish dominance. In porn, *woman* is a glut of options, available for squander. "Virgin" tops search terms because man loves to lay waste to innocence. "Rosebud," because he loves to lay waste to the human body.

The catharsis I've found in porn exacts a human cost, even if I've too often turned a blind eye. It may have been your undoing. It drives human trafficking; it dwells in the realm of death.

When the discussion winds down, and the group disperses for red wine and lemon bars, the newcomer makes a beeline for Cameron's vacated chair and introduces herself as Kim. "You must be a writer," she says in a smoky voice, alluding to my citations. She's an art student, she tells me, and she's looking for a collaborator for her graphic novel. We exchange contact information, but when I rise to leave, she touches my arm. I could swear she's *hitting on me*.

"I'm attracted to women," she finds a reason to say, in the midst of a monologue about her boyfriend and her taste for drugs. "But women aren't attracted to me."

"*I'm* attracted to you," I hear myself say in my out-loud voice. But I don't know what's come over me. I'm dating someone, sort of, and Kim is clearly trouble. Flustered, she returns to the graphic novel, and my face floods with shame for my little foray into wishful thinking.

But then she looks me in the eye and tells me she's flattered.

"When it rains it pours," Cameron says, when we're settled in for the bus ride home. "She was into you."

I shake my head. But then my phone jingles. There's an event at my college, Kim texts. She's going. She wants to know if I'm going. She wants to know if she can stay at my house.

I'm not sure why she's interested. It's just a faculty literary reading. It's a long drive and it's on a weeknight. But I tell her she's welcome to stay. Many have put me up on my travels, and I always try to extend the favor.

"See?" Cameron asks, with an approving nudge. "She's trying to see you again."

"She's so young. And so *hot*. What does she want with a woman pushing fifty?"

Cameron launches a protest: There are lots of reasons to be into me. But I recline my seat and close my eyes, and I go to a dark place. I'm not amused at the universe's cruel little joke. I'm growing old; the window for racy trysts is closing fast. I couldn't be blamed for seizing upon an opportunity like this. I don't even need to decide—I'll just throw myself in the path of temptation. Mistakes are made when people fail to plan ahead. Mistakes can be forgiven. Grace and I probably won't last, anyway—it's just the odds.

And that's the upshot, isn't it? If Grace is the one for me, I'll regret a romp with Kim. If not, I'll regret the missed opportunity. It's a cost/benefit analysis.

I try to count the relevant factors, weigh them, compare them. But too much is unknown. I can't extrapolate my future with Grace from the fourteen days we've spent together. It can't be done.

Your campaign to destroy me does not flag.

"I wasn't going to tell you," one of your allies texts me, when I'm back home. "But then Jamie took it too far." You've been cyberstalking me since the day we parted ways, she says. You created a software bot to spy on me. You know about Eli, and my new job, and my travel plans. You told her I'd adopted a "poisonous worldview." You told her I was online "spewing hate." She asked you for links. When you had none to give, she became suspicious.

You've started a new blog, Cameron tells me later. You speak of me frequently there, referring to me as your "abuser." I shouldn't look, but I do.

In some of your posts, there's a grain of truth.

I called you a "tranny," you write. I did—at *your request*. It made you feel "cute" and "small," as I recall. I used it too flippantly once, and when you objected, I apologized. But *you* brought the word into our lives.

In others, there is no grain of truth.

You claim I called you a "faggot." You put quote marks around the word, as if you're *quoting* me. The word may roll off your tongue, Jamie, but it's never crossed mine. I knew same-sex attraction at a young age, felt the shame in slurs like these. It's *you* who feared "looking gay." Keep your homophobia out of my mouth.

You write that I was "disgusted" by you. *Me.* The one who lusted after Frank-N-Further. The one who's dirty danced with drag queens, and dated butch lesbians, and who once got hot and heavy with someone at a party whose sex was unclear to me. I loved gender nonconformists years before they were on your radar.

You charge me with "disconnecting" from you sexually. But my failure to get aroused was a result of what *you* did—and stopped doing. I tried everything to repair our broken sex life: asking for help, performing without reciprocation, even drinking.

You say I "made it clear" that you shouldn't transition. But I didn't ask you to stop your plans; I only wanted to know what they were. It was *my life too*—remember? I had needs, but I wasn't pushy about them. I scarcely admitted them to *myself.* And is clarity such a bad thing? As far as I can tell, we needed *more* of it. My efforts to spare your feelings only postponed the inevitable. You add that I "extracted" compromises from you. But you made no compromises, compelled or otherwise. You wouldn't even take it slow.

And here's the part that makes me sad. You write that I "weaponized" your niece against you. As if being a female child could be anything but a liability.

I didn't invent sexual assault to get on your nerves or thwart your plans. That it's so theoretical to you, so academic, reveals how shielded you are from its horrors. I've been victimized a dozen times and your niece faces the same risks. It is *you* who uses Nina, as a pawn to sacrifice if it helps you win your game.

And I don't understand why there's a game. I never considered you my opponent. I never thought to raise a weapon, human or otherwise. What has driven you into this corner, compelled you to raise your shields?

"I have a female brain," you assert, in one of your posts.

Lyle backs you up in the comments: "The science is there."

Eunice says I'm a testament to the past—a past you want to disown. It seems she's right. You can't assimilate me into your story. And you can't give up on your story. So, like your old blog, I must be erased—and rewritten.

But you have your own life now; you're a media darling. I see you in the news and on television. You speak at Pride and the Women's

March. And you're dating Caleb. If a new partner won't bring you peace, what will? You said you'd always love me. You said you'd remain at the window of the train, forever watching me.

I guess you got the latter part right.

I know I wasn't perfect, but I didn't mistreat you. For the last year and a half I gave away everything I held dear for you. I brought you my concerns, even as you dismissed them as some sort of affront. I gave you money when you wouldn't work. I played intimate partner after you hobbled our intimacy. I can no longer ignore my suspicion, so long held at arm's length, that you have *utterly lost your moral compass.*

But then I see a post about a conversation we had almost a decade ago, before any of this began. And I see something I didn't see before.

I remember that afternoon well. You and I were channel-surfing on the couch, and we landed on a show where some crafters discussed needlepoint techniques.

"Sometimes I think about becoming a cross-stitcher," you said—but I misheard you.

"A crossdresser?"

"No!" you said with a laugh. "A cross-stitcher. I want to stitch some Christmas ornaments." Then you added: "That's an interesting thought, though—what if I *was* a crossdresser?"

I thought for a moment. "It would be fine. But it would give me pause."

You asked why. I shrugged. I'd known a few crossdressers. They couldn't talk about anything else.

You relay the story very differently.

"Years ago," you write, "Shannon and I were lying in bed, sharing our deepest secrets. Terrified, I asked what she'd think if I were transgender. 'I'd never date a tranny,' she answered. 'Trannies are insane.' I knew, then, I could never come out to her."

You took that conversation, and you placed it on a bed instead of a couch. You removed the television. You cast it as a failed confession, instead of a lighthearted exchange.

You said we were talking about transgender people when we were talking about crossdressers. And that you considered yourself transgender, back then, though you explicitly dismissed the notion until recently.

You accused me of saying "I'd never date" such a person. What I said was, "it would give me pause." You said I used the word "insane," when I most certainly didn't. And "tranny," a word I'd never uttered at the time. You distorted literally *every* nuance of the conversation. Why twist my off-handed remark—which turned out to be prescient, by the way—into some bigoted tirade?

So far I've assumed you're a run-of-the-mill liar—even as your lies grow more malicious. But I see something else, now. There's a quality to your narrative I recognize. Something about its egotism. Something about its conviction.

You *believe* what you're saying.

Because of dysphoria, you see your body in a fun house mirror. That much I've understood. It makes you prefer the pained photo of yourself to the vibrant one. You're focused on your jawline. Your hairs. Your skin. The trees, not the forest.

But you see the things that *happen* to you in a distorted way, too. In retrospect, I see it all over your behavior.

You heard an insult in a compliment at Moon Garden. Then you heard an apology that never occurred.

You saw a nuanced understanding of gender identity in some dudes giving you side-eye at a sports bar.

And that encounter at the Miami airport—it grows more sinister with each retelling. On your new blog, you claim the female officer "groped" you. But you aren't *lying* about that—even though it isn't true. A little stress crack has formed in the memory. It's grown and spread over time.

The officials notice your manner of dress. *Noticing* becomes *discomfort*. *Discomfort* becomes *rejection*. You think you passed that day because you long to pass. You think your genitals are baffling because *you* want them to be.

Our conversations have morphed in the same way. To have my own ideas is to *reject yours*. To reject your ideas is to reject *you*. From there, violence and abuse are a short jaunt.

You think people are spying on you. Thinking about your genitals. Sabotaging you. These are classic *delusions of persecution*. I've seen them before. In a schizophrenic high school friend. In a neighbor with alcohol-induced psychosis. Maybe you think the forces aligned to schedule your laser appointment on Paige's birthday. Maybe you were never photographed at the grocery store. While I've petitioned for your respect, you've watched me grow ugly and strange like the psychedelic cats that flowed from Louis Wain's pen as he lost his mind.

It's something I haven't wanted to see in you. Something I haven't been *allowed* to see in you.

There is one narrative. To be transgender is to embark upon a beautiful journey. Any deviation is verboten. By you. By my nail-polish-wearing classmate. By your activist friends. By the media.

I haven't been allowed to notice your misery, the way it climbs in lockstep with transition. Your sexual dysfunction, so at odds with the healthy, happy relationship your revelation promised to bring. Your addiction to social media. Your intolerance for truth.

I haven't been allowed to notice the irony. Self-hatred masquerading as self-acceptance. The practiced persona as the true one. The purchase and augmentation of body parts as an expression of authenticity.

I haven't been allowed to notice your physical decline, illustrated so starkly in that pair of photos. Once vibrant and fresh-faced with glowing skin. Later, sallow, a ghost of yourself. "Desexualized," like Michael Jackson after his transformation, in the words of culture critic Mark

Fisher. Maybe even "denatured." But Jackson was ill, so I'm not to make the comparison.

I'm not allowed to notice the steep increase in transgender people around me. For the first four decades of my life, I knew only two—both from that drag bar. Now I know more than I can count. Classmates—a couple per class. Three-quarters of the university's Pride group. A share of College Democrats and the bicycling club, too.

The daughter of someone in my Wiccan group, for a while. "She changed her mind," my friend announced at the last ritual. "After breaking up with her boyfriend." The love interest was trans, too.

Someone in my own family. Someone too young.

Most were born female. Most haven't driven a car, kissed someone or set foot in a bar. They share a penchant for undercuts, often dyed blue, and they choose names that evoke Victorian toddlers: Larkin, Duncan. Two Quinns. Two Flynns.

But there are others. Anastasia, formerly Red, is now a woman—and no longer with Willow. "Sometimes you have to cut toxic people out of your life," Anastasia explains in a videotaped makeup tutorial, applying gloss to lips clenched tightly over those still-missing incisors. This is the Red who denounced shaving as patriarchal and store-bought shampoo as a consumerist excess. The critic of the "industrial-medical complex," now injecting hormones. The minimalist, now collecting eye brighteners and a SiliSponge. I'm not allowed to notice Red's two selves—or to wonder which is the true, authentic one.

Cameron tells me you're blowing up social media with news of your "new vag," sharing details about the suture and your favorite brand of sanitary napkins.

At night I dream I'm digging in the back of a closet in a spare room. There I find a shoebox with a baby snake inside. It was once a pet, now forgotten, shriveled and dying of neglect. I offer nourishment but the snake rejects it, even as it writhes in suffering. "You need to kill it," friends advise. "Put it out of its misery." But it would break my heart to do it violence. I can only watch, helplessly, as it dies.

The next evening I trek to Mi Familia in the first light dusting of snow. After a day on the phone with the mechanic, debating a repair bill that exceeds the worth of my vehicle, I'm ready to let someone else make my dinner. Tomorrow I figure out how to pick up my car. Tonight, I eat tacos.

After putting in my order, I browse a refrigerated case stocked with tamarind juice, pulpy sodas, and cold Coronas. Choosing a Mexican cola in a glass bottle, the kind sweetened with cane sugar instead of corn syrup, I retrieve the bottle opener from the coffee can on the counter. I settle into a molded plastic booth, watching Angel toss pork and pineapple on the grill. He sings as he works, to the tune of some happy Latin melody emanating from a boombox nearby, and wipes his hands on a grease-smeared apron. Overhead, a television blasts a glamorous game show. The music competes with contestants' squeals as they smash buzzers before a procession of bikinis and gowns. I barely hear my phone when it jingles.

"I have some sketches to show you," Kim texts. Before I can respond, I get another notification.

"I want to help you pick up your car," texts Grace.

It's a generous offer. It's several hours each way, and the car—which I asked the mechanic to make drivable as cheaply as possible—might not last the trip. I tell her she shouldn't sacrifice her Saturday.

"Darlin'," she texts. "It's OK. We'll bring a towing rope. We'll take it slow." She *means* it. And I could use the help.

I ponder her offer, surveying the paintings that line the walls. Cornucopias. Rolling fields of farmland. Women tending rows of corn, cradling baskets of ripe fruit. Sunflowers and calla lilies. Abundance. Not too-muchness.

"Amiga!" The store's owner, who always greets me, emerges from a door in back carrying a roll of butcher paper. "How are you?"

Reflexively, I shout that I am good.

And then I realize I *am* good.

Somehow, it happened.

I'm good.

Angel's son drops a paper basket on the wood-grain melamine in front of me: tacos al pastor, piled high with cilantro and onions. The best food nine dollars can buy. The best food I've ever taken for granted.

The cakey aroma of freshly made tortillas wafts through. Chicharrones, fried fresh this morning, overflow stainless steel chafers, tongs perched atop. Homemade sauces fill red and green squeeze bottles. Steam from the grill takes the edge off a chill seeping under the door. Friendly faces surround me. Even the piñatas dotting the ceiling seem auspicious: donkeys and stars in Crayola-colored crepe, Spongebob and Dora trailing metallic streamers.

This is abundance. This is the sacred. It's *worlding* here.

Your Buddhist friend calls happiness the ability to feel joy without grasping. I'm flooded with gratitude, despite the car trouble, despite the hectic day. Not so long ago, it seemed I had no friends. But a friend accompanied me to Columbus. Another rescued me when my car broke down. And a third has offered to help me get it back. I have community, here, in my neighborhood, and at the book club, and at school.

My phone jingles with texts from two lovely women who want to spend time with me. For the first time, I see clearly what my dilemma means: I have *more* than I need. I've embarked upon a relationship that's worth cultivating. And I can still turn a head once in a while! Bounty is not burden. It's the crisis of modernity that arouses greed where gratitude is called for.

I can be flattered by Kim's interest instead of resentful of her timing. I don't have to conquer every frontier. I don't need to predict the future. I can, instead, live with grace in the present.

I love Grace. It's a young and naive love, with no guarantee of permanence. But it's a love I enter into intentionally, with my eyes open, ready for all the messy risk of loss that love entails. I'm going to love with my whole heart.

I text Kim and tell her I'm happy to collaborate. But I can't host her while she's in town, after all. Cameron might be able to offer a bed. I'll ask him tonight.

I crush a lime wedge over a taco and take a bite, grateful for life's simple pleasures, for good food and drink, for a warm refuge from winter, for community, for collaboration, for burgeoning love.

When my belly is as full as my soul I rewrap my scarf, step into a cool quiet warmed by the North Star, and call Grace.

Acknowledgments

I owe my deepest thanks to my partner, Grace. She is an Amazon, a Goddess, and a total badass. She's put up with a lot as I brought this book to fruition, and she's been nothing but patient and encouraging. She inspires me to be my best self, and I am more than honored to know her and to love her.

A huge thank you to my beta readers and workshoppers: Tegan, Maria, MJ, Nina, Lois, Elizabeth, Lisa, and Rachel. To Kathleen and Mercedez for editing. To Terry, Kyle and Robbins for professorial wisdom. To Lyn for a tarot reading. To Rich for advice. For support and encouragement: the Goddess women, the Chicago women, the Urbana women, the Michigan women, the Supper Club women, and my mom. Love and "I miss you" to Liz and Lonnie, who departed this world as I wrote this, for the best friendships I've ever known. And a sincere thank you to Carol for utterly immeasurable support.

In My Tote

Adorno, Theodor W., and Max Horkheimer. *Dialectic of Enlightenment*. London: Verso, 2014.

Arcade Fire, "Wake Up," track 7 on *Funeral*, Merge Records, 2004, compact disc.

Austin, J. L. *How to Do Things with Words*. Eastford, CT: Martino Fine, 2018.

Butler, Judith. *Gender Trouble: Feminism and the Subversion of Identity*. New York: Routledge, 2015.

Baron Byron,George Gordon Byron.Lord Byron - *Sardanapalus: "Adversity is the First Path to Truth.".* United Kingdom: Stage Door,2015.

Burton, Tim, director. Beetlejuice. 1988; Geffen Company/Warner Bros. Pictures., 1999. 1 hr., 32 min. DVD.

Camus, Albert. *The Myth of Sisyphus. Translated by Justin O'Brien. Penguin Modern Classics.* London, England: Penguin Classics, 2000.

Coe, David Allan, "You Never Even Called Me By My Name," track 10 on *Once Upon a Rhyme*, 1975, vinyl LP.

Dalai Lama: A Policy of Kindness.India:Motilal Banarsidass Publishers Pvt. Limited,2002.

Debord, Guy. *The Society of the Spectacle*. Berkeley, CA: Bureau of Public Secrets, 2014.

Didion, Joan. *Slouching Towards Bethlehem*. New York: Dell, 1968.

Diehl, Matt. "It's a Joni Mitchell Concert, Says Joni." *LA Times*, April 22, 2010. https://www.latimes.com/archives/la-xpm-2010-apr-22-la-et-jonimitchell-20100422-story.html

Fisher, Mark. *The Resistible Demise of Michael Jackson*. Winchester, UK: Zero Books, 2009.

Fleming, Victor. *Gone with the Wind*. 1939. Selznick International Pictures, 2002. 3 hr., 14 min. DVD.

Foucault,Michel."What is Enlightenment?" *The Foucault Reader*.United Kingdom:Pantheon Books,1984.

Freud,Sigmund.*Beyond the Pleasure Principle*.Austria:International Psycho-Analytical Press,1922.

Fromm, Erich. *War Within Man: A Psychological Enquiry into the Roots of Destructiveness; a Study and Commentary*. Philadelphia: Peace Literature Service of the American Friends Service Committee, 1963.

Giacobetti, Francis, director. Emmanuelle 2. 1975. Parafrance Communication, 2019. 1 hr., 31 min. DVD.

Goffman, Erving. *Presentation of Self in Everyday Life*. S.l.: Penguin Books, 2022.

Grzymkowski,Eric.*The Quotable A**hole: More Than 1,200 Bitter Barbs, Cutting Comments, and Caustic Comebacks for Aspiring and Armchair A**holes Alike*.United States:Adams Media,2011.

Hacker,Joseph, and Abraham Meir Habermann. *The alphabet of Ben Sira: facsimile of the Constantinople 1519 edition*. Verona: Valmadonna Trust Library, 1997.

Hagar, Sammy, "There's Only One Way to Rock," track 2 on *Standing Hampton*, Universal Music Group, 1990, compact disc.

Heidegger, Martin. *Being and Time*. New York, NY: HarperCollins, 2008.

Hoff, Benjamin. *The Tao of Pooh*. New York: E.P. Dutton, 1982.

Jordan, Lawrence, director. *Dress to Kill*. 1999; Vision Video, 1999. 1 hr., 55 min. DVD.

Jung, C. G., Herbert Read, Michael Scott Montague Fordham, and Gerhard Adler. *The Collected Works of C.G. Jung*. London: Routledge & Kegan Paul, 1970.

Keith, Catfish, "Cherry Ball," track 5 on Cherry Ball, Tower Records, 1993, compact disc.

Kenny, Anthony, *Ancient Philosophy, A New History of Western Philosophy, vol. 1*, Oxford, England: Oxford University Press, 2004.

King Missile, "Detachable Penis," track 8 on *Happy Hour*, Atlantic Records, 1992, compact disc.

Lorde, Audre. "Love Poem." *The Collected Poems of Audre Lorde*.United States:W. W. Norton,2000.

Lorde, Audre. *Uses of the Erotic: the Erotic as Power*. Tucson, AZ.: Kore Press, 2000.

Macquarrie,John.,Heidegger,Martin.*Being and Time*.United Kingdom:HarperCollins,2008.

Moran, Caitlin. *How to Be a Woman*. New York: Harper Perennial, 2011.

Mosendz, Polly. "Shadi Petosky, a Transgender Woman, Alleges Unfair Screening by TSA at Orlando Airport." *Newsweek*, September 22, 2015. https://www.newsweek.com/shadi-petosky-transgender-woman-alleges-unfair-screening-tsa-orlando-airport-375220

Namjoshi, Suniti. *Because of India: Selected Poems and Fables*. London: Only woman, 1989.

Nietzsche,Friedrich Wilhelm.*Beyond Good and Evil: Prelude to a Philosophy of the Future*.United States:12th Media Services,2018.

Nietzsche,Friedrich.*The Birth of Tragedy and Other Writings*.United Kingdom:Cambridge University Press,1999.

Nietzsche, Friedrich Wilhelm. *The Gay Science; with a Prelude in Rhymes and an Appendix of Songs*. New York: Vintage Books, 1974.

Oliver, Mary. "The Summer Day." *House of Light*. Boston, Mass: Beacon Press, 1990.

Oliver, Mary. "The Wild Geese." *Dream Work*. Atlantic Monthly Press, 1994.

Onstad, Chris. *Achewood*. Last modified December 25, 2016. https://www.achewood.com.

Paglia, Camille. *Sexual Personae: Art and Decadence from Nefertiti to Emily Dickinson*. New Haven: Yale Nota Bene, 2001.

Pascal, Blaise, 1623-1662. *Pascal's Pensées*. New York :E.P. Dutton, 1958.

Project Runway. 2010. Season 8, Episode 14. "Finale Part 2." Directed by Eli Holzman. Aired October 28, 2010 on Bravo.

Quinn, Daniel, and Anthony Heald. *The Story of B*. New York, N.Y.: Bantam Doubleday Dell Audio Pub, 1996.

Rich,Adrienne."Twenty-One Love Poems [(The Floating Poem, Unnumbered)]." *Collected Poems: 1950-2012*.United States:W. W. Norton,2016.

Rojek, Chris. *Presumed intimacy: Para-Social Relationships in Media, Society and Celebrity Culture*. Cambridge: Polity Press, 2016.

Rossetti,Dante Gabriel. "Body's Beauty." *The House of Life: A Sonnet Sequence*.United States:Thomas B. Mosher,1903.

Roxette, "It Must Have Been Love," track 5 on *Greatest Hits*, International, 2006, compact disc.

Shakespeare, William, and David M. Bevington. *The Complete Works of Shakespeare*. New York: Longman, 1997.

Sharman,Jim, director. The Rocky Horror Picture Show. 1975. 20th Century Fox/Michael White Productions, 2000. 1 hr., 38 min. DVD.

Stone, Merlin. *When God Was a Woman*. Houghton Mifflin Harcourt Trade & Reference Publishers, 2001.

Takahashi, Keita. Katamari Damacy. Namco. Playstation 2. 2004.

Triller, Kaeley. "A Rape Survivor Speaks Out About Transgender Bathrooms." *The Federalist*, November 23, 2015. https://thefederalist.com/2015/11/23/a-rape-survivor-speaks-out-about-transgender-bathrooms

Vijayasree,C..Suniti Namjoshi : *The Artful Transgressor*.India:Rawat Publications,2001.

Williams, Heathcote. *Of Dylan and His Deaths*, Wales Arts Review, 2016

Made in the USA
Monee, IL
19 March 2023

30152558R10184